FINANCING HEALTH CARE: COMPETITION VERSUS REGULATION

FINANCING HEALTH CARE: COMPETITION VERSUS REGULATION

THE PAPERS AND PROCEEDINGS OF THE SIXTH PRIVATE SECTOR CONFERENCE
March 23 and 24, 1981

edited by

DUNCAN YAGGY, Ph.D.
WILLIAM G. ANLYAN, M.D.

foreword by

DAVID A. HAMBURG, M.D.

BALLINGER PUBLISHING COMPANY
Cambridge, Massachusetts
A subsidiary of Harper & Row, Publishers, Inc.

International Standard Book Number: 0-88410-737-X

Library of Congress Catalog Card Number: 81-20629

Printed in the United States of America

Library of Congress Cataloging in Publication Data

Main entry under title:

Financing health care.

Papers from a conference held at the Duke University Medical Center, March 23 and 24, 1981.

Includes index.
1. Medical care—United States—Finance—Congresses. 2. Medical care, Cost of—United States—Congresses. 3. Medical policy—United States—Congresses. I. Yaggy, Duncan. II. Anlyan, William G. III. Duke University. Medical Center. [DNLM: 1. Economics, Medical—United States—Congresses. 2. Insurance, Health—United States—Congresses. W3 PR945F 6th 1981f / W 74 P961 1981f]
RA410.53.F558   338.4'33621'0973   81-20629
ISBN 0-88410-737-X   AACR2

CONTENTS

THE PARTICIPANTS

Presiding

William G. Anlyan, M.D.
  Duke University Medical Center

Giving Papers

J. Alexander McMahon
  American Hospital Association

Uwe E. Reinhardt, Ph.D.
  Woodrow Wilson School of Public and
    International Affairs
  Princeton University

Karen Davis, Ph.D.
  Johns Hopkins University

Paul Ellwood, Jr., M.D.
  InterStudy

John W. Colloton
  University of Iowa

Responding to the Papers

Walter McNerney
Blue Cross Association

Alain C. Enthoven, Ph.D.
Graduate School of Business
Stanford University

David E. Rogers, M.D.
The Robert Wood Johnson Foundation

Richard H. Egdahl, M.D.
Boston University

Commenting

John E. Affeldt, M.D.
Joint Commission on the
Accreditation of Hospitals

Karl Bays
American Hospital Supply
Corporation

William Beers
Kraft, Incorporated

William Bevan, Ph.D.
Duke University

Frederick A. Coe, Jr.
Burroughs Wellcome
Company

John A.D. Cooper, M.D.
Association of American
Medical Colleges

Merlin K. DuVal, M.D.
National Center for Health
Education

C. Douglas Eavenson
General Motors Corporation

E. Harvey Estes, Jr., M.D.
Duke University Medical
Center

Nelson Ford
Department of Health and
Human Services

John G. Freymann, M.D.
National Fund for Medical
Education

Ashley H. Gale, Jr.
The Duke Endowment

David A. Hamburg, M.D.
John F. Kennedy School of
Government
Harvard University

Joseph N. Onek, Esq.
Onek, Klein, and Pharr

C. Rollins Hanlon, M.D.
American College of Surgeons

Paul G. Rogers, Esq.
Hogan & Hartson

Billy McCall
The Duke Endowment

Jack K. Shelton
Ford Motor Company

Jack D. Myers, M.D.
American College of Physicians

Joseph V. Terenzio
United Hospital Fund of
New York

Alan Nelson, M.D.
American Medical Association

Daniel C. Tosteson, M.D.
Harvard Medical School

Gilbert S. Omenn, M.D.
Woodrow Wilson of Public and
International Affairs
Princeton University

Richard S. Wilburn, M.D.
Council of Medical Specialties

The participants spoke for themselves. Their affiliations—as of March 1981—are listed to facilitate identification. A few have changed since.

LIST OF FIGURES

LIST OF TABLES

FOREWORD

Recent commentary has characterized the discussion of American health policy as a debate between the defenders of government regulation and the advocates of a competitive health market. Through most of the 1970s, the United States relied on various forms of regulation for the implementation of its health policy. With the growth of competing prepaid plans, the increasing popularity of legislative proposals designed to bring competition to the American health care market, and the election of Ronald Reagan, the tide turned. The regulators are put to rout.

Or are they? The authors of this book perceive it differently. Competition will have its day, but in most places it will progress gradually over the next decade. To restrain cost increases between now and then, continued regulation will be necessary. To create a competitive health market, new law and regulation will be essential. Regulation will not disappear; it will pursue new objectives.

The choice is not between regulation and competition. The choice is among different approaches to the creation of a competitive health market. Do we want competition carefully controlled or relatively unbridled? Do we want competition between providers, between competing medical plans, or both? Given the progress which competing medical plans are making, do we still have a choice? Or is the decision largely made?

And what of the impact? Competition's advocates talk at length about the benefits to consumers. But what of providers? If the legislation creating a competitive health market strips away the protection which cost reimbursement provides, what will happen to providers who cannot compete on price? The wasteful and inefficient will surely sink, but so may teaching hospitals, whose high charges to private patients carry the costs of charity care, teaching, and research which we can ill afford to lose. Some are concerned that price competition may take away the funds needed to investigate the cost and benefits of diagnostic and therapeutic inventions and to determine their value.

As the papers and proceedings of Duke's Sixth Private Sector Conference demonstrate, those charting the future of American health care disagree at critical points. Their debate clarifies the issues and suggests the positions which consumers, providers, third party payers, and governments are likely to take. The resolution will help to determine the direction of American health policy for the next decade.

The Private Sector conferences were founded on the perception that health policy is the outgrowth of a continually changing interplay among the public sector and the various parts of the private sector. As the first conference opened in 1977, the public sector dominated the formulation of American health policy. The private sector was on the defensive. Its members could agree that the role of government should be reduced and that restraints on the private sector should be relaxed, but they could not agree on constructive alternatives to public sector policies, or even that private sector alternatives were necessary. The first conference was dominated by complaints about government regulation.

As it gradually became clear that public policy sought significant, legitimate objectives and that a policy built largely on public restriction of the private sector would fail, the tone of the conferences changed. Participants began to discuss ways in which the public and private sectors might cooperate, and situations in which appropriate incentives could be substituted for prohibitions and restraints. "If the government would give us the chance . . ." was a phrase repeated several times.

This year it became clear that the private sector will get its chance, and the conference considered the likely result. The question to the private sector used to be, "If you had your way, what would you do?" This year it became "What will you do?" The answers to this question exposed the divisions within the private sector, as well as the difficult problems of the competitive environment.

The Private Sector conferences clearly document the complexity of the problems, the intricacy of the web which they weave, the diversity of perspectives, the frictions which conflicting obligations create, and the appalling difficulty of creating truly constructive change. But the conferences also demonstrate growth in our understanding and in our willingness to accept responsibility and deal thoughtfully with convoluted and highly charged issues.

The nation is served well by Duke University in its fostering of continuing dialogue between private and public sectors in health, and challenging both to face complex problems with respect and imagination.

David A. Hamburg, M.D.
Division of Health Policy Research and Education
Harvard University

ACKNOWLEDGMENT

This is to acknowledge with gratitude the vision and generosity of the Duke Endowment, which has sponsored the Private Sector Conferences at Duke University Medical Center since their initiation in 1977.

William G. Analyan, M.D.

SESSION I: FIRST DAY

1 FINANCING HEALTH CARE: AN HISTORICAL OVERVIEW

In our complex society, solutions to one set of social and economic problems often create a new set, and nowhere is that dynamic more visible than in the evolution of health care financing and delivery in the United States.

During the first three-quarters of this century, public and private sector energies were devoted to increasing the effectiveness and accessibility of the health care system and to developing a financing system that spread the financial burden of serious illness. We have made enormous progress, and we have created new challenges for the nation. With longer life spans come questions about retirement policy, the viability of the Social Security system, and long-term health care. With scientific and technological advances come new and difficult ethical issues. And with the increasing capacity and sophistication of health care and the expansion of third-party financing comes the question: "How can we control health care costs?"

This question is important, and it is being asked by the federal and state governments, by business and industry, and by consumers and providers of health care services. Today, I would like to explain how we got where we are, and then discuss briefly how the growth of health costs might be moderated. I shall start with an historical overview because understanding the events that created the cost problem is essential to thoughtful analysis of future health policy.

HISTORICAL OVERVIEW

The long-term consequences of many events that shaped our health care system would have been difficult to predict. These events have combined to generate a powerful momentum toward more accessible, more effective, and more costly health care.

Pre-1940: Beginnings

As this historical trace begins, the U.S. health care system was at an early stage of development. In the early years of the twentieth century, medical education was uneven, antibiotics were unknown, abdominal and thoracic surgery was limited, and public health measures were only beginning to control infectious disease. The primary role of hospitals was caring for the indigent and terminally ill. Health insurance was largely unknown.

Three events in this era set the stage for later rapid growth in health care spending. First, people began prepaying hospital expenses under risk-sharing plans in 1929, and the Blue Cross concept was born. It gained modest popularity during the Depression; commercial insurers entered the market in the late 1930s. Second, passage of the Wagner Act in 1935 gave workers protected rights to organize unions and bargain collectively through representatives of their own choosing. The simultaneous development of health insurance and collective bargaining produced rapid growth in the number of people covered by health insurance plans. The third event was the 1935 enactment of Old Age and Survivors' Insurance, the first federal effort to create economic security for older Americans and the precursor of the Medicare program enacted thirty years later.

1940-50: Health Insurance as an Employee Benefit

World War II gave a direct impetus to the development of new medical technology and an indirect boost to the popularity of health insurance as an employee benefit. The indirect boost resulted from the operation of two factors. First, wartime wage and price controls did not apply to fringe benefits. Second, the large number of service men and women returning to civilian society were accustomed to health care that was free at the point of delivery. Between 1940 and 1950, the number of people covered by hospitalization insurance increased from 12 million to 77 million. The number of people with other types of health insurance coverage also grew rapidly.

At the same time, there was recognition that the nation needed more health care facilities. In 1946, the Hill-Burton federal matching grant program was enacted to expand access to high-quality, well-planned hospital and nursing home facilities.

During the 1940s, improvement in the effectiveness and accessibility of care and expanding employee health benefits were mutually reinforcing. As medical care became more available, effectiveness grew, and as more hospitals were built, the desire for health care and insurance coverage increased. As health care coverage improved and expanded, the development and dissemination of new medical technology was encouraged. The result was an accelerating demand for health care services, and accelerating cost.

1951-65: Prosperity

The period from 1951 to 1965 was a time of peace and prosperity, and we achieved unprecedented improvements in our standard of living. The personal automobile, home ownership, suburban development, and home appliance purchases were visible signs, but the same dynamic was at work in health insurance. Between 1950 and 1965, the proportion of a quickly growing population with hospital insurance coverage climbed from 50 percent to 70 percent, a total increase of about 60 million covered people.

As health care purchasing power increased, so did access to health care. The use of Hill-Burton program funds expanded the supply of nonfederal short-term hospital beds by 47 percent. More than 365,000 general hospital beds were built or renovated—a number equal to about one-third of our current general hospital bed supply.

Throughout this period, there was increased interest in health care. By 1963, the federal government was providing significant levels of financial support for health personnel education and training. Medical knowledge continued to develop at an accelerating pace, and the mass media expanded their coverage of developments in medical science. All this tended to increase the demand for health care. In addition, the "baby boom" of the late 1940s and 1950s had a fairly immediate impact on the demand for prenatal, maternity, and pediatric care.

1965-Present: Government Financing

Since 1965 government financing has had the largest impact on demand and spending for health services. The landmark event was enactment in 1965 of the Medicare and Medicaid programs, which created access to health care for millions of the elderly, the disabled, and the poor.

Medicare and Medicaid relieved health care providers of much of the pressure associated with providing care for people with limited means. Hospitals and physicians were freed to concentrate on enhancing the comprehensiveness and sophistication of their services. Medicare and Medicaid costs rapidly exceeded early projections, and today these programs play a major role in health care financing. In 1979, 28 million people were enrolled under Medicare, and Medicaid paid benefits on behalf of nearly 23 million recipients. The two programs now account for over 35 percent of hospital payments. As longer life spans increase the proportion of the population age sixty-five and over, the impact of Medicare will grow steadily.

While the health care purchasing power of the employed population grew rapidly between 1940 and 1965 through private health insurance, the elderly and the poor achieved a comparable level of health care purchasing power after 1965 through the Medicare and Medicaid programs. Advances in medical science were accelerated by substantial federal support for medical research, medical spin-offs from the space program, and discoveries in electronics and biochemistry. As before, the various developments reinforced one another.

Impact

The significance of the events in these four periods can be read in the growth of spending for health care. Before 1940, health care spending per capita increased at a significantly slower rate than in later years. The size of average annual increases in per capita spending grew in each subsequent phase. Had the rate of increase between 1965 and 1979 remained at the level of the years 1950 to 1965, health care spending in 1979 would have been 22 percent lower. Had the 1940 to 1950 rate of increase prevailed between 1950 and 1979, per capita spending in 1979 would have been 45 percent lower than it actually was (Figure 1-1). This same acceleration is reflected in health care spending as a percentage of the gross national product (GNP) (Figure 1-2).

In reviewing the historical growth in health care expenditures, I should note that expenditure growth has been accompanied by significant gains in the effectiveness and accessibility of health care. There is, however, a growing consensus among the leaders of business and government that some moderation in the rate of increase is essential. State and federal government budgets are being severely strained by increasing Medicare and Medicaid spending. Corporate

Figure 1-1. Health Care Spending Per Capita, Constant 1967 Dollars.

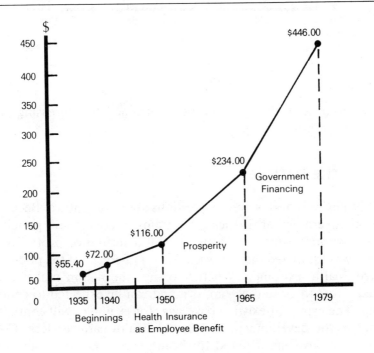

Figure 1-2. Health Care Spending as Percentage of Gross National Product.

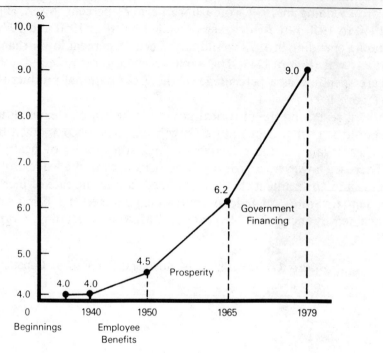

employee benefits budgets are being strained by increasing group health insurance premium costs.

THE FUTURE

This brings us to today and to questions about the future. Because of gaps in governmental financing programs, there are still population groups without adequate levels of health insurance protection. In 1978 it was estimated that between 5 and 11 percent of the population lacked health insurance. Whether or not the nation makes a concerted effort to close that gap, demand can be expected to continue rising. The extent of existing coverage, for example, will continue to stimulate the development and use of health care services. Consequently the growing demand for health care will remain an important—if not the most important—policy issue for the future.

Although there is fairly strong consensus about the need for moderation of health care expenditures, there is disagreement about the way to meet it. We can make more economical use of health care services, but it is not yet clear which restraints will work best. It is also not clear how quickly such restraints can work. To protect hard-won gains, health care consumers and providers, as well as federal and corporate policymakers, must apply considerable creative energy to the development of cost containment strategies.

Policy Alternatives

There are a wide range of policy options that should be considered in the formulation of future health care cost containment strategies. One broad category of options includes more intensive government regulation through such mechanisms as certification of need, recertification of need, state rate-setting commissions, and federal caps on health care costs. Another broad category involves adjustments in the private and governmental financing system designed to promote more voluntary discipline and action on the part of consumers, providers, and health insurers. New incentives might include more financial involvement and more choices for consumers in the selection and use of health benefits. In another approach, government or private carriers and health maintenance organizations (HMOs) could contract with providers on selective or conditional bases, as some Blue Cross plans, HMOs, and the government have already begun to do. Or new payment methods and incentives for providers, such as innovative prospective payment systems and more extensive insurance benefit exclusions for questionable or outmoded procedures, could be instituted.

Within these broad categories are a wide variety of options for providers, employers, insurance carriers, and government. It would help to know more about the probable effects of various cost containment approaches, but the nation does not have the luxury of unlimited time to research and debate courses of action. We must be willing to try new approaches without perfect knowledge. This means more risk taking and risk sharing in the health care field. We must be willing to institute temporary, short-term measures, while viable long-term solutions are being developed.

CONCLUSION

The dramatic growth in health care spending has resulted largely from the interaction between growth in private and governmental health insurance programs and rapid development of the health care system's capabilities. This growth has had many positive aspects, particularly improved access to high-quality health care for all segments of population. With these gains, however, have come new problems: increases in expenditures for health care that strain corporate, public, and personal budgets. We must be creative and flexible in pursuing health care cost containment strategies if we are to contain costs without impairing the willingness and ability of the health care sector to respond imaginatively, quickly, and effectively to changing demands and opportunities.

DISCUSSION

Dick Wilbur: I've had the feeling over the years that, by the time we really get seriously concerned about a problem of this type, it's already beginning to be solved. Rapidly rising expenditures for hospital services may soon be a thing of the past because the number of days of hospital care per thousand population is dropping, even though our population is aging. Aren't we devoting a lot of enthusiasm to a problem that may be solving itself with more physicians, more out-patient care, and less hospital care?

Alex McMahon: Days of care aren't dropping. The Steering Committee for the Voluntary Effort met last Thursday, and we reviewed the numbers then. Total days of care per thousand are still inching up. And when you look at hospital expenditure figures, you discover that after a wonderful year in 1978, we lost ground in 1979, and in 1980 the rate of increase was back up to 16.8 percent. No, I don't think the problem is solving itself. And I'm not sure at this stage how to address it. I do know that until we do something about the demand for care and about the incentives now in place, we're never going to have much impact on hospital costs in this country.

Joe Onek: I would like to suggest that we separate two issues. One is the amount that society should spend on health care. I believe it is very difficult to set any limit on expenditures for health care because, if people in our society choose to spend more, it is going to be hard to stop them. The other is the efficiency of our health care system. If we are careful, I think we can separate those issues. That is, one can believe in a more competitive, more incentive-oriented system without necessarily believing that 9 percent is too high a proportion of our GNP to devote to health care.

Paul Ellwood: Did you ever consider capitating Medicare?

Alex McMahon: I think that holds some promise. Going beyond the demonstrations that are now available to a real voucher system that would capitate makes a lot of sense.

2 TABLE MANNERS AT THE HEALTH CARE FEAST

Uwe E. Reinhardt

"Medicine and deregulation go together like a horse and carriage," declared Susan Stone in her regular column in the *American College of Physicians Observer* upon President Reagan's assumption of the presidency. "Conservatives' promotion of deregulation and *laissez-faire* doctrines foretell an era of reexamination of Great Society programs." She goes on to report: "Traditional Republican marketplace economic theories promise to play a large role in the formulation of National Health Insurance legislation. . . . The name of the game from now on is competitive."[1]

The excitement seems widely shared among commentators on health affairs and, curiously, even among the providers of health services. It is an excitement vaguely reminiscent of the months preceding the outbreak of armed conflict. Everybody involved in such a conflict is certain of victory. While some blood may be spilled along the way, that blood is expected to be someone else's and, in any event, a worthy price for victory. Warfare thrives on such euphoria and so, apparently, does health policy in the 1980s.

But just as armed warfare tends to bring with it many an unpleasant surprise, so may the eagerly awaited economic warfare soon to be unleashed in the health care market. There may be more than a few casualties, and some of the nicest folks may receive direct hits.

At this point it is not at all clear who the ultimate victors in the anticipated scramble for health care dollars will be.

Much will depend, of course, upon the *Conventions*—the rules and regulations—society will impose upon this scramble. If economist Milton Friedman and his disciples have their way, there will be few holds barred.[2] The health care sector will become the analog of the infamous Russian front of World War II. For, unlike the marketeers of the corporate-state school, who believe in competition within what they call "orderly markets," Friedman and his disciples truly believe in unfettered economic warfare. They believe in it just as fiercely as General George Patton believed in shooting wars. Patton's glory, of course, was short-lived, and so may be the glory of the true marketeers who have managed to jump on board the new administration. These true believers will sooner or later come to be despised for their relentless attacks on the pastoral tranquility of "orderly markets." They are dangerous and thus quite probably an endangered species.

In this essay I shall elaborate on these musings. I shall make the point that, in the profane discourse of noneconomists, such hallowed words as "free markets," "laissez-faire," and "competition" have been debased. They mean different things to different people. Only this confusion in terms can explain how a vision so intrinsically controversial as a truly competitive health care market could have produced so much euphoria.

The terms "deregulation," "laissez-faire," and "free markets," for example, are often used simply as code words to describe the *selective* elimination of whatever government regulation one finds burdensome. The emphasis here is on the word "selective," for the advocates of deregulation in medicine do not invariably favor a wholesale retreat of government regulators. Is one to assume, for example, that physicians and dentists who now celebrate the impending deregulation of medicine are implicitly advocating the abolition of mandatory professional licensure? Would they actually favor letting pediatric nurse practitioners and dental hygienists practice independent entrepreneurship and compete head-on with physicians and dentists? Yet this is precisely what "laissez-faire" means in French. The question is an interesting one, surely, and one to which the advocates of competitive health care markets will soon have to respond explicitly, because there is an alternative interpretation of "laissez-faire" and "free markets": for example, the harsh vision projected by

Friedman in *Capitalism and Freedom*, a world in which consumers reign supreme and in which there is absolutely no place for protection of economic turf through the coercive power of government (licensure).

With the rise of the marketeers to political power, those who cheered them on must now be called on to articulate clearly just what they meant, and now mean, by the term "free markets," and what, if any, constraints ought to be placed on competitive forces in health care. It is my purpose to tease the participants in this conference out of their respective closets on this issue. My strategy to that end will be the following.

In the second section I shall describe briefly the emerging competitive pressures in the health care sector and sketch as vividly as I can the economist's vision of laissez-faire and freely competitive markets. I do so with the thought that, if we are to debate the age-old issue of regulation versus competitive markets, we ought to do it in the technically precise language developed by the professionals properly licensed to define such terms—economists.

Furthermore, I present the economist's vision of freely competitive markets in the expectation that the mere description of such a market environment will make most health care providers blanch and run for rescue by—you guessed it—the public sector.

Upon completion of that sadistic exercise, I shall become humane once again and allow, in the third section, that reasonable and honorable persons might prefer "government-regulated competition" to the Friedmanesque vision of the free-for-all. Health care providers will breathe easier in this section. On the other hand, I must at the same time rob them of the illusion that government-regulated competition is an unmixed blessing, that it either can be or ought to be purely provider inspired. Government-regulated competition inevitably invites the government into the health care sector, for better or for worse, if only because feuding providers will look to the government for arbitration of their squabbles.[3] Furthermore, government-regulated competition in health care requires us to reach a political consensus on the extent of government intrusion, and neither reaching nor living with this consensus will be peaceful.

Finally, I shall ask in the fourth section how much competitive economic pressure can be prudently imposed on the key decision-maker in health care, the physician. Do patients really want to have their bodies invaded by persons engaged in fierce economic warfare?

I do not offer any insight on this question; I merely raise it for further debate, and expect to come away enlightened.

Throughout the composition of this essay I have been reminded of a fabulous story attributed to that great observer of the animal world, Konrad Lorenz. Two canines meet face to face through a picket fence. Their ferocious snarls suggest beyond any doubt that they would devour one another, should there ever appear a gap in the fence. A gap does appear. Do the dogs devour one another? They do not. They quickly retreat to territory safely divided by the picket fence, there to growl at one another as fiercely as before, suggesting that, but for the fence, they would devour one another at the first opportunity. I do not know why this story has lingered on my mind ever since the new administration promised competitive markets. I merely tell the story for what it may be worth.

ON THE NATURE OF COMPETITIVE MARKETS

The Dual Social Role of the Health Care Sector

Every economic activity in our economy serves a dual purpose.[4] On the one hand, the activity provides goods or services to a clientele. On the other hand, the activity offers an economic mainstay to the owners of the productive resources used by that activity. Figure 2–1 depicts this dual function schematically.

Figure 2-1 immediately suggests a self-evident but often overlooked tautology that will be helpful in our subsequent discussion. The tautology is the following:

> Every dollar of expenditure on the goods and services yielded by a particular economic activity is automatically transformed into a dollar of income accruing to the owners of the productive resources used in that activity.

On application to the health care sector, for example, this tautology implies the equation

$$\text{National Health Care Expenditure} = \text{National Health Care Income}$$

Figure 2-1.   Economic Sectors as Troughs at Which People Eat.

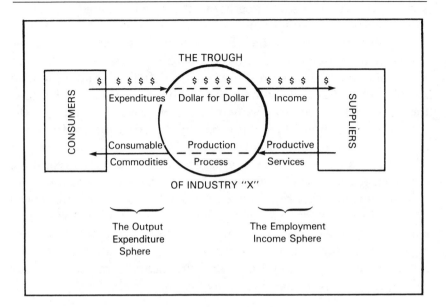

From the tautology follows the further insight that one may analyze the economic activity in question by examining either its output-expenditure sphere (the left-hand side of the figure) or its income-employment sphere (the right-hand side of the figure). Cultural patterns appear to dictate the sphere we select for policy debates. In discussions of the automobile industry, for example, we tend to treat the income-employment function of that industry as its primary social purpose and act accordingly. By contrast, in discussions of the health care sector, we tend to focus strictly on the output-expenditure sphere and to ignore the income-employment sphere. And so it is that we celebrate additional expenditures on automobiles as a sign of economic health, while deploring additional expenditures on hospital care as a sign of economic malady.

In this essay I take temporary leave from the prevailing cultural pattern and focus unabashedly on the income-employment sphere of the health care sector. As Figure 2-1 suggests, it is legitimate, from an analytic viewpoint, to treat the health care sector as one of many alternative troughs to which certain creatures who own productive resources (human labor, land, and capital) come in search of fiscal nourishment. In deference to the elevated status of the health care sector, however, one should perhaps substitute the image of a dinner table for that of a trough, and I shall do so henceforth.

Why the guests at the health care dinner table chose that table rather than an equally laden alternative table—the aerospace table or the hoola-hoop table—is a question best left to psychologists and sociologists. It has to do with intrinsic features of the table other than the fiscal diet served. At this point I merely wish to assert that the search for fiscal nourishment is generally the prime motive for a person's seeking out some dinner table in the economy and that it is neither unrealistic nor offensive to examine the operation even of the health care sector through analysis of its income-employment sphere.

To adopt the novel perspective I propose, we shall obviously need new terminology. Our traditional jargon, tailored as it is to the output-expenditure sphere, just will not do. Table 2-1 presents a modest beginning of the linguistic transformation we shall require. The reader is invited to commit the novel dictionary to memory for our subsequent discussion, and to apply the new terminology to a tradi-

Table 2-1. A New Dictionary for Health Policy Analysts.

Traditional Terminology (based on the service-expenditure facet of the health care sector)	New Terminology (based on the employment-income facet of the health care sector)
1. National health care expenditures	1. National health care incomes
2. The demand for health services	2. The supply of health care incomes
3. The supply of health manpower	3. The demand for health care incomes
4. Containment of health care expenditures	4. Containment of health care incomes
5. Health care cost containment	5. Containment of the income provided per unit of health service
6. Increased efficiency in the production of health services	6. Reduction in employment per unit of health service
7. Federal subsidies to health manpower training	7. Federally stimulated increases in the demand for health care incomes

tional cost containment speech to appreciate more fully the analytic power of the perspective.[5] It is my assertion that we shall understand health policy in the 1980s, and the health care sector's reaction thereto, much better if we learn to substitute the new jargon for traditional terms.

Equipped with these analytic tools, we may now return to the main focus of this essay: the table manners that should be exhibited at the health care feast during the next decade or two. It may be well to begin with a brief look at the past, if only to appreciate why table manners have hitherto received such fleeting attention.

The Health Care Feast: Past and Future

During the past several decades the health care dinner table grew rapidly larger, added many empty chairs, and offered a richer and richer fare. It was widely agreed during the 1950s and 1960s that there was a health personnel shortage all around and that the imperative of national health policy was to bring added guests to the table, whatever the expense.

To entice the added guests, we paid part of their way to the table, through loans and scholarships directly to them and through grants to the institutions that trained them. These policies increased substantially the demand for health care incomes (the supply of health personnel).

To meet this enhanced demand for fiscal nourishment we obviously had to enrich the offerings at the health care dinner table, and this we did—with unprecedented generosity. Table 2-2 illustrates the extent of our generosity. As is shown in line 2b, after adjustment for general price inflation and population growth, our annual appropriations to the health care sector increased by an average annual rate of about 5 percent during the 1970s. These appropriations, it must be noted, were made at a time when real gross national product (GNP) per capita grew by only about 2.5 percent per year.

Our ever larger offerings at the health care dinner table made it possible to seat an ever increasing number of guests at the table and to feed each guest very well indeed. In return for our generosity, these guests comported themselves graciously. There was very little squabbling among the guests, and they treated with courtesy and good care the throngs of patients who brought the fiscal nourishment to table. It was, all in all, a splendid feast.

Table 2-2.   Resource Allocation to the Health Care Sector, United States, 1970–78.

Item	Dollar Expenditure on Health Care		Percentage Increase	
	1970	1978	1970–78	Average Annual Compound Rate
1. National health expenditures (billions of dollars)				
A. Current dollars (undeflated)	74.7	192.6	159	12.6
B. As a percentage of GNP	7.6	9.1		
2. Personal health care expenditures per capita				
A. Current dollars (undeflated)	315.4	753.0	139	11.5
B. Deflated by the implicit price deflator for the GNP	340.9	501.3	47	4.9
C. Deflated by the implicit price deflator for personal health	345.7	456.9	31	3.4

Some of this splendor may disappear from the health care feast in the 1980s. The new administration has declared itself tired of the "coast-to-coast soup line" of which the health care sector has become an ever longer part. Other bearers of fiscal sustenance—for example, the business sector—seem equally fatigued and threaten to be more parsimonious in the future. In short, the supply of health care incomes in the future is unlikely to grow as rapidly as it did during the last decade. The health care table will be lucky to see its share of the national pie grow at all during the next decade, and that pie itself is not growing in size as fast as one would wish.

At the same time, the government continues to send out dinner invitations through direct and indirect subsidies to the training of health professionals and even through continued subsidization of hospital capacity. There may soon come a time when the guests presenting themselves at the health care feast will outnumber the chairs, and when those lucky enough to be seated at the table will scramble for the offerings to be had there. Physicians in ambulatory care, for example, may seek to shoulder aside their fellow guests from the hospital sector by performing one-day ambulatory surgery or one-day ambulatory diagnostic workups hitherto performed in the hospital. The hospital sector may push back by developing more fully its outpatient operation. Next, physicians in ambulatory care may begin to chase away from the table the hungry auxiliary personnel, including physician assistants, whom the governess invited to table. Under current licensure laws—one of the government's more appreciated favors—physicians have the license to chase away these miserables, although the latter may seek to have these licensure laws changed. Finally, there may be shoving matches among duly licensed physicians themselves. The American College of Surgeons, for example, may seek to bar family practitioners from their corner of the table, and the latter may be reluctant to refer patients to any specialist's corner for fear of losing that patient for good.

Initially, of course, such jostling will be accompanied only by hushed murmurs, and these will be not about fiscal sustenance, but about the patient's welfare. Eventually, however, table manners may deteriorate both audibly and visibly, and society will be forced to meet the issue of manners at the health care table head-on. We must then decide who is to enforce good manners at the table, and what book of etiquette is to be used for that purpose. Although these questions have long been settled for most other dinner tables in our economy, we have only just begun to address them in health care.

In the abstract, it can probably be agreed that a good book of etiquette for the health care table should meet at least the following minimal desiderata:

1. It should allow guests free access to the dinner table and prohibit strong ruffians from chasing away daintier guests when the offerings at the table are sparse.
2. It should force the guests at table to treat the bearers of fiscal nourishment—the patients—courteously and with good care. Indeed, the richness of the fare should depend directly on the patients' satisfaction with their treatment.
3. The guests should observe some propriety in determining the size of the portions they scoop for themselves at the table. Heavy eaters who dip their arms up to their elbows into the salad bowl ought to be sanctioned somehow.

Do these desiderata suggest one evidently superior approach to the issue of table manners? Economists may think so, but, in fact at least three alternative approaches have been advanced as the "perfect" solution:

1. Table manners in health care should be defined and enforced by that great governess, the government, who alone can know the common good. The governess will hover over the table at all times. She will plan the menu and the guest list, and generally supervise the deportment at table.
2. Table manners in health care should be defined by the dinner guests themselves, who alone can know the common good in this sector and who will enforce the code of etiquette selflessly through self-regulation, with only occasional help from the great governess (e.g., in determining the seating order at table through licensure).
3. The health care table will be so organized that both the dinner guests and the bearers of fiscal sustenance (the patients) are forced to act out the manners prescribed for a truly competitive market.

It is now said that we have tried approach (1) and that it has failed. This conclusion appears to have emerged after countless conferences on the topic of regulation versus markets. The complaints against the governess have been that she was fickle, often unduly enamored with one or the other group of dinner guests, or just plain unsophisticated in the articulation of rules.

Economists were widely used—and willingly let themselves be used— as a spearhead in the assault on the much despised great governess. Never known for their political savvy, these fighters for economic efficiency generally believed that their relentless attacks on the governess paved the way for approach (3), the economist's vision of a preferred social order. Oddly enough, in its travail the economic brigade was cheered on by the guests at the dinner table—health care providers. That circumstance alone should have given a thoughtful person pause, for obvious reasons.

A competitive market system is, after all, a social arrangement whereby life is made hell for providers to make life cheap and easy for consumers. That this should be the natural order of things is probably obvious only to economists, who are rarely suppliers of anything. Surely where one stands on issues of this sort must depend on where one sits,[6] and where the providers of health care sit on this particular issue is perfectly clear. The question is how economists could ever have regarded health care providers as their natural allies in the campaign for competitive health care markets. Perhaps they thought that health care providers would deem virtually any book of etiquette preferable to that written by the great governess. But somehow I cannot escape the nagging suspicion that, in the end, the economists will have been tested in their good fight—that they were cheered on by providers who expected all along that, once the great governess was slain, they would be able to implement their preferred strategy (2)—that is, that a sort of Platonian health care state with "orderly markets" managed by a highly trained priesthood for the common good would emerge.

With the demise of the big, bad governess, economists may soon find themselves put out to pasture on this issue, unless they muster the strength and the courage to tip lances with the very folks they sought to liberate from the bad beast.[7] In this connection, it is illuminating to read the adventures of our latter day Don Quixote—Professor Alain Enthoven—whose "Does Anyone Want Competition? The Politics of NHI" describes in mournful tones the underwhelming enthusiasm with which the health care sector has responded to his valorous ideas about competition.[8]

On the Rigors of Competitive Markets

To see why the second, and probably much tougher, stage of the battle for competition in health care is now upon us, one need only articulate the conditions that must be met before purists would declare a market freely competitive. A review of these conditions will be particularly instructive for physicians, who have always thought of themselves as the living symbols of free enterprise and who find it difficult to see what more could be done to make their corner of the market more competitive.

Key among the conditions for a competitive market are:

1.   That there be free entry into that market
2.   That consumers be free to choose among alternative providers

These conditions, most any physician will tell you, are clearly met in medicine as long as the great governess keeps out of it. But are they? To gain perspective on this point, let us review what Milton Friedman, the free marketeer par excellence, observes on this particular point. In connection with occupational licensure, Friedman remarks that:

> It is clear that licensure has been at the core of the restriction of entry [into the health care field] and that this involves a heavy social cost, both to the individuals who want to practice medicine but are prevented from doing so and to the public deprived of the medical care it wants to buy and is prevented from buying.[9]

Friedman's more extended analysis of occupational licensure makes clear that he is not concerned solely with entry into the medical profession. By "entry" he has in mind entry into the practice of medicine, even by persons who do not have a formal medical degree. To guarantee the individual the right of entry into medical practice, Friedman would replace the current system of mandatory licensure, which prohibits medical practice by anyone not properly licensed, with mere certification, known technically as "permissive licensure."

Under permissive licensure, a person is prohibited from claiming possession of a professional title unless he or she has been certified to possess the competencies implied by that title. But he or she could still render professional services without the title. Writes Friedman:

> If the argument [for mandatory licensure] is that we [consumers] are too ignorant to judge good practitioners, all that is needed is to make the relevant information available. If, in full knowledge, we still want to go to someone who is not certified, that is our business.[10]

This passage clearly indicates what economists of Friedman's persuasion mean by "free choice among providers." To physicians, the term "free choice" implies the patient's freedom to choose among duly licensed physicians. To a true believer in laissez-faire markets, the term embraces also the freedom to choose medical care from either medical or nonmedical personnel. In practice, the concept would permit two consenting adults—one a dental hygienist and one a consumer—to contract freely for the cleaning or scaling of teeth, with or without a dentist's supervision. It would allow a consumer to consent to the dilation of his or her pupils by an optometrist. It would permit a consenting adult to purchase well-baby care from a pediatric nurse in independent practice. It would allow consumers to have their teeth drilled and filled by dental nurses engaged in independent practice, as in New Zealand. The free marketeer's preferred order would accord patients the right to pick from the entire array of price and quality combinations the market would make available in the absence of mandatory professional licensure. It would never occur to a free marketeer to give physicians the right to limit the consumer's choices in this respect, if only because physicians could not devise such limits free of a direct economic conflict of interest.

Fundamental to the Friedmanesque vision of a freely competitive health care market are two further conditions that must be met:

1. Consumers must be able, technically, to choose rationally among the price and quality options available to them in the health care market.
2. Consumers must have available to them all the information essential to a rational choice.

Serious people sincerely believe that condition (1) is so commonly violated in health care that it is pointless to meet condition (2), and that the Friedmanesque vision of consumer choice itself is laughable. This belief appears to have wide currency among members of the medical profession and, remarkably, among the profession's harshest critics. Naturally, the two groups draw from their belief diametrically opposed policy implications.

To the medical profession it seems self-evident that, if consumers are unable to choose sensibly among alternative price and quality combinations in health care, physicians must presort these combinations for the consumer and eliminate the risky ones from view (through the mechanism of licensure). "Who is better equipped to make such judgments," asks the profession, "than physicians whose technical expertise in these matters is unsurpassed and whose motives are properly constrained by the Hippocratic Oath?" "Who would be the last group on earth one would give this responsibility," retort the critics, "but the very persons who stand to gain financially from the limitations they would impose on consumers' choices?" As economist Paul Feldstein has recently observed:

> It would appear . . . that the concern of the medical profession (as well as of other health professions) with quality is selective. Quality measures that might adversely affect the incomes of their members are opposed, such as reexamination, relicensing, continuing education, and any measures that attempt to monitor the quality of care. The hypothesis that quality measures [such as licensure laws] are instituted to raise the return of practicing physicians appears to be consistent with the position on quality taken by the medical profession.[11]

Obviously, we have here a dilemma that we have solved so far by letting the medical profession have its way. Given an ever growing supply of physicians and society's apparent desire to rechannel resources away from social programs into military and industrial hardware, we may want to consider different solutions. Those who would be loath to leave the matter in the hands of the medical profession propose one of two alternatives. The free marketeers among them, as we have seen, would dump the matter into consumers' laps in the belief—and a belief it is—that consumers are quite able to fend for themselves. Those who do not share that belief—that is, those who judge consumers incompetent to choose intelligently in health care—would presumably leave the matter in the hands of the great governess. To whom else could one turn?

ON GOVERNMENT-REGULATED COMPETITION

I began this essay with a jubilant quotation from a medical journal according to which laissez-faire and medicine go together like horse and carriage or like love and marriage. To understand more fully that journal's joy, I depicted, in the second section, the precise meaning of the terms "deregulation," "laissez-faire," and "competitive markets." In the search for purity, I turned to the writings of Milton Friedman, widely acknowledged as one of the deans of the free-market school. After exploring Friedman's vision of a freely competitive health care market, I conclude that celebrants either endow the technical term "laissez-faire" with an unconventional interpretation or belong to the chain-and-leather crowd. Friedman's vision should send shivers up the spine of any straight-thinking physician.

To crystallize their attitudes on this issue, readers may wish to complete, and possibly extend, the litmus test for the true marketeer given in Figure 2–2. If the noes predominate among the answers, the reader obviously does not favor a freely competitive health care market, as true believers understand that term. He or she favors a regulated market environment, one in which the forces of competition are reined in for specific purposes. He or she is then left with the following questions:

1. What limits to free competition should be drawn in the health care sector?
2. Who shall set and enforce these limits?

We shall be debating the first of these questions throughout the coming decade and reach, at best, an uneasy compromise. As to the second question, I have no doubt that we shall ultimately settle once again on the great governess. We were rather silly to debate the issue of table manners in recent years under the heading "Government Regulation *versus* Competition." The options actually before us were government regulation *for*:

1. Direct government control of decisions in the health care sector
2. Government-controlled competition in the health care sector
3. Complete laissez-faire competition in the health care sector

Figure 2-2.   Litmus Test for True Marketeers.

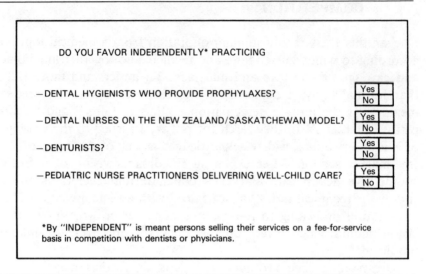

DO YOU FAVOR INDEPENDENTLY* PRACTICING

—DENTAL HYGIENISTS WHO PROVIDE PROPHYLAXES?   Yes ☐ / No ☐

—DENTAL NURSES ON THE NEW ZEALAND/SASKATCHEWAN MODEL?   Yes ☐ / No ☐

—DENTURISTS?   Yes ☐ / No ☐

—PEDIATRIC NURSE PRACTITIONERS DELIVERING WELL-CHILD CARE?   Yes ☐ / No ☐

*By "INDEPENDENT" is meant persons selling their services on a fee-for-service basis in competition with dentists or physicians.

Here it may be noted parenthetically that even the free markets envisaged by classical economists—and by Friedman and his disciples today—generally cannot flourish in the absence of vigorous government supervision. There has to be a statutory framework that preserves the conditions essential to the proper functioning of free markets—for example, rules on the dissemination of accurate information, and rules prohibiting anticompetitive collusion among agents in the market.[12]

It seems unlikely that health care providers would favor a move in the direction of option (3). On the contrary, I suspect that, if health care providers were truly put to the test of living under raw, laissez-faire competition, most of them would yearn once again for the more orderly world of option (1)—a world, after all, the regulated have always somehow learned to control in the end.

The current mood in Congress, and in the new administration, seems to be a swing away from (1) and toward (2). The task at hand, therefore, is the development of government regulations for carefully controlled competition in the health care market. To appreciate the complexity of that task, one need only enumerate the many government regulations that will be required to make Professor Enthoven's consumer choice health plan (CCHP) operational. A foretaste of these regulations can be had in the several procompetitive health insurance bills now before Congress. The regulations in these bills are but an augury of things likely to be required upon full implementation of the CCHP concept.

What overall social objectives might one posit for government-regulated competition in the health care sector? The bulk of the discussion on this question has focused on three goals:

1.   The arrangement should bestow on patients high-quality care and leave them satisfied.
2.   The arrangement should encourage a careful juxtaposition of costs and benefits each time services are rendered to patients.
3.   The arrangement should slow the rapid growth in health care expenditures.

Here it may be thought that achievement of the second goal automatically implies achievement of the third, but that is not necessarily so. Indeed, one can question the legitimacy of the third goal altogether, as I have in the past.[13]

Controlled competitive forces could be brought to bear on health care decisions at: (1) the nexus between patient and health care providers and (2) the nexus between patient and third-party payer.

The first of these is emphasized in the traditional catastrophic health insurance plans—for example, Martin Feldstein's maximum liability risk insurance (MLRI) plan. The central idea underlying these plans is that cost-effectiveness in health care will be achieved only if patients themselves have a direct financial stake in efficient health care delivery. This financial stake is assured through heavy cost sharing, up to a maximum risk exposure per year. Obviously these schemes place a good deal of trust on the ability of consumers to fend for themselves in the health care market and to force competition on price and quality among health care providers. In fact, so strong is the implicit faith in the market power of consumers that these plans rarely suggest any explicit measures policymakers might suggest to enforce competitive behavior on the part of health care providers. Perhaps this oversight—or undue faith in the consumer—has contributed to the rather lukewarm reception catastrophic insurance plans have received among health experts.

The second nexus is, of course, the prime focus of Alain Enthoven's CCHP, which, in turn, has spawned what has come to be called the "procompetitive health bills" now before Congress.[14] The central idea underlying these plans is that cost sharing by patients, while helpful at the margin, is unlikely to furnish the countervailing market power required to force providers into competitive, cost-effective behavior. To encourage such behavior, the CCHP would encourage the formation of closed-panel insurance plans in which a limited set of providers ally themselves with a given plan which in turn sells comprehensive insurance coverage to patients. There would emerge, it is hoped, competing high-cost and low-cost panels, permitting patients to trade off certain perceived dimensions of quality—for example, the degree of freedom to choose among physicians, or highly resource-intensive treatments—for the sake of lower insurance costs. Cost sharing may be a feature of particular plans, but it is not the central workhorse of the concept. The central workhorses are, on the one hand, competition among closed-panel plans for insured members and, on the other, competition among health care providers for alliances with particular plans.

As already noted, the reception of the CCHP plans by health care providers, by consumers and by the business world in general has so far been mixed and, by and large, cautious to unenthusiastic.[15] In some quarters, there is uncertainty over the precise set of rules and regulations implied by the idea. In other quarters, there is probably great certainty about the deleterious effect this type of plan could have on entrenched economic positions. Other speakers at this conference will address these problems in detail, and I shall not dwell on them here.

There is, however, one other goal which neither of the procompetitive insurance plans address explicitly: the development of opportunities for entrepreneurs. It is rarely mentioned in our debates on health policy because the goals traditionally posed for government-regulated competition in health care usually involve only the quality and cost of the output. As I have argued earlier, however, there is another important function performed by the nation's health care sector: the provision of economic opportunities to the owners of productive resources.

One can argue that, wherever technically feasible, a given economic sector should seek to maximize the range of economic opportunities it offers members of society. By "economic opportunity" is meant not only the ability to earn an income in the health care sector, but also the ability to do so on the terms preferred by the recipient.

The freedom to exercise entrepreneurship in health care is now severely circumscribed. It is restricted to the owners of inpatient facilities, pharmacies, and licenses to practice medicine and dentistry. The desirability of delegating tasks from dental or medical to paradental or paramedical personnel is typically assessed, even by policymakers, strictly in terms of the impact of this delegation on the quality and cost of health services. If substantial cost savings at constant levels of quality cannot be demonstrated, the case for task delegation is closed. In thinking about competitive markets, however, one might inquire also into the desirability of offering, through task delegation, added outlets for entrepreneurial talent, even if the cost savings from the patient's viewpoint seem modest. We should explore the social merits and demerits of permitting independent paramedical and paradental practice. Although this is unquestionably a proposal fraught with a problem or two, I consider it worthy of open debate.[16]

CONCLUDING REMARKS

For most of the postwar period, commentators on the American health care sector tended to describe it as rather backward by international standards—a cottage industry that kept our infant mortality rate just above that of Portugal. Actually, that image has always been misleading. Although our health insurance system still leaves too much fiscal agony at the fringes and saddles enormous loads of paperwork on almost everyone, it is the complement of a highly innovative health care delivery system—a system that is advanced by international standards, not only in medical technology, but also in the technology of health care organization and marketing.

In few if any other nations does one find the sheer range of alternative production and marketing schemes in health care we have come to take for granted in this country. Indeed, the statutes of most other nations would not even permit experimentation with alternative delivery systems such as HMOs or individual practice associations (IPAs). And few if any other nations have been quite so bold as the United States in experimenting with competitive market forces in the organization of health care delivery. On this score alone, the United States health care sector will undoubtedly attract many foreign observers to these shores in the decade to come.

For American observers of the health care sector, the coming decade is apt to be one of the most fascinating in memory, as corporate, financial, and managerial muscle begins to penetrate hitherto tranquil health care markets, and as the competitive scramble for the health care dollar unfolds. Health care providers undoubtedly will be uncomfortable. The question is: How much discomfort is enough and how much is too much?

Economists are of the persuasion that a constant threat from competitors and the daily struggle to protect one's economic flanks bring out the best in people. The only way to build one's defenses, the reasoning goes, is to please one's customers. And thus, spoke Adam Smith, is private avarice converted to the common good.

The argument has enormous intuitive appeal when applied to the markets for shoelaces and hoola-hoops. Here we can be sure that, the more competitive pressure there is on the supplier, the better the customer will fare. Curiously, Adam Smith himself stopped short of applying this line of reasoning to physicians:

> The wages of labour vary according to the small or great trust which must be reposed in the workmen. . . . We trust our health to the physician; our fortune and sometimes our life and reputation to the lawyer and attorney. Such confidence could not safely be reposed in people of a very mean or low condition. Their reward must be such, therefore, as may give them that rank in the society which so important trust requires. The long time and the great expence which must be laid out in their education, when combined with this circumstance, necessarily enhance still further the price of their labour.[17]

Adam Smith quite clearly believes that ethical conduct—including medical ethics—is a luxury good of which proportionally more will be consumed as income rises. One doubts, therefore, that Adam Smith would favor the immersion of medical practitioners into daily cutthroat competition with their peers.

By contrast, Milton Friedman has the following observation on this point:

> When [physicians] explicitly comment on the desirability of limiting numbers to raise incomes they will always justify the policy on the grounds that if "too" many people are let in, this will lower their incomes so that they will be driven to resort to unethical practices in order

to earn a "proper" income. The only way, they argue, in which ethical practices can be maintained is by keeping people at a standard of income which is adequate to the merits and needs of the medical profession. I must confess that this has always seemed to me objectionable on both ethical and factual grounds. It is extraordinary that leaders of medicine should proclaim publicly that they and their colleagues must be paid to be ethical. And if it were so, I doubt that the price would have any limit. There seems little correlation between poverty and honesty. One would rather expect the opposite: dishonesty may not always pay but surely it sometimes does.[18]

Milton Friedman, then, believes that medical ethics would be unlikely to be eroded by fierce price competition among physicians. Presumably he would argue that, the fiercer the competition among physicians, the better their patients will fare.

Once again two prominent economists disagree. We are faced here with an empirical question, and one to which, quite candidly, I do not have an answer. I can but expose the problem for debate and hope to come away properly instructed.

NOTES

1. Susan Stone, "For Medicine, Deregulation Is on the Way," *American College of Physicians Observer* 1, nos. 1 and 2 (January/February 1981): 5.
2. See Milton Friedman, *Capitalism and Freedom* (Chicago: University of Chicago Press, 1962), Chapter 9, "Occupational Licensure."
3. To illustrate, in the state of Washington feuding ophthalmologists and optometrists are currently carrying their squabble to the state legislators. The state's ophthalmologists there seek to enlist the coercive power of state government to bar optometrists from their economic turf.
4. This section draws on several of my earlier papers, especially, "Health Care Expenditures and the Economics of the Health Care Trough" (Paper presented to the National Health Leadership Conference on American Health Policy, Washington, D.C., April 29-30, 1976).
5. A speech beginning "We must reduce health care expenditures through greater efficiency in the delivery of hospital care" becomes: "We must eliminate some health care incomes by reducing the employment opportunities per patient day in the hospital." These are analytically equivalent statements.

6.   The famous Rufus Miles law.
7.   Their strength is already being sapped by deep cuts in the budgets for health services research.
8.   C.M. Lindsay, ed., *New Directions in Public Health Care* (New Brunswick, N.J.: Transaction Books, 1980), pp. 227-50.
9.   Friedman, *Capitalism and Freedom*, p. 155.
10. *Ibid.*, p. 149.
11. Paul J. Feldstein, *Health Care Economics* (New York: John Wiley and Sons, 1979), p. 327.
12. Ironically, but certainly not surprisingly, the Federal Trade Commission came under severe attack from the private sector just as the thrust of its activities shifted from direct control of production and marketing decisions to concern merely over full disclosure of pertinent information.
13. See U.E. Reinhardt, "Health Care Expenditures and the Economics of the Health Care Trough" (1976), and "Health Manpower Policy and the Cost of Health Care," *Nursing Dimensions* 7, no. 3 (Fall 1979): 60-68.
14. Both Richard Schweiker, Secretary of Health and Human Services, and David Stockman, director of the Office of Management and Budget had, as legislators, introduced procompetitive health bills. Similar legislation has been introduced by Congressman Richard Gephardt, Senator David Durenberger, and Senator Orrin Hatch.
15. See Alain Enthoven, "How Interested Groups Have Responded to a Proposal for Economic Competition in Health Services," *The American Economic Review* 70, no. 2: 142.
16. For a more extensive exploration of this issue, see U.E. Reinhardt "Health Manpower Substitution in Dental Care," *Journal of Dental Education* (in press).
17. Adam Smith, *The Wealth of Nations* (New York: Random House, 1937), p. 105.
18. See Friedman, *Capitalism and Freedom*, p. 152.

DISCUSSION

Alex McMahon: There can be no question that we treat expenditures for health care differently from expenditures for automobiles or transportation. We think about them differently, we analyze them differently, and Uwe Reinhardt asked why.

It seems to me that the reason why is the pool. Expenditures for health care are made from a pool, and there are two big contributors to that pool: business for its employees and government for the poor and the elderly. There's no such pool for automobiles or transportation. If transportation were a fringe benefit, instead of an individual responsibility, we'd be having the same discussions about transportation that we are having about health care. The big payers are saying, "You have outrun our ability to finance care for the aged and indigent and for employees. Do something."

Uwe Reinhardt: Let me answer business first. I think it really rather unfortunate that we chose to finance health care through payroll taxes. Doing it that way totally distorts the way decisions get made, particularly when fringe benefits such as employer-paid health insurance premiums come out of the recipient's pretax income. I can well understand why business wants to find another way to finance health care. After all, American business has to compete with companies from other countries (e.g., Canada and Japan) where health care may be financed differently.

I consider the government's objections less legitimate. In a speech he gave in Florida shortly after he won the election in 1976, Jimmy Carter said that he always found people willing to pay more taxes for one thing—health care. A recent survey of Canadians pointed to the same conclusion. When asked what they thought of the various uses made of their tax money, Canadians said that spending for health care was one use that seemed worthwhile. So if Stockman decides that we should have less health care, I'm not so sure he will have the people with him.

Alain Enthoven: Why is the cost of health care a problem? First, because governments—federal, state, and local—are together paying about 42 percent of the total, and that's creating problems at every level, beginning with deficits at the federal level, which cause inflation. At the state and local levels, expenditures for other purposes are being cut back to allow for the increase in Medicaid, health care programs, fringe benefits for government employees, and so on. And, while there may be no evidence that people want to pay less for health care or for health insurance, it is pretty clear that people want to pay less taxes.

Second is the loss in efficiency that results from the way the financing mechanisms work and the incentives that they create. In the health care market, we are not talking about transactions between consenting adults choosing how to spend their own money. Instead, we are talking about transactions between providers and consumers taking place in the absence of significant financial restraints on either, and I cannot help but think that that ties in with a widespread recognition that there is a great deal of waste in our health care system. Some of us manage to live very happily as members of organized medical care systems that seem to do the job even though they hospitalize people half as much and cost, overall, 10 percent to 40 percent less. Why is it that Medicare beneficiaries in New York spend twice as much time in the hospital as Medicare beneficiaries in California? Is it because New Yorkers are twice as sick? I don't think anybody around this table thinks that. I think it is because the health care system in New York is more wasteful.

Uwe Reinhardt: I think it is true that we are tired of taxes in this country even though, by international standards, we are not that heavily taxed. But the fact that we are against more taxes in general doesn't mean that we are against more taxes for health care, and I was really talking about that. Even so, you may be right. Perhaps I am mistaken in assuming that people are prepared to tolerate further increases in Medicare and Medicaid expenditures.

I also think that you are right about the cost of inefficiency. I share your hypothesis that, if people were to pay directly for health care, their expenditures on health care would go down. I am not so certain that merely the competitive marketing of *health insurance* will act as a constraint on overall expenditures. That remains an empirical question. For all we know, when facing the choice, most households who can will opt for the Cadillac policies, and health care providers would probably cheer them on in that choice. Let us wait and see.

3 REGULATION OF HOSPITAL COSTS: THE EVIDENCE ON PERFORMANCE

Karen Davis

In recent years it has become fashionable to argue that regulation cannot control health care costs and that the only way to curb excessive increases is to restore competition to the health care marketplace. Rarely has the discussion of competition and regulation been guided by empirical evidence. Rather it has rested on theory, faith, and ideological persuasion.

The existing empirical evidence is spotty. Most regulatory approaches were instituted in the middle and late 1970s. Given the lags in data generation and the time required for detailed analysis, definitive conclusions about the efficiency of regulation are several years away. Competitive approaches are largely untested. Except for the experience of health maintenance organizations, which is well documented, little is known about the possible effect of shifts toward competition in employer health insurance or in Medicare and Medicaid.

There is agreement, however, that the health care market exhibits a basic lack of restraint. In the absence of regulation or reforms restoring competition to the market, spiralling health care costs are a virtual certainty. Given the implications of these cost increases for federal and state governments and for businesses, the debate about regulation and competition is a serious matter. Before deciding which approach to choose, we should determine the impact each approach is likely to have, and when.

This paper analyzes the current evidence on trends in health care costs, the effectiveness of regulatory approaches, and the promise of competition proposals. It concludes with recommendations that propose reforming some regulatory approaches, abolishing others, restructuring incentives through reimbursement reform, and supporting organized delivery systems that serve as an alternative to traditional forms of health care delivery.

TRENDS IN HOSPITAL COSTS

In the absence of regulation or effective competition, hospital costs are certain to increase rapidly. There are no effective constraints to rising costs. Instead, the health care market is made to order for inflation because:

- Over 90 percent of all hospital revenues come from third-party sources, rather than directly from patients. In most markets, it is the limit on the consumer's willingness and ability to pay which enforces restraint on buyers and sellers. In the hospital market, this limit does not operate.
- Third parties who pay for hospital care do not play an active role in influencing what services are bought from whom or in negotiating the prices to be paid for services rendered. Instead, public programs such as Medicare and Medicaid pay whatever costs hospitals incur. Blue Cross and Blue Shield plans do not pay on the basis of costs, but they rarely question the rates set by hospitals, and they pay all or a fixed percentage of any charges assessed. Exceptions to these general practices are few, and they are largely the result of regulatory intervention.
- Physicians generally decide whether to hospitalize patients, how long patients should remain in the hospital, and what services they should receive while hospitalized. Existing economic incentives encourage physicians to provide and order more rather than less services and more rather than less costly services. The more procedures physicians perform, the more they are reimbursed. The more resources hospitals devote to the provision of care, the more income physicians can earn from hospital-based services.
- Patients have little information on which to base decisions regarding hospital care. Hospitalization frequently occurs at a time of

stress and dependency when patients have good reason not to challenge the judgment of those on whom they depend.

The impact of these conditions on hospital costs has been apparent for some time. It is certain that hospital costs began to rise significantly with the growth of private insurance; Medicare and Medicaid have served to extend this trend.[1] The only interruption was created by the Economic Stabilization Program (ESP), which imposed nationwide wage and price controls, including special restraints on hospital care, between 1971 and 1974. Taylor has demonstrated that major reductions in hospital cost increases occurred during this period.[2]

In the analysis of trends in hospital costs, it is important to identify and take into account the effect of inflation in the economy that drives up the unit cost of goods and services purchased as inputs by the hospital. The unit cost of hospital inputs is captured by a price index referred to as the hospital market basket price index. This index is a weighted average of hospital input prices, with weights corresponding to the fraction of total hospital costs accounted for by each type of input. Adjustment for these factors makes clear that there have been brief periods of abatement in the growth of hospital costs.

As shown in Table 3-1, hospital costs increased by 14.8 percent annually in the period from 1971 to 1977. This period includes the years 1971 to 1974, when the Economic Stabilization Program kept increases very low, and the years 1975 to 1977, when the hospitals recouped any increases foregone during ESP. The rate of increase over the entire period was similar to the rate of increase during the late 1960s. In 1978, hospital cost increases slowed to 12.8 percent, then turned upward to 13.4 percent in 1979, to 15.7 percent in the first half of 1980, and to 17.8 percent in the third quarter of 1980.

More important than the overall increase, however, is the increase over and above increases in the hospital market basket. As shown in Table 3-1, hospital market basket prices have increased in recent years, reflecting accelerating inflation in the economy as a whole. But between 1971 and 1977 hospital costs increased by 5.2 percent more than increases in the hospital market basket and population growth. This additional increase, commonly called the net service intensity increase, reflects the cost increase associated with the provision of additional services per day of hospital care, with increases in the hos-

Table 3-1. Percentage Increases in Community Hospital
Expenses and Hospital Market Basket Index, 1970-80.

	Hospital Expenses	Hospital Market Basket	Population Growth	Net Service Intensity
1971-77 average annual increase	14.8	8.8	0.8	5.2
1978	12.8	8.2	0.8	3.8
1979	13.4	9.9	0.8	2.7
1980				
I	15.7	12.3	0.8	2.6
II	15.7	13.1	0.8	1.8
III	17.8	12.3	0.8	4.7

Source: American Hospital Association, Panel indicator data. U.S. Department of Health and Human Services, Office of the deputy assistant secretary for planning and evaluation/health— Market basket data.

pital patient days per capita, and with changes in the efficiency of the provision of hospital services. If hospital utilization per capita increases, net service intensity will be higher. If hospitals improve productivity or efficiency, net service intensity will be lower. If hospitals add technology that expands the number or complexity of services provided per patient day, net service intensity will be higher.

Table 3-1 indicates that the increase in net service intensity dropped from its 1971 to 1977 average of 5.2 percent to 3.8 percent in 1978, 2.7 percent in 1979, and 1.8 percent in the second quarter of 1980. The third quarter of 1980, however, shows a marked swing upward— with an overall increase in hospital costs of 17.8 percent and a net service intensity increase of 4.7 percent. If these trends continue, the rate of increase in hospital costs will return to historical levels or go even higher.

Various explanations of recent trends have been suggested. In April 1977, the Carter administration introduced a hospital cost containment bill to control rising hospital costs. This bill was seriously considered by Congress and passed in the Senate in 1978. The bill was reintroduced in the Ninety-sixth Congress in March 1979, passed by the two House committees with jurisdiction, and defeated by the full House in the fall of 1979. The possibility of favorable action continued through the first half of 1980 as Congress grappled with a budget reconciliation bill to achieve significant savings in the federal budget. It is possible that the slowdown in hospital cost increases in 1978, 1979, and the first half of 1980 may reflect fear of hospital cost containment legislation. Conversely, the conclusive defeat of the legislation and the shifting political winds of the 1980 presidential campaign may have led to a relaxation of restraint.

Some insight into the moderation of hospital cost increases and the acceleration that followed can be gained by reviewing trends in hospital utilization (Table 3-2). Over the period from 1970 to 1977 hospital inpatient days increased at an annual rate of 1.2 percent. In 1978 and 1979, the increase in hospital patient days fell below 1.2 percent. But in 1980 hospital patient days increased at an annual rate of 2.4 percent during the first quarter, 2.7 percent during the second quarter, and 3.5 percent during the third quarter.

Some changes in utilization are clearly beyond the control of hospital administrators and physicians. Births, for example, increased more between 1978 and the present than between 1971 and 1977. Births, however, account for only about 10 percent of hospital admissions, and they are relatively inexpensive cases. Outpatient visits increased at a much lower rate, perhaps because of an expanding physician supply, improved access to ambulatory care at publicly funded, free-standing ambulatory care centers, or an effort by hospitals to reduce a less "profitable" patient care activity. Other changes, however, such as the overall slowing of admissions and surgical rates in 1978 and their marked acceleration after that time may reflect hospital and medical staff policy to slow cost trends in response to public pressure and congressional consideration of hospital cost containment legislation.

Trends in hospital expenses per patient day are also revealing. As shown in Table 3-3, the average annual increase in hospital expense per patient day (adjusted for out-patient care) was 12.9 percent for the period from 1971 to 1977. In 1978, this rate of increase slowed to 12.1 percent, to 11.5 percent in 1979, and to 10.7 percent in the first quarter of 1980. In the third quarter of 1980, however, hospital costs per patient day were increasing at an annual rate of 13.7 percent. Deflating hospital expenses per adjusted patient day by the hospital market basket price index, we find real increases in hospital expenses per day of care of 3.6 percent in 1971–77, 3.6 percent in 1978, and 1.4 percent in 1979.

Table 3-2 Percentage Changes in Community Hospital Utilization, 1970–80.

	Inpatient Days	Admissions	Outpatient Visits	Births	Surgical Operations
1970–77 average annual increase	1.2	2.3	6.4	–1.1	3.0
1978	0.7	1.5	3.1	1.8	1.7
1979	0.9	1.9	–0.5	3.5	3.5
1980:					
I	2.4	3.0	1.1	3.8	3.6
II	2.7	3.2	1.8	3.2	3.6
III	3.5	2.7	3.1	4.2	4.6

Source: American Hospital Association, Panel Indicator data.

Table 3-3.   Percentage Increases in Community Hospital Expenses per Patient Day, 1970-80.

	Adjusted Expenses per Patient Day	Hospital Expenses per Adjusted Patient Day Deflated by Market Basket
1971-77: average annual increase	12.9	3.6
1978	12.1	3.6
1979	11.5	1.4
1980		
I	10.7	not available
II	13.1	not available
III	13.7	not available

Source: American Hospital Association, Panel Indicator data. U.S. Department of Health and Human Services, Office of the deputy assistant secretary for planning and evaluation/health.

Another explanation for recent trends in hospital costs is that hospitals have been responding to requests for voluntary restraint by both the hospital industry and the Carter administration. In December 1977, the hospital industry, the American Medical Association, business, consumers, and the Blue Cross and Blue Shield Association formed the Voluntary Effort (VE) and set voluntary goals for increases in hospital costs. As shown in Table 3-4, the VE urged a 2 percent deceleration from the 1977 rate of increase (15.6 percent) in 1978, and another 2 percent deceleration in 1979. Hospitals successfully met the 13.6 percent goal for 1978, but they did not meet the 11.6 percent goal for 1979. The VE argued that the acceleration of inflation in the overall economy was responsible for this failure, and that hospital performance should be adjusted for inflation.

The Carter administration also issued voluntary guidelines for the hospital industry as part of its wage and price guidelines for the whole economy. In December 1978, the administration called for a 1979 increase set at 1.8 percent above hospital market basket increases, or a goal of 11.7 percent in 1979. Hospital industry performance fell considerably short of this goal.

In 1980, by coincidence, the goals of the hospital industry and the Carter administration were approximately the same. The Carter ad-

Table 3-4. Community Hospital Cost Performance, 1978-80 (%).

	Hospital Expenses	HHS-COWPS Guidelines	VE Goal
1978	12.8	—	13.6
1979	13.4	11.7	11.6
1980			
I	15.7	14.1	a
II	15.7	14.9	a
III	17.8	14.1	a

[a]VE goal in 1980 is a 1.5 percent real deceleration in hospital inpatient expenses from 1979.

Source: American Hospital Association, Panel Indicator data. Voluntary Effort statements. U.S. Department of Health and Human Services, Office of the deputy assistant secretary for planning and evaluation/health.

ministration goal was again 1.8 percent more than the hospital market basket; the VE goal was 1.5 percent real deceleration in 1980 from 1979. Both prescribed a net service intensity increase of approximately 1.0 percent in 1980 (1.2 percent in the case of VE). It is already clear that the industry will fail by a wide margin to meet this goal.

Medicare cost reports for the period from January 1979 to March 1980 provide some insight into the responses of different types of hospitals to the call for voluntary restraint. As shown in Table 3-5, hospitals with accounting periods ending during this period had increases of 2.6 percent over the Carter administration guidelines. Hospitals performing the best were state and local governmental hospitals, teaching hospitals, and moderately large hospitals (those with 405 to 684 beds). The worst performers were for-profit hospitals, which exceeded the guideline by a margin of 4.7 percent. That is scarcely surprising, of course. It seems reasonable that those hospitals under the budgetary control of other institutions, such as governmental hospitals and teaching hospitals, would respond best to the call for voluntary action, while those hospitals with the most independence and the least to gain, such as for-profit hospitals, might respond least well.

Whether the deceleration in hospital costs during 1978 and 1979 was a reaction to the threat of hospital cost containment legislation or a public-spirited response to the call for voluntary restraint, the

Table 3-5. Excess of Hospital Expense Increase over Department of Health and Human Services—Council on Wage and Price Standardization (HHS-COWPS) Guidelines by Type of Hospital, Accounting Year, January 1979 to March 1980.

Type of Hospital	Excess above HHS-COWPS Guideline (%)
All hospitals	2.6
By control	
Nonprofit	2.7
For-profit	4.7
Government	1.6
By location	
SMSA[a]	2.5
Non-SMSA	2.9
By teaching status	
Teaching	1.5
Nonteaching	2.8
By bed size	
1–100	2.6
101–404	3.1
405–684	1.5
685+	2.8

[a]Standard metropolitan statistical area.

Source: U.S. Department of Health and Human Services, Health Care Financing Administration, Report on Hospital Compliance with Administration Guidelines on Increases in Hospital Expenditures, second quarter 1980.

most recent data give cause for alarm. The rate of increase in hospital costs greeting the incoming Reagan administration is equal to that which greeted the Carter administration, and it is likely to have equally serious consequences for the federal budget and the economy.

REGULATORY APPROACHES: THE EVIDENCE ON PERFORMANCE

The debate about the relative merits of regulation and competition is not known for its specificity. The evil of regulation and the promise of competition are easier to convey as broad concepts than as specific programs. When applied to the health industry, the terms somehow lose their precise meanings. "Promoting competition in the health care sector," for example, typically means increasing the patient's share of medical bills and health insurance premiums, and not reducing barriers to entry, enforcing antitrust laws, or improving consumer information.

Hospitals are regulated in many ways, but those who would "reduce the burden" of regulation are usually complaining about one of three programs: state hospital rate setting or cost commissions; certificate-of-need programs that review the necessity of hospital capital expenditures; and professional standards review organizations (PSROs), which review the necessity of hospital inpatient days for Medicare and Medicaid patients.

State Cost Commission

Regulation of hospital costs by state cost commissions is a relatively new phenomenon. Although a number of states passed enabling legislation in the early 1970s, most state programs did not initiate regulatory activities until 1975.[3] It is scarcely surprising that some studies using data from 1975 and 1976 did not find significant effects of state cost commissions (for example, see Sloan and Steinwald[4]). Other analyses found that state programs reduced the rate of increase in hospital costs by 1 to 4 percent per year.[5]

Studies using more current data have found that state cost commissions have had a marked impact on the rate of increases in hospital costs. Biles[6] et al. find that, for the period from 1975 to 1978, states with rate-setting programs averaged annual increases of 11.2 percent in hospital costs, while states without programs experienced increases of 14.3 percent. A U.S. General Accounting Office (GAO) study found similar effects and concluded that hospital rate regulation offers promise as a means of restraining future cost increases.[7] GAO recommended that Medicare participation in state hospital rate regulation programs be expanded because they provide strong incentives for improved hospital management.

The sustained performance of states with rate-setting programs over the years from 1976 to 1979 is documented in data collected by the American Hospital Association: eight states with mandatory rate-setting programs averaged annual rates of increase 3.4 percent to 6.0 percent below those of states without such programs (see Table 3–6).

Table 3-6. Percentage Increases in Hospital Expenses, Eight Rate-setting States and All Other States, 1976-79.

	1976	1977	1978	1979
United States	16.1	14.2	12.6	13.4
Eight rate-setting states	13.1	9.8	8.6	10.8
Connecticut	16.3	11.4	10.5	9.9
Maryland	17.2	11.8	12.3	14.8
Massachusetts	13.7	13.7	7.1	9.6
New Jersey	15.4	11.8	8.7	11.4
New York	9.5	6.2	7.2	10.1
Rhode Island	11.7	11.1	8.6	11.7
Washington	17.1	15.1	11.6	12.9
Wisconsin	19.6	12.3	12.6	12.0
All other states	17.1	15.8	14.0	14.2

Source: American Hospital Association, Annual Hospital Statistics.

Medicare cost report data for hospital accounting periods ending between January 1979 and March 1980 also demonstrate that hospital cost increases are more moderate in states with rate-setting programs. During this period, hospital costs increased 11.7 percent in the eight rate-setting states and 14.0 percent in states without such programs.[8] Furthermore, a higher proportion of hospitals in rate-setting states were within the Carter administration voluntary guidelines. In states with commissions, 53 percent of hospitals achieved compliance with the guidelines, compared with 39 percent in other states.

It is always possible that the effect of state rate-setting commissions will be vitiated by political pressure or by the cleverness of hospitals. But the experience to date is fairly conclusive that state rate-setting commissions can and do have a marked impact on rising hospital costs.

Certificate of Need

A second major regulatory effort aimed at curbing increases in hospital costs is the certificate-of-need program. It is the regulatory arm of the health-planning program, which plans the growth and allocation of health resources at the local level. The 1974 Health Planning and Resources Development Act required that each state enact certificate-of-need legislation meeting federal standards. Final regulations

Table 3-7. State Estimates of Hospital Bed Surpluses, 1978 and 1976.

State	1976 Excess	1978 Excess[a]	Change in Excess: 1976 to 1978	Percentage Change
Alabama	3,207	3,290	+83	2.6
Alaska	(685)	(815)		
Arizona	(711)	(832)		
Arkansas	1,639	1,447	−192	−11.7
California	(3,124)	(4,703)		
Colorado	749	297	−452	−60.3
Connecticut	(1,544)	(1,352)		
Delaware	(276)	(154)		
District of Columbia	2,220	2,184	−36	−1.6
Florida	8,226	8,391	+165	2.0
Georgia	2,199	3,451	+1,252	56.9
Hawaii	(938)	(1,365)		
Idaho	(153)	(678)		
Illinois	10,490	11,063	+573	5.5
Indiana	2,336	2,154	−182	−7.8
Iowa	5,331	4,131	−1200	−22.5
Kansas	3,831	3,044	−787	−20.5
Kentucky	1,090	846	−244	−22.4
Louisiana	2,248	2,096	−152	−6.8
Maine	659	235	−424	−64.3
Maryland	(2,979)	(2,698)		
Massachusetts	3,094	3,243	+149	4.8
Michigan	3,879	3,007	−872	−22.5
Minnesota	7,773	4,822	−2,951	−38.0
Mississippi	2,371	1,804	−567	−23.9
Missouri	7,517	7,631	+114	1.5
Montana	881	365	−516	−58.6
Nebraska	3,302	1,933	−1,369	−41.5
Nevada	144	(28)	−144	−100.0
New Hampshire	65	(187)	−65	−100.0
New Jersey	758	308	−450	−59.4
New Mexico	(818)	(1,208)		
New York	12,588	7,762	−4,826	−38.3
North Carolina	(143)	403	+403	—
North Dakota	1,691	1,417	−274	−16.2
Ohio	6,863	7,863	+1,000	14.6
Oklahoma	1,614	1,684	+70	4.3

Oregon	(253)	(696)		
Pennsylvania	9,033	8,493	−540	−6.0
Rhode Island	(241)	(185)		
South Carolina	(953)	(886)		
South Dakota	1,060	828	−232	−21.9
Tennessee	6,271	5,778	−493	−7.9
Texas	8,314	8,511	+197	2.4
Utah	(994)	(1,281)		
Vermont	360	21	−339	−94.2
Virginia	7	(458)	−7	−100.0
Washington	(2,492)	(3,050)		
West Virginia	3,263	2,589	−674	−20.7
Wisconsin	5,885	3,273	−2,612	−44.4
Wyoming	152	(79)	−152	−100.0
Total	131,110	114,364	−16,746	
	(15,804)	(20,655)		

aParentheses indicate deficits of hospital beds.

were published in 1977, and states were given until 1980 (later extended to 1981) to create acceptable programs.

Some preliminary evaluations have been conducted. The most prominent of these studies was performed by Policy Analysis, Inc. The evaluation is thorough, but it is based on data from years ending in 1976, and it cannot shed any light on the effectiveness of the federally mandated certificate-of-need program.[9]

More recent data suggest two major changes in hospital capital investment: (1) the number of excess beds is declining, particularly in those states with tough certificate-of-need programs; and (2) real expenditures for hospital construction are declining. Explaining these trends will take considerable work, but they strongly suggest that evaluations of certificate-of-need programs may show the same results as evaluations of state cost commissions: little impact in the early years and a powerful effect in the later years.

Table 3–7 indicates trends in excess beds from 1976 to 1978. Excess beds are defined on a statewide basis as hospital beds in excess of 4 beds per 1,000 population. Over this period the number of excess beds declined from 130,000 in 1976 to 114,000 in 1978. States with tough programs such as New York and Minnesota experienced declines of 38 percent each. States with a pattern of overriding local planning agency decisions such as Ohio show an increase in excess beds of 15 percent over this period.

Table 3–8 indicates that real expenditures for hospital construction declined slightly from 1972 to 1976, and then plummeted between 1976 and 1979, experiencing an average annual rate of decline of 9.7 percent over this period. The Bureau of Health Planning in the Health Resources Administration, U.S. Department of Health and Human Services, notes that:

> The reasons for this decrease in the value of annual health facilities construction over the past eight years are doubtless varied and complex. The tightness of the money market and high interest rates in the last several years probably have had an effect. The significant cut-back in direct Federal assistance for facilities construction, especially the practical elimination of the Hill-Burton grant and loan programs by the mid-seventies, also may have been a contributing factor. And the presence of Federally-mandated State capital expenditure review programs under Title XV of the PHS Act [certificate-of-need] and section 1122 of the Social Security Act may have had a dampening effect as well, particularly in the more recent years.[10]

Whatever the many explanations of this decline, it seems likely that the health-planning effort, including the certificate-of-need program, has played a significant part.

Case studies of particular programs give some clue as to the impact. "Constraining Health Care Costs in Hawaii" found that the actions taken by the Hawaii State Health Planning and Development Agency during 1977 and 1978 resulted in:

The elimination or deferral of approximately $23.5 million in proposed capital expenditures
Savings of roughly $7 million in annual operating costs
Savings of about $1.4 million in annual Medicaid expenditures.[11]

Total costs of the health-planning effort in Hawaii over this period were $1.7 million.

A similar study in the Northwest covered the states of Alaska, Idaho, Oregon, and Washington and documented $143 million in capital cost savings and $329 million in operating cost savings over the 1977–79 period. These economics were achieved with a total ex-

Table 3-8.   Expenditures for Health Facilities Construction, 1972-79.

	Annual Change (millions)		Annual Percentage Change	
	Constant 1981 Dollars	Constant 1972 Dollars	Constant 1981 Dollars	Constant 1972 Dollars
1972	4,180	4,180	—	—
1973	4,154	3,834	− 0.6	− 8.3
1974	4,439	3,422	+ 6.9	+ 10.7
1975	4,954	3,579	+11.6	+ 4.6
1976	5,266	3,732	+ 6.3	+ 4.3
1977	5,023	3,372	− 4.6	− 9.6
1978	5,169	3,090	+ 2.9	− 8.4
1979	5,342	2,751	+ 3.3	−11.0
Average 1972–1979	4,816	3,495	+ 3.7	− 5.6
Average 1977–1979	5,178	3,071	+ 0.5	− 9.7

Source: U.S. Department of Commerce.

penditure of $24 million for the health-planning and certificate-of-need programs in these four states over the same period.[12]

A 1979 survey by the American Hospital Association shows that 20 percent of hospital expansion plans were discontinued or postponed with a large majority citing certificate-of-need or 1122 reimbursement contingent upon planning agency approval as the reason (see Table 3-9).

The jury is still out on the certificate-of-need program. Preliminary evaluations of state programs operating prior to implementation of federal legislation tend to find little or no effect. But more current data indicate that hospital capital expenditure patterns are swinging sharply. While it is premature to attribute these changes solely to the certificate-of-need program, it suggests that later studies may detect marked effects.

Professional Standards Review Organizations

Professional Standards Review Organizations were created by the 1972 Amendments to the Social Security Act to assure the quality and necessity of care provided to Medicare and Medicaid beneficiaries. In each area of the country, PSROs consisting of physicians practicing in the community review inpatient hospital services provided to Medicare and Medicaid beneficiaries. The program is politically controversial, and it is viewed by many physicians as federal encroachment on the independent practice of medicine.

PSROs do not prohibit the provision of care, but they can deny payment from federal programs for care adjudged unnecessary. PSROs are not required to review services provided to privately financed patients, but businesses and private insurance companies may contract with PSROs for that service. PSROs do not fit some of the characteristics applicable to other forms of regulation: They do not prohibit activities of health care providers, and they are not mandated to extend their activities to cover private sector activities. Nevertheless, PSROs are usually included under the rubric of governmental regulation in the popular debate.

The PSRO program is one of the most thoroughly evaluated federal programs. For the past three years, the Health Care Financing

Administration (HCFA), U.S. Department of Health and Human Services, and the Congressional Budget Office (CBO) have conducted independent evaluations of the PSRO program.[13] Their conclusions conflict:

- HCFA finds that the program is cost-effective, with each $1 of program costs resulting in $1.27 of savings to the federal budget. CBO finds that the program is not cost-effective, with each $1 of program costs resulting in $0.40 of total system savings.
- PSROs have reduced the days of care provided to Medicare beneficiaries. HCFA estimates the reduction at 1.7 percent, CBO at 1.5 percent.
- Performance varies substantially by region. Both HCFA and CBO find that PSROs in the South are generally ineffective, while those in the Northeast have produced substantial savings.

HCFA and CBO use the same basic data in their evaluations. The differences between their conclusions arise from differences between their assumptions. HCFA translates the reduction in Medicare patient days into savings in federal governmental budgetary outlays. CBO argues that, in the short term, the only true system savings are the marginal costs of the unnecessary care that is reduced. The fixed costs remain and are presumably shifted to privately insured patient charges. This difference explains the difference between the benefit-to-cost ratios (1.27:1 for HCFA; 0.6:1 for CBO).

As an evaluation of the PSRO program, the CBO analysis is clearly faulty. The relevant measure is either the federal budgetary impact (used by HCFA on the grounds that the purpose of the program is to reduce federal outlays by avoiding payment for unnecessary care) or the long-term system savings (once the hospital industry had adjusted to a new lower level of Medicare utilization). In either case, the benefit-to-cost ratio would be 1.27:1, rather than the short-term benefit-to-cost ratio estimated by CBO. To urge elimination of the program on the ground that it is ineffective when there are short-term budgetary savings and long-term system savings that more than outweigh the cost of the program is plainly specious.

Other differences between the CBO and HCFA results reflect differing assumptions about the way experience should be projected and the way days saved should be valued. Both sets of assumptions sound plausible. HCFA systematically selects those assumptions most ad-

Table 3-9. Hospitals Reporting Discontinuance or Postponement of Plans for Service or Facility Expansion by Cause.

Cause	Public	Private
Less than 400 beds		
Number of hospitals with expansion plans	359	1,364
Number reporting discontinuance or postponement of plans (%)	84 (23.4)	290 (21.3)
Percentage reporting various reasons for discontinuance or postponement		
A certificate of need	41.1	55.8
Planning agency approval required by P. 92–603, Section 112, for reimbursement of expenses pertaining to facility or service expansion under Medicare and Medicaid	36.2	36.0
Planning agency approval required by Blue Cross as a condition for reimbursement of expenses pertaining to facility or service expansion	7.7	13.8

	400 or more beds	
Number of hospitals with expansion plans	74	371
Number reporting discontinuance or postponement of plans (%)	16 (21.6)	60 (16.2)
Percentage reporting various reasons for discontinuance or postponement		
A certificate of need	66.8	49.2
Planning agency approval required by PL 92-603, Section 112, for reimbursement of expenses pertaining to facility or service expansion under Medicare and Medicaid	29.0	28.6
Planning agency approval required by Blue Cross as a condition for reimbursement of expenses pertaining to facility or service expansion	39.9	9.8

vantageous to the program; CBO systematically selects those most deleterious. Splitting the difference would result in a benefit-to-cost ratio of approximately 1.18:1.

The evaluations conducted to date have not looked at other benefits of the PSRO program, such as savings to the Medicaid program or improvements in the quality of care. Consideration of these benefits would boost the benefit-to-cost ratio.

The empirical evidence supports the view that the PSROs have worked. This does not imply that modifications to the PSRO program could not improve its effectiveness, or even that this is the best way to assure the appropriate expenditure of governmental funds. But those who would abolish the program must suggest a viable alternative. It would be unreasonable to require the federal government to pay for all care rendered to publicly financed beneficiaries without review to assure the necessity and quality of such services.

THE PROMISE OF COMPETITIVE PROPOSALS: HOW MUCH, HOW SOON?

There are many ways to promote competition in the health care sector. More information could be provided to consumers; providers could be encouraged to participate in cost-efficient organized delivery settings; alternative modes of delivery (such as expanded use of nurse practitioners) could be emphasized; or providers could be made more conscious of the costs associated with the services they provide.

However, the legislative proposals bearing the label "procompetitive" are not much concerned with the supply side of the health care market. Instead, they aim to change patient behavior by increasing the amounts that patients are required to pay for health care services or for health insurance. Some advocates of competition would like to replace current comprehensive insurance coverage with catastrophic or low-option health insurance containing sizable deductibles or coinsurance. Other competition advocates are interested in encouraging more patients to choose health maintenance organizations (HMOs) or other prepaid health plans. Some of the same proposals are supported by both groups.

The legislative proposals contain two basic features: limits on tax-exempt employer contributions to health insurance for employees and increased employee choice among health insurance plans, with incentives for employees to choose lower cost plans.

Limits on Tax-Exempt Employer Contributions

Currently, employer contributions to health insurance coverage for employees are treated like other fringe benefits: they are tax free to the employee. As a result, employees in high marginal tax brackets may find it cheaper to have comprehensive health insurance coverage purchased by their employers than to receive higher but taxable wages to spend on medical bills. This substitution results in a substantial loss of tax revenue to the federal treasury.[14]

The proposal to limit employer tax-exempt contributions to $120 or $125 per month for a family is not advanced on the grounds that it will tighten a loophole in the tax laws, but on the grounds that it will reduce the increase in health care costs. This effect is to result from operation of the domino principle: If employer contributions to health insurance above a fixed amount are subject to taxes, unions and other employee groups will over time purchase less comprehensive insurance plans. Less comprehensive plans could eliminate benefits (like drugs and dental services) or increase deductibles or coinsurance requirements. If the less comprehensive plans purchased by employees require higher out-of-pocket payments for hospital care, then patients will make less use of hospital care. Hospitals will then lower their costs in order to compete for patients. There are a number of flaws and unknowns here:

- There are no data describing the effects of varying tax provisions on the choice of health insurance plans made by employer groups.
- Less comprehensive health insurance is more likely to drop benefits such as ambulatory care than to increase cost-sharing for hospital care. For this reason, CBO estimates that the proposal will have no effect on hospital costs.[15] And if out-of-hospital care becomes less well covered, some care may shift to the hospital setting.
- While there are data indicating that deductibles and low-insurance requirements reduce utilization, there is no evidence that hospitals will respond to increased cost sharing by lowering the unit cost of care.

As tax policy, the proposal has appeal: it would increase the tax yield. But so would any tax increase. The merits of this particular way of increasing taxes should be evaluated against alternatives using traditional tax analysis. The tax issue is whether the entire contribution should be taxable and not whether the amount above some ceiling should be taxed.

As health policy, a limitation on the subsidy for the employer's contribution raises serious problems. Most health insurance is sold on an experience-rated basis, and premiums reflect the anticipated utilization of services by a specific employer group. An employment group that includes a high proportion of older workers or women pays more for the same package of benefits than a group dominated by men and younger workers. Premiums also vary among geographic areas, reflecting geographic differences in utilization and health care costs. Ginsburg argues that these problems could be solved by varying the employer contribution limit by age of covered worker and by geographic location to reflect the actuarial cost of coverage.[16] This would, however, greatly increase the complexity of the proposal and eliminate many of the economies of group health insurance. Too, enforcement of the provision would require a significant regulatory effort.

Implementation of a limitation on the employee's subsidy may also reduce employer concern about health care costs, and that is a serious drawback. Employers can be a potent force in combating health care inflation. They can actively encourage the growth of health maintenance organizations and negotiate with insurance carriers for more efficient operation. Limiting to a fixed-dollar amount the employer's contribution that qualified for tax exclusion could reduce the employer's incentive to be concerned about rising health care costs.

This particular proposal would yield federal budgetary revenues (as would any proposed tax increase), but it would not achieve any significant reduction in hospital costs. Clearly, it is not a substitute for regulation.

Multiple Choice in Employer Health Insurance Plans

The other major "procompetition" proposal would require employers to offer employees a choice among several health insurance plans, health maintenance organizations, or other prepaid group plans. Employers would be required to make the same dollar contribution toward the cost of each plan offered. An employee selecting a plan costing less than the employer's contribution would be entitled to a cash rebate equal to the difference. Legislative proposals treat the tax status of this cash rebate in various ways.

Different competition advocates support this proposal for different reasons. Some feel that requiring employers to offer HMOs and letting employees benefit financially from any savings would increase the number of employees choosing HMOs. Other competition advocates would require that one of the choices be a low-option plan. They hope that the availability of this option will induce employees to select insurance with high deductibles and coinsurance, with the domino effect outlined above (although the expected degree of cost sharing is greater in this proposal than in the employer contribution limit proposal).

If this provision were to increase enrollment in HMOs, it could be expected to have an impact on hospital costs because the hospitalization rates of HMO members are 10 to 40 percent lower than for non-HMO enrollees.[17] But it is unlikely that this provision would greatly alter current patterns of HMO enrollment. Current HMO legislation requires employers to offer a choice of HMOs where they exist and to make a comparable financial contribution. Most HMOs are not less costly than comprehensive insurance plans, so few individuals selecting the HMO option would receive cash rebates. In fact, the larger cash rebates for low-option plans may discourage employees from choosing HMOs. Only 4 percent of the U.S. population currently chooses to belong to HMOs; even with continued funding of HMO development, it seems unlikely that more than 10 percent of the U.S. population would be enrolled by 1990. The hospital cost savings resulting from implementation of this proposal are likely to be modest and to appear only after considerable delay.

Requiring employees to offer choices among several traditional insurance plans and low-option plans may create new problems:

- Less efficient carriers may be assured a market they are now denied. So long as employers offer only one traditional insurance plan, carriers are induced to offer the best prices and benefit structures they can. Choices will create opportunities for the less efficient.
- The price advantages of group insurance would be reduced if members of the employment group were split among a number

of plans. Carriers may have to increase premiums in order to protect against adverse selection.

- Employers who self-insure to reduce costs may not do so if they are required to offer two plans from traditional insurance carriers as well.
- Offering several plans may lead to adverse risk selection and unstable premiums for different groups. Younger, healthier workers may choose low-option plans, driving the cost of experience-rated premiums for older workers steadily upward.
- If cash rebates are not made taxable, employers may increase the maximum health insurance contribution in order to shelter more employee compensation.
- Enforcement of the multiple-choice and equal employer contribution option would require extensive regulation.

Recommendations for Future Action

Many health care provider organizations have jumped on the competition bandwagon. They claim to prefer competition to existing regulation (and to meaningful hospital cost containment in those states that have not created state cost commissions). Politically, they have seen competition as a way of thwarting regulation.

To propose competition as a substitute for regulation puts a greater burden on competition proposals than they can currently bear. The proposals designed to increase competition and contain health care costs are new and largely untried. There is little evidence that their enactment can provide substantial immediate relief from health care inflation or that competitive approaches can effect more than marginal change in the health care system. Many of the competition proposals merit limited demonstrations or experiments. But they cannot serve as substitutes for regulation in the short run, and it is unlikely that they will be effective as alternatives to regulation in the long run.

In the meantime, rapidly increasing hospital costs continue to drive up federal and state governmental budgets and employer fringe benefit costs. The strain on government is now so tight that people are looking for ways to shift costs elsewhere. A Medicaid cap and block grant at the federal level would shift the problem to the states, which in turn are likely to shift the costs to the poor. A more productive approach would be to build on the experience with regulatory approaches, modify them, and create new incentives for curtailing costs without burdensome regulatory measures.

Prospective Hospital Payment Reform.   One of the most promising approaches involves reforming current methods of reimbursement in public programs and private health insurance plans by establishing a system which creates incentives for efficiency in the provision and utilization of hospital services. Such an approach should be designed to slow increases in hospital expenditures per capita and to pay similar hospitals equal rates for the same services.

The weaknesses of the cost-based, retrospective reimbursement system are well known. Instead of promoting efficiency, it encourages hospitals to expand services, increase utilization, and spend more. The current method is also inequitable: with indirect costs allocated across services according to statistical formulas, hospitals may be paid a different rate for the same service. The system also requires detailed reporting and cost-finding procedures, since both public and private payers wish to limit their liability to costs associated with their patients.

The elements of a reform proposal are intended to give geographic areas and hospitals reasonable flexibility to attain their goals without sacrificing quality or access to care. The proposed plan includes the following features:

- National and areawide goals for per capita hospital expenditures. Goals would be projected to 1990.
- Prospective payment for individual hospitals, with payment rates set in order to achieve the specified per capita expenditure goals by 1990.
- Application to all payers, public and private. Federal programs would pay hospitals according to the prospective rates. Hospitals could not receive total revenues in excess of that allowable under the prospective rates—thereby assuring that private payments would not be out of line with public payments.
- States wishing to develop their own approaches and willing to assume the financial risk could opt out of the federal program, so long as state programs met specified standards. This arrangement would allow states to develop budget review systems and other methods of rate setting more appropriate to their particular circumstances.

- On a limited demonstration basis, local health-planning agencies (or other areawide groups) could develop alternative plans for their areas. These plans would have to achieve the areawide goal for per capita hospital expenditures, meeting specified criteria and accepting financial risk if the goal was not met.
- On a limited demonstration basis, hospitals, health maintenance organizations, community health centers or physician groups could develop an alternative plan for achieving the per capita expenditure goal for an enrolled population, with appropriate adjustment of the goal for any differences between the enrolled population and the area population. The organization would be required to be at financial risk for meeting the goal.
- The plan would include incentives to reward hospitals and areas which managed to keep costs down.
- The program would be phased in over a period of ten years.

Organized Delivery Systems.   It is clear that the delivery of health care services can be organized to result in lower costs than the traditional fee-for-service system of care. HMOs lower hospital utilization significantly. Evidence is accumulating that community health centers also significantly reduce hospital utilization.

Continued support for the startup costs of alternative delivery systems like HMOs and community health centers is essential to assure their continued growth. In addition, reform of current reimbursement practices in Medicare and Medicaid could further promote their growth. Legislation to base Medicare reimbursement on 95 percent of the per capita cost of caring for patients in the fee-for-service system was passed by the House of Representatives in 1980, and it should be given high priority on the legislative calendar. This legislation would include much needed incentives for the elderly to join HMOs, since the difference between the HMO community rate premium and the 95 percent rate would be returned to the elderly in expanded benefits or reduced cost sharing. It would also induce HMOs to enroll the elderly patients as they earn serving other patients.

Systematic demonstrations of various multiple-choice and employer contribution provisions could demonstrate whether such provisions could persuade more individuals to join efficient health care delivery systems.

Certificate of Need.   While the growth in hospital capital expenditures appears to be moderating, some improvements in the certificate-of-need program could increase its cost-effectiveness. In some areas, planning agencies devote considerable review to projects unrelated to patient care (e.g., parking garages and chapels). These projects could be exempted. An upward revision of the $150,000 threshold may also be in order. Projects in the $150,000-$500,000 range should be examined to see if the time required for their review is worth the return.

It is clear that certificate-of-need programs would be considerably more effective if they operated subject to an overall capital expenditure limit for a given geographic area, if such limits could be devised. Additional research and experimentation in this area would be helpful.

Professional Standards Review Organizations. Evaluations of the PSRO programs indicate that the program saves at least as much money as it costs. However, this is a weak claim to fame. The PSRO approach to utilization review does not include the latest quality assurance techniques used by businesses. Instead of developing and using protocols for the identification and analysis of aberrant or substandard practice, the PSRO program reviews all hospital admissions of Medicare and Medicaid patients. Through improved management of the program, PSROs have been able to focus more extensive review on certain cases, but PSROs are still required by law to review all cases. In addition, the PSRO program relies on local physicians who have little economic incentive to identify and report the poor medical practices of their peers.

An alternative to the PSRO approvals could take the form of computerized algorithms identifying physicians, hospitals, patients, or selected classes of diagnoses or procedures for which there is a pattern of unnecessary or substandard quality care. The review teams could review these cases and deny reimbursement under public programs for any care identified as unnecessary or substandard. Such a targeted approach could well prove more cost-beneficial than the current approach.

NOTES

1. Karen Davis, "Hospital Costs and the Medicare Program," *Social Security Bulletin*, no. 8 (August 1973): 18–36.
2. Amy K. Taylor, "Government Health Policy and Hospital Labor Costs: The Effects of Wage and Price Controls on Hospital Wage

Rates and Employment," *Public Policy* 27, no. 2 (Spring 1979): 203–25.

3. See, for example, Brian Biles, Carl J. Schramm, and J. Graham Atkinson, "Hospital Cost Inflation under State Rate-Setting Programs," *New England Journal of Medicine* 330 (September 18, 1980): 664–668.

4. Frank A. Sloan and Bruce Steinwald, "Effects of Regulation on Hospital Costs and Input Use" (Paper presented to American Economic Association annual meetings, Chicago, August 29, 1978).

5. U.S. Department of Health, Education and Welfare, *Research in Health Care Financing* (Spring-Summer 1977) HEW pub. no. (SSA) 77–11901.

6. Biles, Schramm, and Atkinson, "Hospital Cost Inflation."

7. U.S. Comptroller General, *Rising Hospital Costs Can be Restrained by Regulating Payments and Improving Management* (Washington, D.C.: Government Printing Office, September 19, 1980).

8. U.S. Department of Health and Human Services, Health Care Financing Administration, *Report on Hospital Compliance with Administration Guidelines on Increases in Hospital Expenditures, Second Quarter* (Washington, D.C.: Government Printing Office, 1980).

9. For an excellent review of certificate-of-need research and other studies through 1977 see, "Certificate-of-Need Programs: A Review, Analysis, and Annotated Bibliography of the Research Literature," (November 1978) DHEW Pub. No. (HRA) 79–14006.

   For a preliminary evaluation of the certificate-of-need program, see Policy Analysis Inc., "Final Report: Evaluation of the Effects of Certificate-of-Need Programs," Contract No. 231–77–0114, submitted to the Health Resources Administration, U.S. Department of Health Services, January 29, 1981.

10. U.S. Department of Health and Human Services, Health Resources Administration, Bureau of Health Planning, "CON and Health Planning," p. 4. Staff Paper (December 15, 1980).

11. U.S. Department of Health and Human Services, Health Resources Administration, Bureau of Health Planning, "Health Planning in Action," (Washington, D.C.: Government Printing Office, forthcoming).

12. *Ibid.*

13. Health Care Financing Administration, Health Care Financing Research Report, preliminary issuance; and Congressional Budget Office, "1979 PSRO Program Evaluation, The Impact on Health Care Costs: 1980 Update of the CBO Evaluation," May 2, 1980.

14. Martin S. Feldstein and B. Friedman, "Tax Subsidies, the Rational Demand for Insurance and the Health Care Crisis," *Journal of Public Economics* 7 (1977): 155–78.

15. Congressional Budget Office, "Cost Estimate of H.R. 5740," March 18, 1980. CBO estimates that by fiscal year 1985 private spending for in-hospital services such as physician, dental services, and mental health services would be $5 to $8 billion lower.

16. Paul B. Ginsburg, "Altering the Tax Treatment of Employment-based Plans," December 22, 1980. (Unpublished.)

17. Harold S. Luft, "How do Health Maintenance Organizations Achieve Their Savings," *New England Journal of Medicine* 298 no. 24 (June 15, 1978): 1336–43.

DISCUSSION

Joe Onek: One thing that has disturbed me in the last few weeks is the either/or character of the public debate. Regulatory approaches are new enough and promising enough that it may not make sense to abandon them entirely, and competitive approaches are new enough and untested enough that we cannot rely on them totally. Moreover, most of the regulatory approaches that Karen Davis mentioned are not incompatible with a commitment to competitive alternatives. It has been argued that, in some jurisdictions, state agencies have impaired the ability of HMOs to enter the market, but I doubt it. And I think it much harder to argue that state rate-setting commissions stand in the way of competition; indeed, they could be made to facilitate it. PSROs could not have impeded the development of competition, if only because they have been so ineffective. Stockman and others seem to regard the matter as an either/or proposition, as a choice between competition, on the one hand, and regulation on the other. I don't think we should view it that way. I think we could continue to support and study the effectiveness of state rate-making commissions, continue to support planning and study its effectiveness, and press ahead with competitive approaches. The two are not, at this point anyway, in such opposition that we have to choose one or the other at a time when neither has been adequately tested.

Karl Bays: I was going to ask about points at which we might improve the regulatory process. Karen Davis cites a study of planning in four northwestern states that produced savings of $143 million in capital costs and $349 million in operating costs. That sounded great to me, until I saw that we had spent $24 million to get that done. That made me think that it might be easier to keep some of these regulations in effect if we could make the regulatory process more efficient.

Ashley Gale: We have talked repeatedly this morning about the fact that the cost of health care is increasing at 17 or 18 percent a year against an inflation rate of 12 percent. I wonder if that is a fair comparison. Medicine is characterized by a continuing effort to improve the quality of care while in most other industries quality appears to be diminishing. This should not be overlooked and could well be an explanation for the higher rate of increase in health care.

Monte DuVal: Since their elimination is now being discussed, I would like to talk for a moment about PSROs. Although they were put in place as cost control devices, there is a point beyond which they cannot be effective. PSROs can eliminate unnecessary and inappropriate services only once. Once those have been weeded out, PSROs can help to maintain high standards but they will not further reduce costs. The other point I would stress is that they have educated us about the mismatch between needs and services. PSRO statistics have, for example, alerted us to the shortage of nursing home beds in certain parts of New York State by identifying lengths of hospital stay out of all proportion to patient needs. If PSROs can help us understand better the kinds of services and facilities that we need, they will have made an important contribution.

Karen Davis: You all have raised a number of good points, and I will try to respond to them. One question concerned an overall limit on health care expenditures. Whatever the level at which it were set, I think such a limit less helpful than negotiation between payers and providers about rates. We now have an untenable situation in which providers can simpy charge whatever they choose, or whatever their costs turn out to be, and that is just inherently inflationary. State rate-setting commissions can help us cope with that problem. It is true that many of the states where commissions have apparently succeeded were already high cost states by the time their commissions began work. Indeed, that is why the commissions were created. But the fact is that rate-setting commissions have slowed the rate of increase; in high-cost states that don't have rate-setting commissions we don't see the same moderation. So, whether you do a before-and-after study of states with commissions or compare the commission states with other high-costs states, you see a more favorable result in states with commissions. Alex McMahon argues that their effectiveness may not last. I think that is possible, but we have data for four consecutive years which show that it can last at least that long. The threat to the commissions is primarily political: when you lose a governor like Michael Dukakis in Massachusetts and get a governor like Edward King in his place, you have to anticipate a decline in the effectiveness of the state's program.

I should make it clear that I am not questioning the fact that HMOs reduce hospitalization. I think the evidence on that point is very compelling. My question concerns the likely growth of HMOs. My guess is that if we do everything we can to increase membership, we may have 10 percent of the population enrolled by 1990. The fact we all have to confront is that 60 million people live in nonmetropolitan areas, which aren't easily served by HMOs. If by 1990 we got the rest of the country up to the level that Minneapolis has now achieved, we would still have fewer than 40 million people enrolled.

Could there be improvements in the regulatory process? I think we could improve the certificate of need process dramatically by exempting all capital investment projects unrelated to patient care—like parking garages and chapels—and by raising the threshold for project review from $150,000 to $500,000. I agree with Monte that the PSROs are limited in the savings that they can achieve, but their elimination would allow inappropriate utilization to increase one again. Finally, I think we must face the fact that the far-reaching reforms under discussion here will take ten or fifteen years to achieve, and I think we must devote at least as much attention to prospective rate setting, negotiations between providers and payers, and other proposals for more immediate relief.

4 COMPETITION: MEDICINE'S CREEPING REVOLUTION

Paul Ellwood, Jr.

Competition in medical care is not a winner, it is a survivor! Competition is a concept of health care reform that has survived zealous friends, powerful opposition, and political support. Now it appears poised to move ahead of regulation as the American health reform policy. Can it survive the nurturing of another batch of politicians? Can it survive another voluntary effort? Can it survive another Duke Private Sector Conference?

A strategy of reliance on market forces to improve the health sector requires such massive change that a new rhetoric has evolved: health maintenance organizations (HMOs), individual practice associations (IPAs), fair market choice, consumer choice health plan (CCHP), major risk insurance, and preferred provider organizations (PPOs) now dot our discourse. The names of some of the new competitive medical plans sound more like brands of soap than sources of professional services. The rapidly expanding "care" family of health plans is headed by just plain CARE, but namesakes like Take Care, Comprecare, Prucare, Primacare, Northcare, and about forty others are spread throughout the country. There isn't a Don't Care or a Care Last, but there is a Care First.

For the past ten years, I have thought, written, and talked almost nonstop about a competitive approach to health care reform, and yet I struggle to find a generic label for the wide variety of medical care arrangements that can compete. As a matter of fact, when I first coined the term "health maintenance organization," it was to be just such a label. But momentum and fate limited its use to a highly specific arrangement delineated in the HMO Act of 1973. In turn, the act, and the marketplace, have produced price-competitive health plans that are virtually all HMOs, in some form or another. This turn of events has handicapped discussions of competition ever since. Because discussions about competing medical plans were naturally focused on HMOs, many individuals who advocated competition were labeled HMO proponents, and the fact that HMOs are simply prototype competitors, the first of a breed, was sometimes overlooked.

Since labels are easier to change than the health delivery system, I will apply the term "competitive medical plan" (CMP) to all combinations of physician and hospital services that are purchased on a price-competitive basis. CMPs range from preferred provider organizations to closed-panel HMOs. The "competitive health system" refers to the whole concept of a medical marketplace organized around competition and the interplay of market forces.

This paper discusses some of the changes the competitive health system idea has undergone in the past decade and presents some of my thoughts on where it is likely to go from here. The idea now has significant private sector momentum, and a reconfiguration of the health system along competitive lines is at this point inevitable. Some of what's coming may include such trends as:

- The structure of the health industry will change dramatically as the incentives and mode of payment change.
- Multispecialty group practices will have significant advantages in the CMP business, and they will form the basis of large, integrated medical care firms operating in multiple regions throughout the country.
- Solo practitioners may be squeezed out of the medical market unless they can devise arrangements that will allow them to achieve group utilization rates without actually joining groups. (Administrative arrangements with good information systems and utilization controls may provide the necessary mechanisms.)
- Hospitals must find a way to profit from predictable shrinkages in inpatient use by becoming involved in the areas to which the action is shifting—primary outpatient care, ambulatory surgery, and so on. Like solo practitioners, hospitals will need to find

CMP models that will help them achieve group practice performance standards.

- Some of the gaps in our knowledge about what makes for efficiency and high quality in medical care organizations will need to be filled. Health services research will become critically important as the new bottom line becomes "health produced per dollar spent." Opportunities to study health outcomes and to devise a balance sheet for health will be present in organized systems linking defined populations with specific providers for total care.
- A competitive market in health care introduces new responsibilities and problems for the buyers and consumers of health services as well. Measuring and assuring quality will become more important. The sellers of health services are capable of segmenting the health care market, and may be encouraged to do so under competitive conditions. Advertising is just arriving on the health care scene, and has the potential to affect consumer behavior powerfully and to further segment the market.
- Enrollment growth in CMPs will be steady, but competitive reform of the health system will take fifteen to twenty years.

DEFINITION OF A COMPETITIVE HEALTH SYSTEM

In a competitive health system most consumers will be given a choice among several competing plans by their employer (or by Medicare or Medicaid). Employers (or government) will contribute a more or less fixed amount, with consumers paying or being paid the difference between that amount and the premium for the plans of their choice. Most areas will have a diversity of competing provider and insurer plans.

The Roots of a Competitive Health System

Desperate for a policy to meet what President Nixon labeled "the health crisis of America," his administration tentatively adopted the competitive health system idea in early 1970. This new and uniquely American approach was designed to preclude the need for increasing government regulation. The distinction between competition and regulation was first drawn in a memorandum from the Department of Health, Education and Welfare (DHEW) to the White House Council: "This paper proposes that we shift from the federal regulatory investment planning strategy to a second alternative strategy to promote a health maintenance industry."[1] Throughout these early communications, the administration used the expression "health maintenance strategy" or "health maintenance" to describe the competition idea. Although its implementation would entail substantial reform of the existing health delivery system, endorsing the idea of competition was consistent with Republican free-market ideology.

The initial strategy was to promote a competitive health system through persuasion, startup grants for competitive plans, and capitated Medicare contracts. Consumers were to be given an equally subsidized choice between traditional insurance plans and competitive medical plans (then limited to HMOs). The administration planned to explain the broad goals of this reform and leave the implementation to the private sector. Lewis H. Butler, Assistant Secretary of Health, Education and Welfare explained: "Let's specify what we want it to do. And we don't give a damn how they put it together. They can make it a partnership, a corporation, they can make it one of fifty-five different organizational forms. Let's describe the thing by what we want it to do, not how it's formed."[2]

At the outset, it was decided that the Secretary of Health, Education and Welfare, rather than the president, should test the reaction to such a radical shift in American health policy. The first public announcements of the new policy were made in March 1970, when Secretary Robert Finch issued a statement endorsing the idea of introducing competition to the provision of Medicare and Medicaid services:

> Our goal is that every elderly or poor person covered by Medicare or Medicaid be given the right to choose between receiving services under such a contract (i.e., capitation contract) and receiving individual hospital and physician services in the traditional manner. We must promote diversity, choice, and health competition in American medicine if we are to escape from the grip of spiralling costs.[3]

In a formal health message eleven months later, Richard Nixon articulated the competition strategy and the philosophy of its implementation:

One effective way of influencing the system is by structuring *incentives* which reward people for helping to achieve national goals without forcing their decision or dictating the way they are carried out. The American people have always shown a unique capacity to move toward common goals in varied ways. Our efforts to reform health care in America will be more effective if they build on this strength.[4]

The competition strategy was never implemented as envisioned. Internal disagreements over the policy within the administration and an increasingly tenuous relationship between the administration and Congress stifled it. First, Congress prohibited the administration from continuing to spend previously earmarked money on competitive medical plans. Senator Edward Kennedy supported the idea of an act to promote HMOs as a model health delivery system and forerunner of his national health insurance plan, but he disagreed with the economic principles of a competitive health system. At the same time, the concept of nationwide health delivery reform encountered stiff opposition from organized medicine.

These events forced the administration and the Congress to reconsider their support of competition as the centerpiece of national health policy. The resulting HMO Act of 1973 was a far cry from the flexible medical care organizations initially sought by the administration's market-oriented health advisers. The act, through its narrow definition of a medical plan, promoted only one type of HMO, rather than various types able to compete with each other. Finally, competition advocates could not muster enough support to overcome the opposition to a Medicare capitation system that surfaced in the staff of the Senate Finance Committee and the Medicare bureaucracy.

In 1977, Alain Enthoven advanced the competitive health system concept as a public policy by proposing a complete national health insurance scheme built on competition. Enthoven's consumer choice health plan was conceived for DHEW Secretary Joseph Califano.[5] The Carter administration failed to see the merits of the Enthoven plan, but several members of Congress were quick to recognize its value as a public policy that could contain costs and improve financial protection. In rapid order, a whole series of "procompetition" health bills were introduced by both Republicans and Democrats in the House and Senate. Procompetition bills introduced in the Ninety-sixth Congress include:

Al Ullman	Health Cost Restraint Act of 1981
David Durenberger	Health Incentives Reform Act of 1981
Richard Gephardt and	
David Stockman	National Health Care Reform Act
Orrin Hatch and	
Richard Schweiker	Comprehensive Health Care Reform Act of 1981
Sam Gibbons and	
James Jones	Consumer Health Expense Control Act

As of early 1981, the competition idea appears poised to move forward once again as a major national health policy. A remarkable number of competition proponents have moved into positions of power in Congress and in the administration. Jim Jones is chairman of the House Budget Committee and a key member of the Ways and Means Committee; Dave Durenberger has become chairman of the Senate Finance Committee's Health Subcommittee; Orrin Hatch is the chairman of the Committee on Labor and Public Welfare; Richard Schweiker has become the secretary of Health and Human Services; and Dave Stockman is the hard-hitting director of the Office of Management and Budget.

But even without future government action, competition will advance on its own momentum, stimulated by:

- The antigovernment and antiregulation sentiment reflected in the tax revolts, the election of Ronald Reagan, and the deregulation of the transportation and communications industry.
- The success of many evolving competitive health systems, led by the Minneapolis-St. Paul and California markets.
- The continued expansion of 244 existing competitive medical plans.
- The emergence of well-capitalized national firms that should elicit competitive responses from the traditional system.
- The coming surplus of physicians and the continuing surplus of hospital beds, which will increase the disparity in costs between the traditional system and a competitive system.
- The evolution of new methods of organizing CMPs that are less costly to establish and potentially more acceptable to doctors and consumers.

Competition is inevitable. In fact, it is difficult to envision a public policy that could completely stifle competition at this point. The questions that remain are:

- What will a competitive system look like?
- How far will competition go?
- How fast will it spread?
- How will it affect buyers and consumers?
- How long will it take market forces to become the dominant influence on the health system?

The Components: Competitive Plans and Fair-Market Choice

Though the competitive health system idea has only recently found favor in national health policy circles, its components have been developing since the birth of the American Republic. Corporation-sponsored, multispecialty, prepaid, and just plain group practice are all at least seventy-five years old. One of the earliest precursors to modern CMPs, the Boston Dispensary, was founded in 1770 to provide group-based medical care for the poor.[6] In 1883, the Southern Pacific Railroad opened corporate-sponsored group practice facilities for its workers in San Francisco and Sacramento.[7] The Mayo brothers began the model Mayo Clinic, a modern multispecialty group practice, in 1887.[8] The Ross-Loos Clinic opened a prepaid group practice in Los Angeles in 1929.[9] And in the 1940s, the Kaiser-Permanente Medical Care Program became the first prepaid group practice to have multiregional locations.

These early plans formed for quite different reasons than CMPs form now. The Mayo Clinic was started as a means of gathering specialists when specialists were rare. The Southern Pacific Railroad and Henry Kaiser formed medical care organizations to improve access to care for their employees. Like the competitive health system idea, each of these innovations in health care delivery was viewed with skepticism and criticized sharply. They made a strong impression during the depression years, however, when prepaid health plans were praised for providing more doctor visits and hospital days than the health system at large. By the 1950s, when economy was becoming a byword, prepaid groups were making less use of health care resources than the traditional system.

Even the latest twist in medical care delivery had its roots several decades ago. The newly formed preferred provider organizations, now competing in the Denver, San Francisco, and Los Angeles markets, got their start when a group of Dallas teachers made a predetermined monthly rate contract with the Baylor Hospital for hospital room, board, and specified ancillary services in 1929.[10] This ultimately led to the development of Blue Cross and Blue Shield. For those unfamiliar with PPOs, selected doctors and hospitals are recommended by employers or third parties to employees as preferred over other providers. Any employee using these preferred providers receives more extensive health insurance coverage than the standard company plan. The preferred physicians typically agree to a fee schedule and some sort of utilization control scheme, while the hospitals agree to lower rates. In return, the providers get their bills paid more promptly and attract more patients. The PPOs differ from the HMOs in that consumers are not locked into one set of providers; they can opt in or out of the PPO each time they need medical care. As PPOs are currently organized, there is no guaranteed availability of services, there is no standard government prescribed benefit package, and the providers are not put at financial risk.

The idea of fair-market choice received its first widespread test under the Federal Employees Health Benefit Program in 1960. Today, 10 million federal employees continue to have a choice of several health plans and health insurance vendors. They receive a fixed dollar contribution toward the plan of their choice and thus are rewarded for choosing less costly care.

FORM FOLLOWS DOLLARS
The Old Rules

In 1970, Ernest B. Howard, executive vice-president of the American Medical Association (AMA), was approached for the AMA's support of the competitive health system idea, but he said, "There's one nonnegotiable demand: fee for service." Burt is a wise man!

The fee-for-service payment of doctors, cost reimbursement of hospitals, and third-party coverage are the DNA of the present health system. Given the highly specialized and interdependent nature of modern medical care, nothing less than a professional obsession with autonomy, backed by a fee-for-service payment system, would allow 58 percent of physicians to continue to practice alone (34 percent are in small groups, and only 8 percent of physicians practice in groups of more than ten[11]). Multispecialty groups, while perhaps enjoying some qualitative advantages over solo practice, have certainly enjoyed no economic advantage and have grown slowly. Cost-charge reimbursement of hospitals has led to larger hospitals and more recently to horizontal integration of hospitals, but not to vertical integration. Wise hospital administrators are not going to get into any arrangement that would offend their independent doctor constituents.

The suppliers to the health industry—drug companies and the health products manufacturers—have also grown steadily larger, in part because size was necessary to afford costly government safety and efficiency regulations. Their high profit margins have made them prime takeover targets, and important segments of that industry are now subsidiaries of larger, diversified corporations. While some of these suppliers have been cautiously edging into the service side of the health industry (e.g., by operating laboratories and marketing health promotion programs and home care programs), they too have been careful not to go too far, for fear of appearing to compete with doctors and hospitals.

The other important component of the current structure is passive large buyers consisting of employers and unions, and their intermediaries—the insurers, Taft Hartley Trusts—who tend to be reluctant to exercise power in dealing with the health professions. Medical care inflation is forcing them to change their focus from neutrally passing health care dollars through insurers to actually buying medical care. Most of them are not prepared for the caveat emptor atmosphere of the reformed medical marketplace.

In summary, while some segments of the health industry are becoming larger and more competitive, the key element—physicians—remains locked in small units that do not compete on price. Physician opposition to overt price competition has inhibited many better capitalized and managed firms associated with the health industry (e.g., hospitals, drug and product manufacturers) from establishing CMPs. Some health insurers have broken ranks and are beginning to establish CMPs, but they are still the exception.

The New Rules

The mutant incentives unleashed by price competition will dramatically change the shape of medicine. With the advent of price competition, small, relatively simple local firms will increasingly give way to large, complex medical care corporations. The process is already beginning with mergers and acquisitions of individual CMPs and with the entry of large insurers into the health delivery business. (So far, no major industrial corporation has signified an intent to deliver acute health services on anything other than a local basis.) The expansion and consolidation of smaller units will lead to a series of increasingly large regional and national CMPs.

The CMP models themselves will be based increasingly on multispecialty group practices, either fee-for-service or prepaid. Other CMP models, primarily fee-for-service, will be designed to accommodate solo and small group physicians, but the aim of those organizations will be to enable nongroup providers to function like groups. The fate of solo and small group doctors, like conventional hospitals, will depend on their ability to create such loose-knit CMPs and make them work.

Resource allocation in CMPs will be determined to a greater extent by the demands of large buyers and consumers than has been true in the past, resulting in improved distribution and availability of health services. Since CMPs depend on members' premiums for revenues, the financial strength of the organizations will be in large part determined by their ability to satisfy their members' demands.

Here Come the Groups

In a competitive system, multispecialty group practices will for the first time realize some economic advantages over other modes of health care delivery. Groups have certain characteristics which allow them to deliver a comprehensive range of services more efficiently than nongroups. Because of those structural advantages, nongroups will have a difficult time matching the performance of group-based CMPs.

Competitive medical plans have, thus far, achieved their greatest economic advantage by hospitalizing less than the traditional health system. Rates of hospital use—measured in days, admissions, and length of stay—have become the shortcut measure for comparing various CMPs to each other and to the system at large. Recent studies, for example, show that group-based HMOs tend to hospitalize less than nongroup IPA-HMO models. The rate of admissions for IPA enrollees is 41 percent higher than for groups, while the number of IPA hospital days per 1,000 is 23 percent higher than the number for group model enrollees. [12]

Before fee-for-service multispecialty groups added prepayment on a significant scale, it was assumed that putting the provider at risk for hospital costs was the incentive that led prepaid group practices to make comparatively less use of the hospital. The relationship was never proved because the absence of a separately defined population exclusively served by a single fee-for-service medical group effectively prevented hospital use comparisons between fee-for-service and prepaid multispecialty groups. In the 1970s, such comparisons became possible when a number of fee-for-service groups began adding prepaid enrollees to their fee-for-service practices.

The St. Louis Park Medical Center, a highly regarded 140-physician fee-for-service multispecialty group, found, after adding prepayment, that from the outset its HMO enrollees were being hospitalized at a rate comparable to that of established pure prepaid group practices. This group had apparently been achieving 300 to 400 days of hospital utilization per 1,000 per year in its fee-for-service practice without relying on any direct financial incentives to physicians or utilization control schemes. The clinic is now conducting a cohort study of its fee-for-service and prepaid patients. The results thus far show that the style of practice is the same in each group. A recent study by the Mayo Clinic, where the population was accurately defined, not by enrollment in an HMO but because Rochester residents receive virtually all their health care through local providers, confirmed that the Mayo Clinic hospitalizes at rates that are far below the United States average (40 percent lower) and reasonably comparable to those of the more mature and successful prepaid groups. [13] An analysis conducted by InterStudy of twenty fee-for-service groups which added prepayment, however, indicated that some of those groups experienced high initial rates of hospital use. These fee-for-service groups have found it necessary to add various controls to reduce hospital utilization from their previous levels in order to be effective prepaid competitors. [14]

We do not know the reasons why some multispecialty groups have succeeded in providing comprehensive medical care at lower costs than IPAs or the traditional health system. A descriptive study of the effects of reimbursement on physician hospitalizing behavior concluded that a cost-effective orientation of physicians could be better accomplished through peer interaction, fostered by effective medical leadership, than it could by negative financial sanctions.[15] Groups have other advantages for achieving cost-effective practice, including:

The ability to select each member of the medical group
The incentive to match the needs of the group's patient population to the numbers and specialties of the group's physicians and other health professionals, so that they all work at or near capacity in their own fields
Easy, formal, and informal consultation in the office, which can often prevent unnecessary hospitalization
Extensive resources for outpatient services, including group-owned radiology and clinical laboratory facilities, which make it easier for physicians to do many procedures in their offices

What causes some groups to make greater use of the hospital than others is less well understood. One might speculate that some groups are more procedure oriented, hospital oriented, and profit maximizing than others, while other multispecialty groups are professionally oriented toward conservative diagnosis and treatment. Whatever the full set of explanations, loosely organized CMPs that cannot be selective about how many and which physicians participate in their plans are unlikely to be able to compete effectively against the well-managed groups. If nongroup CMPs are to compete on price, they need powerful incentives, as well as unequivocally effective and often onerous hospital utilization controls. Only the primary physician-based nongroup CMPs, like those pioneered by SAFECO Insurance, have succeeded in matching the performance of groups without resorting to direct hospital utilization controls. In this case, primary physicians function as small groups, controlling the selection of specialists who see their patients and authorizing their hospitalization. This solo or small group practice CMP arrangement could be further strengthened with a computerized medical record system that would allow the same kind of quick communication and unit records that exist in multispecialty groups. This system, in fact, could go one step further by providing the primary physician with comparative information on the performance of various specialists to whom patients might be referred.

Even at this early stage of CMP development, the competitive advantages of group models are evident. As of July, 1981, 161 group practice HMOs had enrolled 8,281,589 people, while 89 independent practice HMOs had enrolled 1,404,104 people. Well-managed IPAs should be able to grow more rapidly over the next few years than group models, given consumers' natural reluctance to leave their own physicians to join a new health plan. However, the balance is likely to shift toward groups. If fee for service was invented for solo practice, then prepaid competition was invented for groups.

Corporate Takeover

One of the most significant developments in recent years—and one with far-reaching implications for the future of a competitive health system—has been the emergence of large firms that own or manage CMPs in more than one state. Nine such "national medical care firms" already exist, and they account for over 50 percent of the total CMP enrollment nationwide: 4.9 out of the total 9.7 million CMP enrollees are enrolled in national firm branches, 3.9 million in the Kaiser plans alone. If the 1.36 million enrollees in Blue Cross and Blue Shield-associated CMPs are added, 64 percent of total enrollment is in national firms (Table 4-1).

The trend toward regional and national CMPs is likely to accelerate as pressure from major buyers of health care to contain costs puts an increasing premium on operational efficiency and managerial strength. The factors that contribute to success in competitive medical plans favor large-scale operations. Success requires good management, a recognizable and respected name, strong marketing, capital, and the ability to develop and install sophisticated information systems. Additionally, while large insurers initially began to develop CMPs in order to protect their existing market shares, the HMO Act's dual-choice mandate created new market opportunities by requiring health care buyers to offer HMOs.

The impact of national firms on local health markets, and on the delivery system as a whole, differs from the impact of small, first-start CMPs in a number of important ways. Since national firms will

Table 4-1. National Medical Care Firms.

HMO	Location	December, 1980 Enrollment	Percentage Change 1979-80
Kaiser Health Plan	Southern and northern California; Denver; Washington, D.C.; Hawaii; Cleveland; Portland; Dallas (with Prudential)	3,937,400 (Dallas enrollment included)	3.0
Insurance Co. of North America (INA)	Phoenix; Los Angeles; Spokane; Dallas (option to buy two Florida plans)	400,021	3.0
Prudential	Houston; Austin; Nashville; Dallas (with Kaiser) (Developing in Atlanta; Oklahoma City; four others in feasibility stage)	57,850 (Dallas enrollment not included, 15,628)	75.6
Connecticut General	Phoenix; Columbia, Maryland	93,467	22.9
SAFECO	Seattle; Sacramento; Salt Lake City	40,682	13.6
CNA	Illinois; Indiana (developing in Tucson)	55,800	66.7
American Medical International (AMI)	Los Angeles; Salt Lake City; Guam	107,933	6.5
Charter Medical Corp.	Minneapolis; Dayton; Cincinnati; Columbus, Ohio (Developing in Austin)	139,370	100.1
Medserco	St. Louis; Pontiac, Michigan; (developing in Rhode Island; Chicago)	46,611	429.7
Total		4,879,134	6.8

select locations on the basis of market potential, the distribution of CMPs will become more predictable. Until recently, development of the first CMP in a market was often quite serendipitous, dependent on idealists receiving federal funding, or the interest of an existing group practice in developing a new line of business, or medical society acquiescence. National firms believe the most promising markets are those where medical care costs and hospital utilization rates are high, where large numbers of doctors and hospitals are already in the market, where the population is growing, and where prevailing health benefit levels are fairly rich. Prudential, for instance, plans to open CMPs in Dallas, Houston, Tulsa, Oklahoma City, Atlanta, Nashville, and Birmingham. In a number of these cities, the opposition of the medical community has previously inhibited the organization of CMPs.

National firms have higher enrollment expectations than most individual plans. The Kaiser Health Plan, for example has attained memberships of 100,000 in each of its major medical markets except for the newest branches in Dallas and Washington, D.C. Because of their capital strength and growth expectations, national firms have the potential to trigger more serious and faster competitive responses from existing providers in the markets they enter. In fact, this pattern of competitive response, rather than intellectual acceptance of the idea, is the key to the spread of the entire CMP concept. In Denver, for example, Kaiser's entry into the market precipitated the almost immediate formation of a number of other CMPs. Dallas merits close scrutiny since three national firms—Insurance Company of North America (INA), Kaiser, and Prudential—have already begun providing services there.

The enthusiasm of insurers or any other for-profit corporation for future CMPs will depend on their earnings. Since most of the current national CMP firms are relatively new and growing rapidly through acquisition or investment, their profitability remains uncertain. Only Kaiser, a not-for-profit firm, has survived long enough and with enough success to prove that large-scale health care corporations are economically feasible. Kaiser's own growth has been inhibited by capital formation problems inherent in not-for-profit organizations, combined with the resistance of physicians to the idea of transferring capital and management expertise from one region to another when they had little to gain by the organization's overall growth.

For-profit firms are likely to be more aggressive in their pursuit of growth. However, with the exception of SAFECO, insurer sponsors have not experimented in the structure of their medical care organizations, and they have shown little inclination to conduct the kinds of health services research that could lead to major improvements in health care delivery. Perhaps if corporations with strong traditions of research and development (particularly high-technology information firms) were to enter the CMP field, research and development activities would receive more emphasis and innovations in health care delivery would follow.

As Relman's thought-provoking article in the *New England Journal of Medicine* pointed out, there is some reason to be wary of a shift in dominance from non-profit to for-profit organizations.[17] However, the giant for-profit insurance corporations that have entered the CMP field have done so in highly visible ways, and they have reputations to protect. They certainly have the capital to make good on their commitments, and the means to succeed in this business, if they have the appropriate long-range objectives.

The national firms that already exist will continue to expand as rapidly as profitability and the supply of promising markets warrant. New national firms will be created. Individual CMPs may merge, essentially creating their own new regional or national firms, or be acquired by the major nationals as part of their expansion strategies.

Hospitals as Big Cars

Hospitals appear likely to become the "big cars" of the health industry. In fact, a health system dominated by CMPs, and operating at their current age-adjusted levels of utilization, would drop U.S. hospital use from the present 1,206 hospital days per 1,000 population to less than 750 days per 1,000. Beds needed would fall from 4.5 to 3.0 per 1,000. Like the auto manufacturers, hospitals must find some means of down-sizing that allows them to gain while undergoing a reduction in inpatient utilization. This will entail vertical integration and the development of a full array of services to produce and maintain health.

The ability of hospitals to lead the formation of CMPs may depend on their ability to develop CMP models that their medical staffs find comfortable. These models must allow staff members to keep or gain patients in the face of competition from other CMPs and the growing supply of physicians. In the past, hospitals have been reluctant to establish CMPs, presumably because they lower hospital utilization and create dissension among physicians when the entire medical staff is not included. Strong hospitals, however, have some decided advantages in starting health plans: they have management, capital formation ability, high visibility, and facilities that can be used either for inpatients or for outpatients. The role that hospitals choose to play in establishing CMPs will be an important early determinant of the extent to which competitive systems will be vertically integrated.

Given the oversupply of hospital facilities, most CMPs will choose not to own their own facilities. CMPs are finding that they can entice hospitals in overbedded communities to compete on price for their business. As a matter of fact, some CMP managers say that, given the severe overbedding that exists in some communities, they are simply waiting for hospitals to become bankrupt before acquiring them. Just as the past financial difficulties of some hospitals led to their acquisition by multihospital systems, hospital difficulty in the future could lead to widespread vertical integration of the health industry as troubled hospitals are acquired by CMPs.

The vertical integration process would be accelerated if the larger existing multihospital systems were to decide to establish CMPs. INA, which owns Hospital Affiliates, has moved aggressively into the CMP field, but it has yet to integrate the services of its hospitals with those of its medical plans. Except for Los Angeles, INA's hospitals and medical plans are located in different communities. The largest CMP, the Kaiser Health Plan, is vertically integrated in part and owns several hospitals in California. But in its three newest regions, Washington, D.C., Dallas, and Denver, the Kaiser organization has not found it necessary to acquire a hospital.

Management Deficiencies

Remarkably little is known about group practices, even though multispecialty groups and national medical corporations seem to enjoy substantial advantages in the delivery of health care. While documentation of group characteristics is increasing, notably through studies like the recent one conducted by Mathematica,[18] our lack of understanding of the factors that contribute to superior performance is a serious problem. It will impede the development of CMPs and make replication of their best features in a national organization difficult. The packages will probably look the same, but, in the absence of effective tools to manage groups, the results could be radically different.

The health business needs a Peter Drucker to write a "concept of the medical group." The production of medical care (Dare we call it health?) has not been viewed in management terms. At one insurance company which owns a single successful CMP, the chief executive officer has expressed reluctance to go national with the plan because he feels the success of that CMP was too dependent on the mysterious abilities of one particular physician manager, and he doubts that the success is replicable.

Some of the unanswered questions about successful medical care organizations are fundamental:

How are medical care organizations best governed?

- How should the friction between health professionals and nonmedical managers be alleviated?
- Is there any logic to the current division of labor among physicians of various specialties and between licensed physicians and other health care professionals?
- Do successful medical care organizations require physicians as top managers?

How should health professionals be selected, motivated, paid, and managed?

- What kinds of physicians work well on a team?
- How can health care professionals be motivated to plan the futures of their organizations?
- What system of compensation will reward productivity and clinical excellence without tilting toward each new high-technology fad?
- Will the big medical corporations' profit motive and drive for quality control adversely affect the quality of care?

Most important, each medical care organization needs a health care management information system and balance sheet. The management of large corporations depends on the availability of impersonal, quantitative information describing the business' performance. Medical care corporations that seek to deliver high-quality care at reasonable costs need an analogous management tool, one which will measure something more than the dollar return on premiums, patient visits, hospital admissions, or episodes of illness. What appears to be needed is an enrollment-based, computerized medical information system that:

- Permits comparison and control of the quality of medical services delivered at dispersed treatment sites
- Provides immediate feedback to management and individual providers
- Compares diagnostic and treatment methods
- Facilitates the development and application of measures promoting cost-effectiveness

Such a management information system would measure constantly the ability of the CMP to produce or maintain health among its users and to reinforce ideal professional behavior. Perhaps more important, it would enable the CMP to quantify progress toward quality objectives, so that profit margins will not be the only measure of plan performance. This ultimate information system will function as an educational device as well as a management tool.

Significant investments in health services research and education will be necessary to develop and test improved methods for organizing and managing giant medical care organizations. The group practice arrangements and the management tools sustaining today's competitive medical plans are at least fifty years old. If this "revolution" in medical care is to amount to anything more than prepaying and proliferating conventionally organized group practices, then a new tradition must be established. This new tradition must recognize the economic and social utility of investing in and improving the process of medical care delivery.

Dan Tosteson, speaking on competition and medical education, stated that:

Each clinical encounter is, in an important sense, unique and requires of the doctor an act of learning. The quality of learning determines the quality of care, and, conversely, the quality of care determines the quality of learning. This characteristic of medicine underlies the close association between teaching, research, and service in medical education. This triangle has been sustained by the special dedication of teaching hospitals to all three of its sides. It will persist in the future only.if some HMOs and other corporations delivering medical services are also committed to the fundamental unity of these dimensions of medicine. In short, it will require some *teaching* HMOs. Such organizations would have a great opportunity to address important issues that have been relatively neglected by academic medicine during recent decades.[19]

Tosteson then went on to say that it would be proper for some of the cost to be borne by HMO subscribers, so that academic activities could be treated as a legitimate cost of supplying medical services. I would go one step beyond, to say that the market of the future will not only sustain investments in research and education, it will require them.

THE CONSUMER SIDE OF THE HEALTH CARE MARKET

Traditional notions of competitive markets place ultimate power and responsibility in the hands of the consuming public. A competitive market in health care, however, poses some unique questions:

1. Who will choose to join competitive medical plans and why? Who will be excluded?
2. Does medical care lend itself to rational economic choices?
3. How can risk be equitably distributed among plans which are competing on price, where prices are determined by the risks posed by the enrolled populations?
4. What is the appropriate role of large intermediary buyers— business and the government—in representing large groups of consumers?

Certain trends in the economy and in the increasingly sophisticated marketing practices of competitive medical plans will highlight the potential seriousness of these problems. Major shifts in consumer response to competitive plans will be determined by changes in coverage levels and price sensitivity to health benefits; public policies that will affect CMPs' ability to segment the health care market; and CMPs' willingness to invest in market research, new product development, and advertising. All will entail changes in the traditional concerns and priorities of health plans.

Most of what is known about consumer response to competitive medical plans comes from studies of HMO members and their motives in joining. Our own research focuses on the Minneapolis-St. Paul HMO market, partly because the Twin Cities area offers the best example of a competitive environment. The response of consumers to the range of health plan choices in this market suggests what may happen across the country as competitive forces grow stronger.

Who Joins CMPs and Why?

Some theorists have argued that extensive third-party coverage discourages people from seeking out less expensive medical care. The Twin Cities' experience suggests that even heavily insured employed populations will join CMPs, if given the choice. Seven Minneappolis-St. Paul HMOs now enroll about 23 percent of the metropolitan population, almost exclusively through employers. People join CMPs because they are attracted by the scope of benefits and the characteristics of the delivery system. The promise of savings on total health care expenditures is paramount. Closely tied to cost are issues of access: CMPs attract patients in large part by removing the financial barriers to care and by guaranteeing entry into a coordinated system when needed. Increasing economic pressure on the individual should increase the power of this attraction.

If the prices of various competing plans are about the same (as they are in the Twin Cities), they will compete over other things that consumers value—specific benefits, delivery sites, locations, hours of service, and quality, for instance. Competition ultimately results in an attempt to fill the gaps in health benefits. It is conceivable that health care organizations could begin to extend their services into nonhealth areas (e.g., legal and financial services), especially if total fringe benefit levels were to be capped.

It has been widely speculated that CMPs attain lower hospital use rates partly because they attract better risk patients needing less care. Research to date indicates, however, no appreciable difference in health status between HMO members and traditionally insured populations matched for sex and age.[20] In fact, the comprehensive benefits offered by CMPs can be attractive to higher risk individuals precisely because they expect to need and use more health services: the higher premiums of CMPs are then "worthwhile."[21]

Conversely, individual plans suspect that those who do not use many services tend to disenroll from CMPs earlier than higher users, apparently deciding that their use of services is not sufficient to justify the higher initial cost of membership. (Research data to confirm or refute this common perception are not presently available.)

The experiences of several large Twin Cities' employers demonstrate the willingness of consumers to enroll in CMPs when given the chance. In several cases, over 40 percent of employee groups have enrolled in CMPs in the first few offerings; in one case, 70 percent signed up. Once people join, they become attached to the CMP approach to health care delivery. Sometimes they switch loyalties from personal physicians to a specific health plan, or to the CMP concept generally. When one physician group dropped out of a St. Paul health plan, the majority of the patients which that group had been seeing chose to remain with the plan and switch physicians. The fact that Twin Cities' HMO enrollment has grown from 5 percent of the population to 23 percent in five years attests to the kind of momentum that can build in a competitive market. Such rapid growth only comes, however, after some period of much slower growth, when CMPs are establishing their reputations and community awareness is building.

The Twin Cities' experience also suggests that the potential for large enrollments in CMPs is much improved when large numbers of physicians are participating in CMP arrangements. Here, consumers joining HMOs have about 80 percent of the local physicians to choose from in one or another of the plans. In fact, the much higher rate of physicians participating suggests that the provider side of the market may well be transformed before a majority of consumers are enrolled in CMPs.

On a national scale, the economic factors that make CMPs attractive to consumers—lower total costs for health care and the elimination of unexpected medical expenses—can only become more important as the economy tightens. Some of the other factors that distinguish CMPs from traditional indemnity insurance—a coordinated delivery system, more convenient access, greater responsiveness to consumer demands, and ultimately, greater ability to measure and assure quality—will also serve to strengthen the market position of CMPs. In general, consumer demand for CMPs is a slow growing but inexorable force that will generate increasing competition in the health care system.

If the entire system is to be shaped by competitive forces, attention must be paid to those portions of the market which are presently excluded from CMPs. Because of the high level of coverage (and concomitant high premiums) characteristic of CMPs, many employee groups whose health benefit levels are lower are excluded. New competitive arrangements which, perhaps like the PPOs described earlier, have the flexibility to tailor benefit packages to the need of individual groups and local market conditions might be better able to enroll that part of the market.

The other major groups to whom CMPs are not widely available are Medicare and Medicaid beneficiaries. The intermittent eligibility of Medicaid recipients has effectively precluded their participation in arrangements requiring year-long contracts. Medicare has not allowed capitation contracts, and providers are not able to pass on any efficiencies to Medicare recipients in the form of greater benefits. Fixed capitation contracts are being tested in a number of demonstration projects, including one in the Twin Cities. Here, four HMOs will compete for Medicare enrollees. Preliminary evidence from other communities indicates that CMPs can cut Medicare hospitalization by about two days per person per year.[22] If these savings are converted to more benefits, CMPs should prove extremely attractive to Medicare beneficiaries.

Can Consumers Make Wise Health Care Choices?

When the feasibility of a marketplace approach to health care is discussed, someone usually asks whether consumers can be trusted to make wise choices. Traditionally, "purchases" of medical care services have been made under adverse circumstances; sick people have no inclination to comparison shop. HMOs deal with this problem by enrolling people in advance of the provision of services (when they are well). (The lack of such an advance purchase feature may be a principal weakness of PPOs, and of major risk insurance as well.)

Consumers find it difficult to choose between health plans, especially when deciding for the first time. While it is hard to know how consumers assess the quality of the care they receive, it is clearly important to them. Some people choose a CMP because they perceive its care as better than that provided by the traditional system. Conversely, some people who choose not to enroll in a CMP cite their perceptions that CMPs provide an inferior quality of care. Until more precise ways of measuring quality are developed and made available to the public, decisions based on perceptions of quality will remain highly subjective and unpredictable.

The reactions of HMO members are easier to assess. Some HMOs have experienced very sharp drops in enrollment following large premium increases or management changes that led to perceptible shifts in providers' attitudes toward the plan and its subscribers. Overall, consumers' own ratings of their satisfaction with their medical care and their reenrollment behavior provide the best indicators of their opinions. Consumer surveys conducted by individual plans, by employers, and recently by Louis Harris and Associates, indicate a high level of satisfaction with the CMP style of medical care delivery. The Harris survey found in a national sample that a slightly higher percentage of HMO members than members of the general public were "very satisfied" with their care. Reenrollment statistics provide a valuable measure: only 3 percent of the Harris HMO member sample reported that they did not intend to reenroll, most for eligibility reasons.[23]

It is virtually certain that known and significant differences in quality will not be tolerated as a matter of health policy. Once we have the means to measure quality, we will insist that it be measured and uniformly assured. It will not be left up to individuals to discover poor quality for themselves. I personally believe that we can attribute the fact that we have no good quality assurance sytsems to date to the absence of defined populations to study. The expansion of CMPs will provide new quality assurance and research opportunities.

Market Segmentation and Equitable Risk Distribution

Another historically inviolable principle of national health policy is that medical care must be available to all, regardless of age, health status, or ability to pay. Achievement of that objective has meant that risk must be evenly distributed across groups so that lower risk populations subsidize higher risk ones. A health system organized around CMPs should achieve the same result; separate CMPs for the healthy and for the sick would not. The incentives under a competitive scheme, however, may encourage just such a separation. From a financial standpoint, CMPs will want to enroll the lowest risk populations, and consumers will want to join the plan offering the lowest premium cost.

Market research is providing increasingly precise information about the different services which different segments of the population value and require. Such information will allow CMPs to develop products (i.e., a variety of benefit packages or a basic benefit package and supplemental riders) and market them to the segments they are in the best position to attract. Some "natural" segmentation of the health care market is created by demographic factors (age, sex, employment, income, etc.). More segmentation is created by traditional insurance practices (e.g., experience rating) and employer policies (e.g., level of health premium contribution rates, benefits, and specific offering methods). Legislated benefit levels can also segment the market.

In developing their marketing strategies, CMPs can segment the market further, intentionally or inadvertently. The location of delivery sites is one obvious way to take advantage of geographic segmentation. A plan's premium structure and benefit packages can be designed to attract certain segments of the market. (There is evidence to suggest that higher consumer premium contributions result in the enrollment of higher risk subscribers,[24] and conversely that the lower the cost to the consumer, the lower the health risk of those who enroll.) The makeup of a plan's physician panel also determines who joins: large IPAs contend that they attract a higher risk population than closed-panel group practice plans.

Advertising campaigns can be designed to attract certain market segments, although sometimes the effect is unforeseen. In Minneapolis, the 1,600-physician IPA has built its marketing efforts around the ability of potential enrollees to retain their preexisting physician relationship. The plan's management now contends that many high utilizers are being attracted to the plan through their established ties to specialty physicians. Those enrollees have also been willing to pay somewhat higher premiums to retain their own physicians (which provides further confirmation of the consumer contribution-risk relationship mentioned above).

Some CMPs (Kaiser and others) have chosen out of principle to attract a broad cross section of the market. Some of the worst-risk segments of the populations may be attractive to physicians from a professional challenge standpoint, setting up a valuable counterbalance between a plan's professional and financial objectives.

It is clear that, whatever the specific causes, segmentation of the health care market does take place, to the advantage of some CMPs and individuals and the disadvantage of others. Until now, the public policy response to market segmentation has been to require CMPs to hold open enrollment and to community-rate. However, carefully designed marketing strategies will enable CMPs to reduce their financial risks while complying with open enrollment and community rating requirements. The impact of sophisticated advertising techiniques—never before a relevant factor in medical care—on consumer choices and market segmentation could be dramatic and should be closely watched.

The Role of Large Buyers: Business and Government

The best countervailing force in balancing market segmentation with broad policy objectives is an increasingly sophisticated cadre of large buyers—chiefly corporations acting on behalf of their employees and government on behalf of the elderly and the poor. These large buyers are absolutely critical to the process, but they are ill equipped to exercise their responsibility.

Employers have little expertise in dealing with the health care delivery system. Employee benefits departments have historically administered benefits simply by negotiating with brokers, and they have not had to deal with difficult issues like employee health status and risk. When corporations decide to take an active role in managing their health care costs, they often find at the outset that they are completely without the information they require. In some cases they have no data on the people they are covering or on the services being provided.

Corporations are, however, attempting to adjust to their responsibility in very hopeful ways. They are designing information systems with which to manage health benefits programs; once that information is available, it will be useful in monitoring fee-for-service performance as well as CMPs. They are studying their employees' enrollment behavior and experiences while in CMPs, with attention to the impact on absenteeism, productivity, and direct health care expenditures.

They are developing methods of evaluating health plans to improve the services and options available to their employees.

The aged and the poor will continue to need an intermediary, presumably the government. If Medicare recipients were allowed to enroll in CMPs, many formerly employed members of CMPs would be likely to remain in their plans upon retirement. (They might be able to do so even if they moved to Florida because the CMP field is likely to be dominated by national firms with branches in key areas.) Perhaps our best safeguard against a two-class medical care system is to require that the poor account for no more than a fixed proportion of any health plan's enrollment.

RADICAL CHANGE SLOWLY

Competition will transform the health care industry slowly. Even under the best of conditions, it will take fifteen to twenty years for price competition to become the major economic force governing the performance of the industry. Scenarios assuming extraordinary rates of growth project that less than one-third of the U.S. population will be enrolled in CMPs by 1990. Furthermore, the required structural reforms will prove so difficult to achieve that it behooves us to move slowly. The long-term quality of the components of a new competitive health system could be jeopardized by vigorous, artificial acceleration. Without caution, intended reforms could be an invitation to "quick-buck" artists, as happened in California with the Medicaid-induced prepaid health plans.

The process of growth could be naturally accelerated by the successful development of new types of CMPs like PPOs, or by an increase in the public's desire to find less costly sources of medical care. If, however, the expansion of competition depends on classical HMO plans, then the market for expansion in the number and size of plans, will be confined to the more liberally insured segment of workers. Growth under these conditions will be slow, but it will achieve substantial momentum by 1990. At that point, the powerful impact of a continuing exponential rate of growth will take effect. A study conducted for the Health Industry Manufacturers Association by Inter-Study estimated that 36 million people will be obtaining their medical care from CMPs by 1990. This projection assumed a 12 percent compound annual growth rate to existing CMPs, 6 million enrollees in plans yet to be formed, and the Medicare market being opened to CMPs. It should be noted that the opening of the Medicare market would provide a tremendous boost to CMP development. Revenue per capita for the Medicare population would be approximately four times revenue per capita for a typical employed population. While CMP experience with the elderly population is limited, it is apparent that CMPs can be expected to cut hospital use by 1,000 to 2,000 days per year for every 1,000 elderly enrollees, a considerable potential cost savings for the plans. Medicare enrollment in CMPs might thus be expected to have an even greater impact on the health care system than the enrollment of employed groups.

Patterns of Growth in CMPs

Despite the variety of their varying organizational and sponsorship arrangements, highly successful group practice CMPs in diverse parts of the country (Boston, Minneapolis, Denver) are showing similar patterns of growth. Each of these plans has enrolled 80,000 to 100,000 over a period of around ten years (see Figures 4-1, 4-2, and 4-3).

Figure 4-1. Harvard Community Health Plan Enrollment, 1969-80.

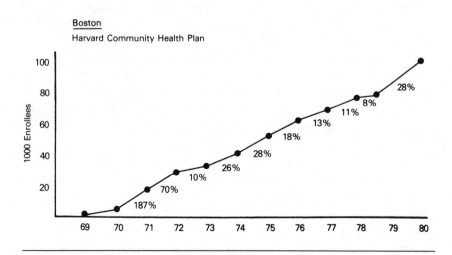

Harvard Community Health Plan is a pure prepaid group practice, staffed by doctors hired by the health plan.
Source: Harvard Community Health Plan.

Figure 4-2. MedCenter Health Plan Enrollment, 1971–80.

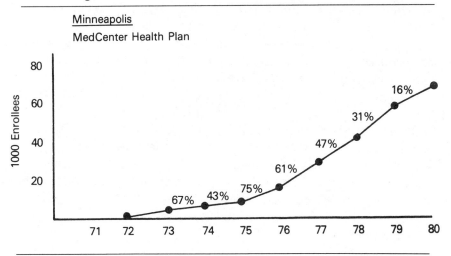

The MedCenter Health Plan is the prepaid component of the St. Louis Park Clinic, a well established, fee-for-service group practice.
Source: HMO Annual Reports of the Minnesota Department of Health, and InterStudy.

Figure 4-3. Kaiser Health Plan Enrollment in Denver, 1969-80.

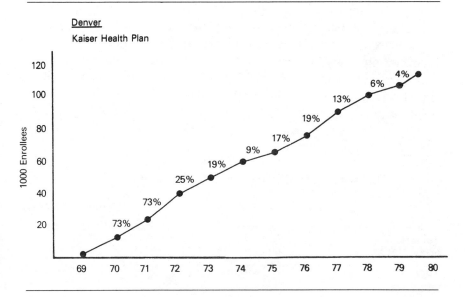

Kaiser-Denver is a regional division of a national medical care organization; the medical group is an independent partnership that contracts with the health plan.
Source: Kaiser Foundation Health Plan of Colorado.

As plans become older, their growth rates drop, but they continue to exhibit increases in numbers of enrollees that are truly impressive. Kaiser in northern California, for example, is now growing at an annual rate of only 6.4 percent, but over the past three years the number of enrollees has increased by 336,000. In a plan like Kaiser, which must invest in both office and hospital facilities for each new enrollee, the capital investment associated with growth amounts to $600,000 in new facilities for every 1,000 people enrolled per year.

Some of the IPA-model CMPs made up of 1,000 or more independent practitioners have exhibited more rapid rates of growth and, apparently, shorter takeoff periods, though none has yet attained the size of some of the older, well-established group practice plans. The largest IPA in the country, Wisconsin Physician Services, enrolls approximately 165,000 people, and the largest groups include more than 1.6 million.[25]

Growth in Local Markets

The composite growth patterns of CMPs for entire communities exhibit few common characteristics, except that successful CMPs seem to trigger the formation of additional plans. This proliferation of plans sets in motion the kind of rapid growth we have seen in the Twin Cities market.

While enrollment growth in competitive medical plans is slow at first, its exponential character leads to substantial increases later on. If several plans are operating in a given community, impressive overall growth rates can be achieved fairly rapidly. This tendency is illustrated on a community-wide basis in the Twin Cities, where enrollment doubles about every three years (see Table 4-2 and Figure 4-4).

Table 4-2. HMO Enrollment in the Twin Cities.

Year	HMO Enrollment	Number of HMOs
1977	43,000	1
1974	83,000	6
1977	187,000	7
1980	423,000	7

Figure 4-4. Minneapolis-St. Paul Metropolitan Area, HMO Enrollment, 1971-80

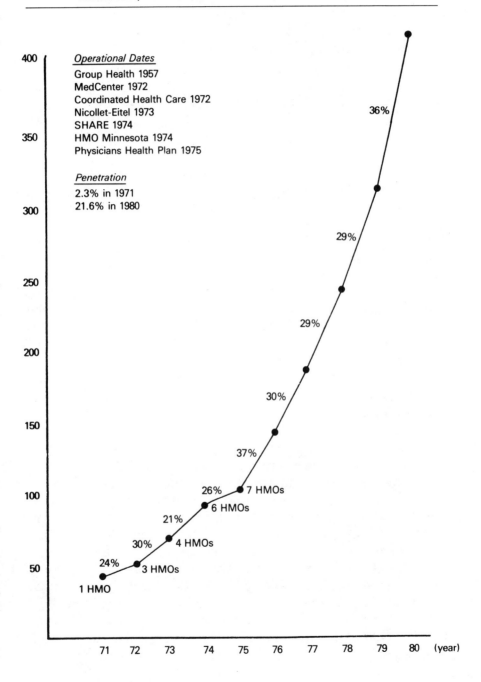

Although the most rapid growth in CMP market share is occuring in the Twin Cities—CMP penetration reached 20 percent eight years after the second plan became operational—ever higher levels of consumer enrollment have been achieved in the San Francisco and Los Angeles areas. Some large cities with multiple plans, however, show inexplicably slow rates of growth. For example, it took the six HMOs in Philadelphia six years and the six HMOs in Chicago ten years to achieve penetrations of 3.1 percent by 1980. The most common explanation for this sluggishness is that CMPs face accessibility problems in sprawling metropolitan areas. Such markets require CMPs to make large capital investments for multiple locations and to pursue aggressive marketing strategies if rapid growth is to occur.

Full-scale competition across the nation will be a long time in coming. In 1970, there were fewer than 40 prepaid health plans. Now, ten years later, there are more than 240 operating HMOs enrolling 9.7 million people (see Figure 4–5). Furthermore, 220 plans are in various stages of development, indicating continued strong growth in the industry. Since only one-third of all the standard metropolitan statistical areas (SMSAs) have even one HMO, it is not unreasonable to assume that the potential for development is strong throughout the 1980s and that by 1990 we might have at least 500 operational HMOs (see Table 4–3).

Making the wild assumption that 260 new plans grow at the same impressive rate MedCenter experienced during its first ten years (85,000), enrollment in the 260 plans would be 28.2 million in 1990. This, added to 30 million enrollees in existing plans, would lead to a total enrollment of 58.2 million.

Another approach to forecasting growth would be to consider local health markets with the highest potential for HMO enrollment—those which now contain at least one plan. These cities, each an individual health care market area, are most likely to experience the proliferation of more competing health plans and to become markets in which the majority of physicians and hospitals compete for patients on the basis of cost. Currently, 114 million people live in the ninety-one cities with one or more HMO. The populations of these cities are likely to grow to 132.2 million by 1990. If competing health plans were to display the same growth rate as those in Minneapolis-St. Paul and achieve a 20 percent penetration in each market, 26.5 million people would be enrolled by 1990. If one assumes that, on average, 5 percent of the population of the cities which now have no HMOs

Figure 4-5. Growth of Prepaid Health Care Plan Enrollment in the United States

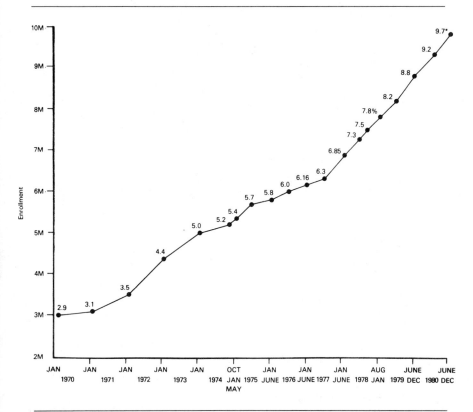

Source: "National HMO Census of Prepaid Plans 1979", OHMO

(now 45.5 million people) enroll in newly emerging plans, an additional 2.6 million people would receive health care from HMOs. That means a total of 29.1 million urban enrollees (see Table 4-3).

Using even more optimistic, market-based assumptions, we would still achieve less than 33 percent CMP penetration of the total U.S. market by 1990. If competing health plans were to achieve a 40 percent penetration in each of the markets where one or more HMOs exist, and if 10 percent of the population in cities where no HMOs exist were to enroll in newly emerging plans, only 57.4 million people (or 31 percent of the population) would be enrolled by 1990 (see Table 4-3).

Table 4-3. HMO Distribution by Standard Metropolitan Statistical Area (SMSA) for 1980 with Projections for 1990.

	SMSAs with One or More HMOs in 1980		SMSAs without an HMO in 1980	
	Number of SMSAs	1978 Total Population (millions)	Number of SMSAs	1978 Total Population (millions)
SMSAs with population over 500,000 (N = 71)	57	104	14	10
SMSAs with 200,000 to 500,000 population (N = 88)	23	7.5	65	21
SMSAs with population under 200,000 (N = 122)	11	2	111	14.5
Total for 1980	91	113.5	190	45.5
1990 population estimates		130.5[a]		52.3[a]
1990 estimated number of CMP enrollees	26.1	26.1 (assumes 20 percent penetration)	2.6	2.6 (assumes 5 percent penetration)
	52.2	52.2 (assumes 40 percent penetration)[b]		5.2 (assumes 10 percent penetration)[b]

[a]Assumes 15 percent population growth rate.
[b]Assumes an unreasonable rate of penetration.

Interim Measures: Utilization Controls

Can we expect the economy to tolerate continued substantial increases in medical care costs for another fifteen to twenty years while competitive market forces take hold? If not, events in the interim may be as important as the ultimate impact of competition. The performance of the traditional side of the health system may be somewhat improved by a ripple effect from CMPs. Several researchers have observed slowing trends in expenditure and cost increases and declines in the overall rate of hospital utilization in communities where CMPs have enrolled 16 percent to 20 percent of the population.[26] It must be noted, however, that strong CMPs have been present in those markets for at least ten years, so the spillover effect probably will not suffice in the short run.

Clearly, then, something more must be done to curb the inflation of health care costs soon. Ideally, interim measures installed now would not interfere with the further development of the competitive system. Of the many cost containment techniques that might be proposed, the most promising appear to be those that attempt to control the amount of hospitalization. There is considerable agreement that excessive hospitalization is currently the norm in most communities, with a national average of 1,206 days per 1,000. Yet rates in San Diego and Honolulu are as low as 724 and 746 days per 1,000, respectively.[27] Furthermore, as previously noted, the Mayo Clinic provides care to residents of Olmsted County, Minnesota, at an age-adjusted rate of 770 days per 1,000.[28] Utilization rates can be lowered by a change in community values, the presence of excellent medical groups, or the introduction of CMPs. If something must be done to cut costs in the short run, there is no more direct way than to eliminate excess hospitalization.

The kind of utilization controls that are being perfected by HMOs, and even their standards for application, could be used by the entire health system without changing the organization of physicians within the delivery system. Several large IPAs, operating under competitive pressure from group-model CMPs, have shown that nonjudgmental systems for cutting admissions and length of stay can be effectively applied. IPAs not faced with strong competition, however, have found it difficult to make onerous controls stick. The PSRO experience certainly suggests the difficulty of enforcing controls based on utilization review.

The principal requirements of effective utilization control schemes appear to be: preadmission review of all nonemergency cases; specification of appropriate length of stay at the time of admission; careful discharge planning and concurrent review; retrospective review to justify longer-than-average stays and to assure quality; financial penalties for failure to comply with admission procedures; and incentives to perform as many services as possible on an outpatient basis. The entire system should require minimal clinical judgment, and should be administrable by nonphysicians, using an automated information system.

For hospital utilization controls to work, physicians must accept them. Finding a way to make controls acceptable will be a major challenge. Perhaps it could be done through a revitalized Voluntary Effort; HMOs and IPAs report that a sense of teamwork and commitment on the part of their physicians is the intangible glue behind successful utilization controls. Once good providers become convinced through exposure to controls that reducing hospitalization will not reduce quality of care (and may even improve it), they will begin to change their behavior. Structurally, utilization control systems could be made available across the country if all insurers were to offer both a traditional insurance plan and a PPO. Participation in the PPO would require compliance with effective utilization controls.

A strategy combining market forces and direct utilization controls seems to be emerging among major employers and traditional insurers in the Twin Cities. When over half of an employer's workforce is enrolled in HMOs, the traditional insurance premiums for the remainder tend to rise. Employers are now asking insurers to install IPA-type utilization controls in their indemnity plans in an effort to curb excess utilization by that residual population.

From the standpoint of the developing market, utilization controls will not prohibit the entry of new competitive medical plans. They are easy to get rid of; in fact, they are so onerous that physicians are delighted to be rid of them. In the worst case for competition advocates, hospital utilization controls could bring the cost of medical care in the conventional system so low in some markets that competitive medical plans would find it difficult to get a foothold.

NOTES

1. Cited in Joseph L. Falkson, *HMOs and the Politics of Health System Reform* (Chicago: American Hospital Association, 1980), pp. 18-19.

2.   *Ibid.*
3.   *Ibid.*
4.   Presidential Health Message, presented to Congress February 18, 1970.
5.   Alain C. Enthoven, *Health Plan* (Reading, Mass.: Addison-Wesley, 1980).
6.   Falkson, *HMOs*, p. 16.
7.   Center for Research in Ambulatory Health Care Administration, *The Organization and Development of a Medical Group Practice* (Cambridge, Mass.: Ballinger Publishing Company, 1976).
8.   Falkson, *HMOs*, p. 16.
9.   *Ibid.*
10. *Ibid.*, p. 18.
11. Arthur Owens, "The Financial Penalty of Solo Practice," *Medical Economics* (December 8, 1980).
12. Lenore Kligman, *July 1980 Survey Results: HMO Enrollment and Utilization in the United States* (Minneapolis: InterStudy, November 1980).
13. F.T. Nobrega, I. Krishan, R.K. Smoldt, W.J. McClure, E. Mohler, "Development of estimates of utilization of health care services in a defined population." Report to the Bureau of Health Planning. DHEW, Contract Number HRA-231-77-0116 (May 22, 1979).
14. Linda Krane Ellwein and Leonore Kligman, *An Overview of Group Practice HMOs: Survey Results, March 1979* (Minneapolis: InterStudy, 1979).
15. G.B. Meier and J. Tillotson, *Physician Reimbursement and Hospital Use in HMOs* (Minneapolis: InterStudy, 1978).
16. Blue Cross and Blue Shield cannot be categorized as a national CMP sponsor because the sixty-five Blue Cross and Blue Shield organizations are autonomous and the affiliated CMPs are not centrally organized.
17. A.S. Relman, "The New Medical Industrial Complex," *New England Journal of Medicine* 303 (1980): 17.
18. P.J. Held and U. Reinhardt, "Analysis of Economic Performance in Medical Group Practice" (July 1979).
19. Daniel Tosteson, "Competition, HMOs, Medicine and Medical Education" (Paper for Conference on HMOs and Academic Medical Centers: Prospects for the Future, Colorado Springs, Colorado, October 23, 1980).
20. Mark S. Blumberg, "Health Status and Health Care Use by Type of Private Health Coverage," *Millbank Memorial Fund Quarterly* 58 (1980): 633.
21. M.I. Roemer, R.W. Hetherington, C.E. Hopkins, A.E. Gerst, E. Parsons, and D.M. Long, *Health Insurance Effects: Services, Expen-*

ditures and Attitudes under Three Types of Plans (Ann Arbor: University of Michigan School of Public Health, 1973).

22. P. Eggers, "Risk Difference between Medicare Beneficiaries Enrolled and Not Enrolled in an HMO," *Health Care Financing Review* 1, no. 3 (Winter 1980): 91–99.

23. Louis Harris and Associates, "American Attitudes toward Health Maintenance Organizations" (Henry J. Kaiser Family Foundation, Study #794021, July 1980).

24. S.L. Susman, "Selectivity among Enrollees in a Prepaid Group Practice Model HMO: The Relationship between the Employee Premium Contribution and Market Penetration and Utilization" (M.P.H. essay, Yale University, 1980).

25. InterStudy Health Systems Demographic Center, "Twin Cities HMO Enrollment" (Minneapolis: InterStudy, February, 1980).

26. M.S. Blumberg, "Morbidity Standardized Hospital Use Ratios by Type of Private Health Coverage" (work paper, 1981); B.R. Chiswick, "Hospital Utilization: An Analysis of SMSA Differences in Occupancy Rates, Admission Rates, and Bed Rates," *Explorations in Economic Research* 3 (1976): 326–78; L.D. Goldberg and W. Greenberg, "Staff Report on the Health Maintenance Organization and Its Effects on Competition" (Federal Trade Commission, Bureau of Economics, 1977); L.K. Ellwein, "Minneapolis-St. Paul Summary Highlights" (InterStudy, August 1979).

27. InterStudy Health Systems Demographic Center, op. cit.

28. F.T. Nobrega, I. Krishan, R.K. Smoldt, W.J. McClure, E. Mohler, op. cit.

RESPONSE
by *Walter J. McNerney*

I should like to comment on Paul's paper from the perspective of a large financing health prepayment group. Let me start with our points of agreement. First, Paul is wise to consider the development of a competitive environment as an evolutionary process lasting fifteen to twenty years. In this context, it is important to be forceful with experiments to achieve breakthroughs. But even if the experiments are bold and uniformly successful, our progress will be slow, and I, like Paul, would hate to see new competition models developed in the expectation that three or five years will suffice.

I also agree with Paul's feeling that the HMO definition got fixed too soon. His first writings described the concept of the health maintenance organization as highly flexible, capable of assuming different forms, and performing different functions, but the federal government chose a specific variant early and encased it in statute and regulation. The result was that we quickly lost room for innovation. We need to recapture it.

Paul is right to urge us to get moving. When Congress and the president first expressed interest in the development of a competitive environment, many thought that we were dealing with a passing fancy. We are not. The thrust for competition has a lot more force behind it than was first apparent. But, if we are to capitalize on the opportunity presently before us, we had better start now to develop the management, marketing, capital and other resources required. The competitive models we have known are small, local units with unsophisticated management and marketing. The transition to larger networks and larger markets requires new organizations and new points of view. Finally, I agree that better care often costs less.

Let me turn to a few issues raised by Paul. First, I should like to see us begin talking more sensibly about the relationship between regulation and competition. As I see it, it is not a question of regulation versus competition, it is a question of blend. And it is not simply the substitution of regulation that facilitates competition for regulation that frustrates it. We must also consider voluntary effort, an effort at self-regulation that makes the interaction of competition and regulation palatable and ultimately workable. Given the extraordinary complexity of the incentives and disincentives we are trying to change, our reference framework must be broad.

Second, I should like to talk about some problems we have to face as we create a competitive environment. If we mishandle it, the effort to create a competitive environment could lead to more regulation, not less. For example, we cannot let people make bad choices, we cannot let people be dropped peremptorily by carriers, and we cannot allow interruptions in protection or significant gaps in coverage. Should we deal with these and other considerations through regulation?

Perhaps the most difficult problem is selection. We have heard considerable discussion about the difficulties that consumers will face in trying to determine the benefits and costs of the options that competition will create for them, but my experience is that people with choices use them shrewdly. This is particularly true of those with the most risk. As older persons and people of poorer health select better coverage during open-enrollment periods, the price of more complete coverage is driven up. Meanwhile, younger persons and people of better health select less coverage and drive its price down. Thus, the risk pool is fragmented. If we are to pursue competition seriously, we must be prepared to face this issue, either with state pools for bad risks who cannot get taken care of otherwise, or tighter control of the options, or both.

A problem that is easy to overlook is marketing. We have to face the fact that there may be more people opposed to the creation of the competitive environment than for it. Much of industry has problems with it; labor does; our competitors do; and I think the American Medical Association is at least skeptical. Private sector inertia will be an important obstacle to the creation of a competitive environment.

It is important to prevent federal intervention, either supportive or obstructive, from handicapping the competitive market. In this connection, it is instructive to consider the history of the HMO Act. That legislation lost sight of the results it was created to achieve. Instead of focusing on the objective of reducing the rate of admissions to hospitals and supporting anyone with a reasonable scheme to achieve that goal, the legislation prescribed a format and structure to be used regardless of the setting, the purpose, or the outcome.

A problem that insurers must face is the fact that the individual customer is a different customer from the group customer. In our work with groups, we have tried to exercise some cost containment controls, and labor and management have usually been supportive, hoping that our success would bring down the cost of production or insurance premiums. On the other hand, a probability sample survey of Federal Employee Program enrollees showed that one of the things that our customers are upset about is that we are challenging inappropriate use patterns. They want protection from us, and not a lot of questions surrounding their protection. That attitude can result in inflated costs, and we will have to find some way to change it. There are other perils and pitfalls to worry about. There isn't time to bring them up here, but those who want to create a competitive environment should examine closely our market experience to date.

Let me add two more observations. Paul underscored the need for facts, but there are a few important ones he ignored. First, saying that multispecialty groups are the best providers is not very helpful.

The fact is that some individual practice associations are doing good jobs and some are doing poor jobs. Which IPA is doing a good job? Is it the IPA that has the fortitude to deal with hospital care prospectively and concurrently as well as retrospectively? The IPA which does that seems to get worthwhile results. Or is it the IPA that puts the primary care physician on capitation payments and runs all referrals through him? That arrangement also seems to get worthwhile results. I think we need a more searching analysis of multispecialty groups; we need to know whether that particular corporate form is superior or whether other forms are deserving of support.

Another unpleasant fact that we have to discuss candidly is the number of HMOs that are in trouble. A lot have gone under, and a lot more are struggling simply to stay afloat. And so many have been propped up by nonmarket forces like government subsidies that it is not clear how many more are in trouble. I think we should find out the reasons why.

Finally, I should like to see Paul address the extraordinary variety of activity now going on. As he pointed out, there is a great deal of ferment among hospitals, where almost a third of the beds are now under shared services and 20 percent are involved in networking. Health insurers are also changing their ways. Along with many of our competitors in the health insurance business, we are constantly looking at new schemes. In Blue Cross and Blue Shield, we are involved in seventy HMOs, and we are looking for new ways of doing things as well. There is no end to the arrangements possible between a consortium of hospitals and a Blue Cross and Blue Shield plan. HMOs are promising, but they are only one of many possibilities. There are many ways of tearing down the walls between the financing and delivery of health care, and we should encourage any which seems responsible and which seems to lead toward less use of the most expensive facilities and greater use of substitute facilities providing good services at less cost.

DISCUSSION

Bill Beers: The primary thing that concerns me is the slow pace at which a competitive system will develop. Costs are rising so fast that a competitive system will have to evolve and succeed quickly to preclude the need for further government intervention. As a business-man, I am a strong believer in the private sector, and I would like to prevent further government intrusion into the field of health care.

I first got interested in health care costs when I became involved with the Voluntary Effort. I began to think about the health insur-ance options offered to Kraft employees, and I realized I didn't even know how much we were spending. So I went to the personnel de-partment and asked. After some research, it was determined that our corporate expenditure was about $1,000 per employee per year, or almost $1 per share of corporate earnings. Now, I can't think of any other phase of our business where there was that amount of money involved and no one working twenty-four hours a day to control the costs. Yet I think you would find the same thing at other corpora-tions, for we all tend to regard the expense of health insurance and benefits as part of the usual and customary package of total employee benefits—and therefore sacred.

Business can do an enormous amount to help control these costs. Businesses can support the Voluntary Effort. Businesses can encour-age their employees to get involved in community health issues, to work in health planning agencies or for the establishment of health maintenance organizations. Businesses can contribute their sophisti-cated systems to the management of health care services and facilities. Businesses can work with their employees to help them develop healthier life-styles, by making available exercise facilities and by discouraging smoking, drugs, and excessive drinking. None of these things is hard. They don't require vast sums of money or the move-ment of thousands of people. They simply require the attention of the people who run our businesses.

How do you get their attention? We can talk on and on about rede-signing corporate benefits, encouraging alternative delivery systems, and promoting new legislation, but the fastest way to get action is to make the business community understand the real cost. When cor-porate leaders see the amount they spend on health, they will quickly begin to figure out ways to get their employees to take some respon-sibility for their own health. And they will bring their first-line management to bear on the financing and delivery of health services. At that point, I think we will begin to make some progress.

David Hamburg: I appreciated Paul Ellwood's thoughtful and forward-looking paper. Having grown up under Alain Enthoven's tutelage, I come to this subject with a sympathetic disposition, and I tried to see to it that the Institute of Medicine would provide a useful forum for elucidating the potentialities of competitive health plans. At the moment, I sit with great interest on the board of the Harvard Community Health Plan. That new responsibility particularly makes me want to face up a little more explicitly to some of the professional and scientific challenges posed by competitive health plans.

One is to make sure that costs are restrained mainly by diminishing unnecessary services, and not by diminishing valuable services. Second is whether, in fact, there is a continuing emphasis on preventive services, as, for instance, the term "health maintenance organization" implies. Third, and perhaps a subset of the second, is whether there is adequate attention to the behavioral medicine component of care, to the enormous problems created by smoking and alcohol, for example. Fourth is whether coverage can be extended beyond the relatively well-educated, middle-class people who have enrolled in these plans up to now. Fifth, and this pursues a point that Paul Ellwood made and that I hope he will draw out, is whether the plans will find ways to foster research and development, both for the direct benefit of the competitive health plans and also for the benefit to society of the information that they have the capability of generating. Sixth, is there an appropriate role for the education of health professionals in the setting of competitive health plans? Finally, it seems to me that the crucial challenge in the next few decades in the technically advanced countries, including our own, is the change in the age composition of the population. I need hardly belabor the fact that the elderly face distinctive problems. Our goal must be to help them cope with those problems and to sustain their functional independence as long as possible. Can the competitive health plans offer us any assistance in that effort?

Fred Coe: I gather that there is considerable support for the idea that corporations be required to offer their employees a choice of health plans. But I gather that the employer must pay the same amount for either one of them, and I don't see how that reduces the cost of health care or how it gets corporations interested in the development of competition.

Alain Enthoven: The problem today is that most employers are, for tax and other reasons, telling their employees, "We will pay the whole thing whatever you do." The most remarkable example is the contract between the automobile companies and the auto workers in Michigan, under which the employer pays the whole cost of either plan the employee chooses. The Blue Cross and Blue Shield plan costs more than the Health Alliance Plan, but employees are given no economic incentive to choose the less costly plan. As a result, the Health Alliance Plan attracts many fewer members than it otherwise might.

On the other hand, there are employers like the state of California and Stanford University which say to their employees, "We will pay a fixed dollar amount toward the cost of the health insurance plan which you choose. You must pay the difference between that amount and the annual premium of the plan which you choose." As I can tell you from personal experience, that arrangement makes you cost conscious. Each year my wife and I look at the options, talk to our friends, and make a choice.

I have talked with doctors involved in this competition, and they can see that the people deciding whether to join their plans are cost conscious. If consumers think that a particular plan doesn't offer them good value, they don't join it. And, since there are not enough patients to keep all the doctors busy all the time, the doctors are organizing themselves and their services to make their product more attractive. There is nothing mysterious about it. It's very straightforward. It's simply bringing health services into the same economic marketplace in which the rest of our private enterprise economy operates.

Karl Bays: We haven't gone as far as that, but we now have an arrangement with our employees under which they must pay something, and we find that they are much more interested and make much more informed choices. We also find that we have been able to lower the rate at which our corporate expenditures for employee health increase.

Paul Rogers: I think the discussion has been excellent today, and it has certainly stimulated my thinking. Competition sounds great. I think it is interesting though that, if you look back, you can see that our government has a way of responding to national needs. After the war, we needed facilities, and somehow private enterprise couldn't produce them. So the federal government got involved, and we passed Hill-Burton. Now we have too many—100,000 beds too many, some people say. Look at our manpower: We had what we perceived to be an acute shortage of physicians, the government advanced some programs, the universities responded magnificently, and today they say we may have enough doctors.

Now the problem is the economy: inflation, rising costs, and the government centrally involved, so people are talking about a competitive system. Now what does that mean? Does it mean more care? Does it mean less care? Does it mean more cost? Or less cost? Well, I think it means that people want the kind of health care they have now, only they want it to cost less. In the discussion today I didn't hear people say that they're basically dissatisfied with health care in America. No one said, "I can't get care if and when I need it." There are some problems of course, but I didn't hear any criticism of the quality or the availability of care in the country, so I gather that the problem is cost. And perhaps these competitive medical plans are the answer to that national need. I just hope we won't try to move too rapidly. I don't think anyone objects to the development of a competitive system—no one should—but I think we need to keep our real goal in view. If our goal is to cut cost, then we ought to gear our thinking to that. I hope that competition will help us do that, but I think we've got to be cautious and not expect too much too soon.

Karen Davis: I want to make a few comments about the management of health care institutions—first about HMOs. Some concern was expressed about the rate of failure among HMOs. So far the experience hasn't been that bad: of 113 federally qualified HMOs, only 7 have gotten into financial difficulties, and 3 of those were taken over by other organizations that are still functioning. That is not a bad default rate, but there are certain to be more failures down the road because HMOs are complex institutions, difficult to organize and difficult to manage.

I liked Mr. Beers's suggestion that the business community provide more technical assistance to nonprofit hospitals, but I think they are generally well managed. What concerns me about the emphasis on competition is that we are talking about saving money by reducing hospitalization, a situation in which competitive medical plans earn profits, while hospitals suffer. My experience is that hospitals respond to incentives. Their incentives now are to keep their beds filled and to provide high volumes of services. By changing the incentives, we could motivate hospitals to develop a full range of health services for their communities and to reduce inpatient services wherever appropriate.

John Cooper: We've talked today about industry and the introduction of competition into the world of medicine. I would like to know the views of the people here about the development of company medical plans. Companies like Ford and General Motors have a history of creating the products and operating the services that they need. Company medical plans would give those corporations the opportunity to introduce their own management into the health care system and to control its operation very tightly. How about that as an alternative to the competitive system?

Doug Eavenson: We have talked about that at General Motors from time to time. The question you have to confront before you take over and begin providing a service which you now buy is whether you can run the service better or more efficiently. We are not at all sure that we could.

The other problem I want to discuss is the reluctance of the unions to discuss alternative health insurance arrangements. We have repeatedly suggested approaches of the kind that Alain Enthoven described, and they are simply not interested. They want first-dollar coverage. They have it now, and they are not interested in giving it up.

Jack Shelton: In 1976, we took a four-week strike at Ford. Co-payments and deductibles were a major issue in the negotiations. The union's problem was and is the transfer of cost: Union leaders cannot approve transferring health care costs from the corporation to the individual, so it is going to be extremely difficult to work any changes in the current arrangements.

We have considered establishing our own health services, but we decided that we would prefer to play a large role in launching a community program for the city of Detroit. We feel that we have a responsibility to the community, as well as to the corporation, and we felt that we could serve our people better by supporting a strong community program. We did it, along with General Motors, Chrysler, and others, and now we have the Health Alliance Plan, an HMO that serves the community at large.

Joe Onek: I am interested in giving competition an immediate boost, and I think the preferred provider organization idea that Paul Ellwood mentioned might prove ideal. It has the great advantage of not requiring a different benefit package: Every insurer and employer can continue using the plans they now have and create second plans by the simple elimination of the most expensive providers. I wonder whether Blue Cross would be willing to try that approach, to have a Blue Cross A and a Blue Cross B that would simply eliminate the most expensive providers available under A. Then people could sign up for Blue Cross B. It would be a tremendous benefit to those people who already use lower cost providers, and it would also be fairer than the current arrangement. In Washington, and I think this is true elsewhere, the upper middle class uses the most expensive health care facilities, while working people go to cheaper community hospitals in the outlying suburbs. But they are all members of the same plan, so that, when I have my child born in George Washington Hospital, I am being subsidized by a GS-8 who lives out in Rockville and has his babies born in a suburban hospital. That is not equitable, and it makes no economic sense. I was wondering whether Blue Cross would be willing to pursue a possibility like PPOs.

Walt McNerney: Yes, I think we should look at it. We have a high-level program, a low-level program, HMOs, and an HMO network. Not everybody knows this, but the best bargain is the low-level program. On the other hand, we haven't experience-rated institutions or doctors, except for the HMO. We would be willing to. Competition is getting so tough that I think we would be willing to try any scheme that had promise. Finding the place to try it would be the key because that's a very tricky provider relationship.

Gil Omenn: Where you stand depends so much on where you sit! I've been recollecting how I was sitting at the Office of Management and Budget just a few months ago, and we were grappling with this same problem. It was clear already that competition was more and more attractive, both intellectually and politically, even though it was not well received within most of the Carter administration. There were several competing objectives. We wanted to assure equity, and we wanted to enhance access. We were well aware that, despite the high costs of health care services, approaching 10 percent of the gross national product, 20 million people supposedly aren't covered at all, and another 40 million have less than adequate health insurance, especially against catastrophic expenses. We were trying to look ahead a few years to see how we could meet the need and still constrain the growth in cost. That led us to try to put together a program in which we were explicit about our objectives and identified some steps that government could take without coming down entirely on the regulation side or on the competition side.

It may surprise you to recall that, in the early part of last year, the Department of Health and Human Services, the American Hospital Association, and the American Medical Association came to virtual agreement on the appropriate increment in cost for calendar year 1980: 13.5 percent. There was a cooperative response from the AHA to proposals for the sharing of information; that was particularly helpful. There has been much discussion here about the power and usefulness of information, and there can be no question that making data about hospital costs (base as well as incremental) more readily available to communities, hospital boards, and other interested parties could help. The government should be pursuing this vigorously, and it should have some kind of a monitoring program of its own.

The question of jawboning is a political one. There are ways of doing it. I've always thought it was more effective to pass out gold stars. Instead of putting out negative information about hospitals that don't perform, give the good performers gold stars and let other people ask why the poor performers didn't get gold stars!

Too, we must recognize that the pluralism and diversity of this country are tremendous. There are lots of experiments now going on, and some are very exciting. But they don't add to much in the short term. The question becomes: How can you get the states excited about a strategy for cost control when there are so many ways of going about it and when you must respect their pluralism and diversity? Besides, the federal government has itself been far too cautious, particularly in not offering Medicare waivers.

Third, the more I think about how to stimulate competition, the more I remember our discussions within the administration about the limit on tax deductibility. We knew we had trouble with the United Auto Workers on that issue; in fact, we lost within the administration on that point. But there is no doubt in my mind that a limit on tax deductibility would grab everyone's attention. It would cut across all the levels, and it would get all layers—the individual, the institutions, the corporations and other large buyers, and, of course, the states—interested in competition.

What's left for regulation? From the OMB point of view, it was dramatic to observe the growth in cost. The federal budget for Medicare and the federal share of Medicaid will grow from a total of $49 billion ($35 billion for Medicare) in 1980 to $67 billion in 1982. Bear in mind that these are estimates, and these estimates have been on the low side. Every three months, they get updated, and they always go up, so take the estimated increase of $18 billion with a grain of salt.

What could be done? I hope Paul Ellwood will come back and discuss how we might use the competition model to effect some really drastic change. We should also have a fall-back position on Voluntary Effort, with a Section 223 cap that respects the differences among our hospitals but imposes a constraint that limits the annual increase in the reimbursement paid to each hospital.

I share these ideas to indicate that people in the government, including many who are still in the executive branch and in Congress, wrestle constantly with these issues. If this and other conferences can propose alternatives that seem compatible with the interests of the various players, there may be some progress. Otherwise, that budget figure will continue to grow by leaps and bounds, the share of the national budget devoted to health care will increase apace, and the risk of some abrupt and drastic change will be considerably enhanced.

Nelson Ford: I have just a couple of comments. First, I think that I'm a little less sanguine than other people here about the future of competition and its impact in the short run. I think other forces will push it off the stage. The two that I'm thinking about are on a collision course. One is the move toward deregulation in the health care sector, and the other is the need to see real reduction in federal outlays for health care services. Two days after we set up the deregulation task force, we got our first letter from somebody with a good idea for deregulation: the elimination of the Maximum Allowable Cost (MAC) regulations. I submit that that change will probably not lower the cost of health care, and neither will a number of other deregulation proposals now being discussed. There are three major pieces of the federal health care dollar: Medicaid, Medicare, and tax expenditures. In recent weeks, we have seen the beginning of an effort to cap Medicaid, and I think that we must expect an effort to get a hold on Medicare costs and to recapture some of the revenues lost to the tax expenditures. The collison of those efforts to control costs with efforts to deregulate the health care sector will push discussions of competition into the background.

Second, a brief comment about the effect of the equal employer contribution. The FEHBP (Federal Employee Health Benefits Plan) has an equal employer contribution. And all of those health care plans require an additional employee contribution of some size. In this environment, 80 percent of the people choose high-option plans. Most of them choose Blue Cross high option, which is demonstrably not the best deal for the vast majority of federal employees. I think that shows that you can't really expect rapid change in the way people choose their health insurance, even when you put accurate information in the street. The programs that have been growing the fastest are not the low-option plans discussed here, but the plans that cover dental care, which are among the most expensive.

John Affeldt: The antiregulatory mood is hitting the Joint Commission on the Accreditation of Hospitals just as it is hitting the government. Although the JCAH is a voluntary, nongovernmental agency, it is nevertheless perceived as having a regulatory function, and its constituency is now complaining about some of our procedures and their effects. They are saying, "We want you to revise your standards, we want you to reduce them in scope, and we want you to relax their implementation. We want you to create a single set of minimal standards and then build in some incentives, so that people will not be satisfied to stay at the minimal level." When you start talking about incentives for facilities to do better, you start talking about ranking hospitals. Someone mentioned the gold star approach; maybe we have to begin ranking hospitals in the way restaurants are ranked. I'm not quite sure how hospitals will respond, but, if they insist on incentives to move them above the minimum, something like that could emerge.

We are also discussing lengthening the accreditation cycle. The Professional Standards Review Organizations (PSRO) are stationed right inside the hospitals and make weekly observations, so the hospitals ask why the JCAH comes as often as every two years. Hospitals are also saying that they want us to look more at quality than at paper compliance. On that point we agree with them, but it is a little hard to figure out how to go about it.

On the other hand, the move toward deregulation seems likely to increase our activities. We have already had calls from Congressional committees considering curtailment of the PSROs and asking about the enforcement of utilization review regulations. They want to know the posture of the JCAH. We remind them that our standards also call for utilization review, so there is an alternative in the private sector.

We are also seeing a lot of action at the state level. Thirty-eight states have arranged or are arranging joint surveys with the JCAH to reduce the amount of state activity. Some states now rely entirely on the JCAH, both for certification and for licensure. States are also starting to talk to us about long-term care because they can see that the federal government is going to reduce its support for the licensure and inspection of nursing homes. They ask whether the JCAH is ready to play a larger role in that area. We don't have the answer to that one yet, but it is clear that the move toward deregulation will have a substantial impact on the JCAH.

Jack Shelton: It seems that we are all in favor of competition. I would hope that we would look carefully before leaping at any kind of legislated competition model. But I think that there are some things that we can do right now to make competition work. First, we can take the wraps off the health maintenance organizations and the other alternative delivery system plans. HMOs have a tough time competing because they have mandated board structures, mandated benefit levels, and strict rating requirements which make it difficult for them to compete in the marketplace with fee-for-service programs. Let's relax those restrictions. Second, HMOs have a tough time gaining access to community hospitals. If we are really sincere about seeing competition develop, we ought to find a way to open up the community hospitals to HMOs. Third, I think we would all prefer to see HMOs develop in the private sector, without government funds. Well, let's create some incentives to get the private sector to develop HMOs. Fourth, we should work to get Medicare and Medicaid beneficiaries into HMO programs so that state governments and the federal government can benefit from cost competition. These are a few things that we could do this year to expand competition, if we are sincere about it.

Monte DuVal: I'd like to extend the discussion of vertical integration. Vertical integration is not an effective or efficient way to distribute services, except where there are constraints of geography or economies of scale that make it work. If vertical integration were efficient outside those special circumstances, it would have been seen more often in the private sector. This has always struck me as one of the reasons—though obviously not the prime reason—that we turn to the public sector for vertical integration to achieve inefficient distribution of services where mission is important—as with the Indians, veterans, or military personnel. I'm very interested in the phenomenon of vertical integration, but I'm discouraged about its prospects in the private sector, except for those special situations where constraints of geography or economies of scale can make it work.

Paul Ellwood: To keep me from repeating my answers, I'll try to batch the questions a little. The first point about the possibility that competition will lead to more regulation, is well taken. The legislative development of some sort of voucher system for Medicare will give us a good idea what's likely to happen. There are three aspects that we're watching there. One is the response of the American Medical Association. That will tell us whether organized medicine is willing to tolerate a competitive health system. The experience we had with organized medicine on the HMO Act suggests that they prefer their competition loaded up like a Christmas tree with requirements and regulations. The second thing to watch is the way the government's price is determined, whether the price is based strictly on capitation or whether there is some sort of cost finding that leads to adjustments. The third point to watch is the eligibility requirements determining which medical care organizations and insurance companies can apply for the capitation payment. If all sorts of requirements are imposed, that will be regulation in another form.

On the matter of market segmentation and selection, I think my remarks may have been too negative. I'd like to be more positive about the ability of employers to do something constructive in wisely purchasing medical care, because it is clear that they can do a lot. In Pennsylvania, for example, the telephone company is now collecting (through Blue Cross) data describing the experience of their employees in various health delivery systems. The company was surprised to discover that much of the increase in their expenditures for medical care in Pennsylvania was attributable to intensive neonatal care. In an analysis of competitive medical plans, the company discovered that one plan has actually led to an increase in hospital utilization and an increase in absenteeism, while another has produced sharp decreases in both. I cite this as an example both because it shows what companies can do and because it is an exception to the rule. Most of the research on the relative efficiency of various health care delivery systems is not based on employee groups because employers have simply not had sufficient data for research. As corporations begin to collect this data, the likelihood that they will begin to manage their health care budgets is very strong.

Some of you want to know what it is about multispecialty practices that leads them to have lower rates of hospitalization. I hope everyone in the room noticed the qualification in my talk: I said "*some* multispecialty groups initiating prepayment have experienced unacceptably high hospitalization rates, at least temporarily." I don't know why that is, and I don't know why groups vary so much in their use of the hospital. I do not think it is related to the way physicians are compensated. It is true that the members of most multispecialty groups are salaried, but those salaries are usually related to fee-for-service productivity. I know of only a couple of groups where physicians are on flat salaries unrelated to productivity. So the financial incentives for physicians in most multispecialty groups are to provide more service and generate more revenue. How that is controlled, and why the control is more effective in some groups than in others, we simply don't know.

Mr. Beers is concerned about health system reforms taking too long. I don't know how to accelerate it, and I'm not sure that it should be accelerated. When you think of 30 or 40 million people receiving a $100 to $150 billion worth of medical services from competitive medical plans by 1990, you cannot help but be impressed by the magnitude and speed of that change. Ironically, one of the things that slows it down most is not the ability of the health system to transform itself, or the willingness of physicians and hospitals to deliver capitated medical care, but consumer acceptance. In the Twin Cities, we have had 80 percent of the doctors and virtually all of the hospitals involved in competitive medical plans for the last six years, and yet we have enrolled only 22 percent of the population. I suppose the process of acceptance might be speeded up if it became fashionable to join a plan, but I suspect that it will take time.

Mr. Beers also discussed bringing the know-how of business into the field of health care. I wonder if detached advice from business can significantly improve the performance of the health industry. It seems to me that, if we're really going to inject the know-how of business into the health industry, businesses will have to go into the medical care field. It's a huge industry, and I have been trying for the last five or six years to encourage companies, particularly high-technology companies, to go into it. The responses I get are full of doubts and objections: "We don't know whether the health business will be profitable for us, we don't know how the government is going to act, and we are not at all sure that we can manage doctors." I suspect that, as competitive medical plans expand, it will become easier to define and predict the economic performance of the health business and estimate the resources required to enter and succeed in it. At that point, conventional firms are much more likely to go into health care as a business.

The John Deere case is a wonderful example. John Deere is adding to its tractor business a small health care business. Deere can do this more easily than some other companies because Deere has been self-insuring for some time. It is of interest that John Deere is using its line managers, people who have been used to running profit centers, to run their health care activities. The head of the John Deere health plan is an engineer who used to run the company foundry, and he looks at the venture in health care as a business opportunity. It will be interesting to see how Deere fares.

Someone asked about the hospital utilization rate of Medicare beneficiaries; the latest figures I have show a rate of 3,767 days per 1,000 for all age groups in 1978. For comparison, let me give you the hospital utilization rate for health plans enrolling sizable numbers of Medicare subscribers. Kaiser of Northern California has 70 thousand enrollees over sixty-five and a hospital utilization rate of 1,700 days per 1,000. Perhaps the most powerful example of the potential appeal of capitated Medicare is to be found in the state of Oregon. Kaiser of Portland has a Medicare experiment under which Kaiser gets paid 95 percent of the area's per capita cost, adjusted for age and sex. There is no way of cheating on age and sex, and Kaiser isn't being permitted to enroll their own members who are already on Medicare. Even so, Kaiser can offer members of the experimental group 365 days of hospitalization, total physician services, drugs, eye glasses, hearing aids, and total dental services, including fillings and prosthesis for $16 a month. By contrast, wrap-around coverage, filling in the deductibles and copayment on Medicare, now costs about $25 a month in Portland. You can imagine how powerful and attractive that kind of scheme is likely to prove.

Finally, I would like to react to Dave Hamburg's questions because I think that they were the most provocative. How do you induce competitive medical plans to be concerned about monitoring the quality of care they provide, or about emphasizing prevention, or about giving adequate attention to behavioral needs, or about providing enough options? What mechanisms will foster research and development? How can you get them to participate in education? Perhaps the most interesting question concerns innovation and research and development. Can you justify, if you are competing on price, spending 1 percent or 2 percent or 3 percent on research and development? What we have seen so far suggests that most plans don't feel that it's justifiable. I suspect that it is because most plans haven't faced competition yet. They have found it easy to reduce hospital utilization below current levels, and that has been sufficient to give them a competitive edge. In the future, they are going to have to compete with one another by managing better and by developing new ways for people to meet their own health care needs through self-diagnosis and treatment. Both of those will require research and development, but the problem is that the kind of products that will come out of that kind of research don't seem very patentable. That is a very interesting question.

Alan Nelson: Paul Ellwood asks what the AMA might think about prepayment for the Medicare population in HMOs. As a fee-for-service practitioner, I'd hate to see that happen because I'm good friends with my Medicare patients. I don't want to lose them as patients, but I can't match the waiver of copayment and deductible in order to keep them and still make a living.

As a participant in this dialogue, I can remove my practitioner hat and have other misgivings. HMOs don't have much experience in taking care of Medicare patients. Where they are successful, I suspect that two conditions are present which may not be prevalent across the country. One is the availability of alternative levels of care and the other is the opportunity which the most successful HMOs have used to develop staffs of efficient physicians. I don't think we have enough experience to know what would happen to the cost of care if Medicare were covered under HMOs at 95 percent. Certainly, I'd like to see more experience with it before that was tried nationwide.

Paul Rogers: I wanted to ask how these competitive medical plans will get started. What is the incentive? The HMO Act allows you to start an HMO right now, and it doesn't have to qualify federally and it doesn't have to meet all the federal standards. If it can be done so easily, why isn't it being done? I'm not sure there are incentives enough, unless you crank in a tight tax incentive. And that might cost governments even more, because you'll still have Medicare, and the states are going to have to carry Medicaid.

Alain Enthoven: It's very tough to start an HMO. Let's say you wanted to start one in San Mateo. Well, the people who live there work all the way from San Francisco to San Jose, and you would have to reach all those employers. It's hard to get one going. It's easier to see how a large one like Kaiser can grow rapidly. As Paul said, I think that the large national medical enterprises hold the key: if they see CMPs as good investment opportunities, they will start them.

Paul Rogers: But how do you get things moving?

Alain Enthoven: By opening up the market. Most employers still don't offer choices.

Paul Rogers: But how do you get them to offer the choices? By regulation?

Alain Enthoven: Yes. I think that a requirement like that incorporated in Section 1310 of the HMO Act is necessary, unless the Congress will enact a limit on the amount of employer contribution an employee can receive tax free. If that were done, employees would demand less costly choices, and employers would be motivated to offer them.

Paul Ellwood: I think I'd answer that a little differently. CMPs are happening anyway. I don't think that much in the way of intervention is necessary now. Most fee-for-service, multispecialty groups find it advantageous to move into this business. They used to depend on primary care physicians referring them patients. Now they find that they have to set up their own network of primary care physicians. If you find yourself in that kind of situation, you might as well lock in a patient population, to use a crude expression, by going into prepayment.

Paul Rogers: You would get rid of the federal support for HMOs? You wouldn't continue using federal support to encourage the establishment of HMOs? Is that right?

Paul Ellwood: My feeling now is that it may not be necessary to continue mandatory multiple choice by employers. Take a firm like General Motors, how many HMOs are you offering now? (*Eavenson:* 72). In company after company, especially large national firms, the machinery is established to offer a multiple choice. If companies find that it saves them money, they'll push it. If they are finding multiple choice isn't saving them money, they can offer an option very passively, and nothing will happen. I'll go back to what I said earlier: I think that you have to take the wraps off the HMOs. Let them compete. Let them write the benefit level that is necessary in the marketplace.

Jack Shelton: It can be done this year. There are certain things we can do this year and get competition moving immediately. We could take the benefit mandate off, we can allow experience rating, we can take the board structure requirement away, and we can begin to get some competitive HMOs.

John Cooper: I want to turn the conversation about competition to the issue of monopoly. I've heard people from multihospital systems say that there are now seventy-five systems and that, within this decade, there will be only twenty-five. That conjures up the image of twenty-five immense multihospital systems, and I have to ask whether that's competition or monopoly.

Alex McMahon: I've heard the same thing, but I don't take it very seriously. What they are talking about is horizontal integration. As long as their integration is strictly horizontal, multihospital systems can't monopolize health care, and there's going to come a time, I think, when they may run out of things to share. They don't know, and we don't know, how big a system should be, or when a system becomes so diverse that its parts can no longer share the accounting, financial management, legal services, and joint purchasing techniques which brought them together because they're so diverse that their merger becomes the combination of centrifugal forces which pull them apart.

The real impact on competition would result from vertical integration, and I don't see that happening. It's too hard to organize, and there are too many obstacles.

Walt McNerney: Paul Rogers asked why things haven't moved more quickly. Employers are cautious today. When certification was an issue, they wanted to go with a certified plan, and they were less than thrilled by the prospect of an uncertified plan. The current bills to amend the HMO Act relax some of the requirements, but they leave others in place, and they prohibit or discourage HMOs as a line of business. We would find them much easier to start if we could make them a line of business, instead of spinning off the subsidiary corporations one after the other. We could start them more easily and operate them more cheaply if they were integral parts of our operation.

This is important because I fervently believe that the only way you can accelerate the development of an alternative delivery system is to make intensive use of your capital, market access, and managerial know-how. The point of view that, "Unless it's old, small, beautiful, and local, it's suspect," is holding us back. If people are worried about our misusing the privilege, I would say incorporate a requirement that we disqualify ourselves if our patient rate per thousand goes beyond a certain level. That's the way to go at it.

Alain Enthoven: Paul Rogers mentioned earlier that nobody says quality of care is no good in this country. I think there is a serious lack of quality control in this industry. There's a lot of bad medical care out there. And I think that one of the things I see in these organized systems of care that I hope we can encourage is greatly improved quality.

Let me give you just one example: The underutilization of surgeons. Recently I was in Santa Monica. In one office building, they told me, there were twelve neurosurgeons. They probably serve a population of 300,000 to 400,000 people. I doubt they have enough cases to remain truly proficient. By contrast Kaiser Northern California, with 1.6 million people to care for, had a total of 7 neurosurgeons, all in one medical center. They are concentrated in one place so that all Kaiser patients requiring their attention get the benefit of a very proficient, experienced team. I think that there's an important qualitative advantage there.

In a *New England Journal of Medicine* issue earlier this month, there were two articles on iatrogenic illness. In one, investigators reported that 36 percent of 815 consecutive patients on a general medical service of a university hospital had an iatrogenic illness. I think it would be appropriate for us to acknowledge that there is considerable room for improvement in the quality of care.

Alex McMahon: I want to go back to a question which Uwe Reinhardt raised this morning. He said the issue isn't a choice between regulation and competition because we will have regulation. The question is regulation for what? I don't think we've paid enough attention to that question. I don't think that there is any question about the fact that under the Carter administration we were headed for more and more regulation of capital expenditures, operating expenditures, and utilization. In that situation, my job was unpleasant but clear: it was to organize my troops to beat the regulators, and I don't think that that would have been very difficult. We knew how to organize politically to beat certificate of need; we proved that over and over again. Rate review was a different kind of problem because in Massachusetts and New York the economic situation was so bad that there was no maneuvering room for anybody. Rate review wasn't fair, but it was going to happen anyway because the governments were in such deep difficulty. Now we're talking about incentive reimbursement. I don't think it can happen. You can install an incentive reimbursement, but we can organize to beat that one as well. And I'm not sure that we wouldn't have found a way to beat the PSROs too. I said this morning that regulatees capture the regulators.

I come back to the fact that we have an opportunity. We may blow it. None of this may work, and we may come back to regulation, but I think we ought to take advantage of the opportunity and look hard at the possibility of making some changes. I wouldn't have any problem answering yes to all four of the questions which Uwe Reinhardt put in his litmus test. I suppose that makes me a marketeer. I don't know whether I'd get lynched or not, but the fact is we talk a lot about protecting the public and it just so happens that the protection of the public and the protection of providers are tweedle dum and tweedle dee, and I'm not sure precisely where we are.

I think it's worth letting the individual get into this game. I'm not sure he needs all the protection that we have argued he ought to have. This may be the last chance to let him in, because if things go awry, if Medicaid continues to present huge financial problems to state governments, if Medicare continues to present huge financial problems to a budget-balancing administration, and if we continue to present business with a pass-through that increases the prices of goods and services that people in the United States buy and threatens our foreign trade as well, then regulation is going to come whether it's the best answer or the worst answer. It's going to come because it's the only answer. Before we take that route, it seems to me that we ought to take this opportunity to rethink regulation and try something different. If we fail, we're going to get more regulation whether we like it or not, and once we start down that road I don't think that there will be any chance to open up the system once again.

SESSION II:
SECOND DAY

5 COMPETITION: THE THREAT TO TEACHING HOSPITALS*

John W. Colloton

INTRODUCTION

The substantial escalation in the cost of health care over the past two decades, coupled with significant increases in the demand for funding of other national needs, has prompted close attention to the issue of health costs. Three basic approaches to this issue have evolved: direct price and cost regulation; reliance on the national voluntary effort of hospitals, physicians, and other health professionals; and competition in the health system. In an effort to minimize the necessity for the regulatory approach, a growing number of health professionals, economists, business groups, and members of congress appear to be favorably disposed toward the establishment of an increased level of competition. Such a system would involve fundamental change in the way health insurance and services are selected and purchased as a means to stimulate cost consciousness among providers and consumers who eventually become patients.

I gratefully acknowledge the assistance of Robert D. Miller, Mary A. Beck, John H. Staley, Carol L. Spradling, and Kenneth H. Yerington, administrative staff members of the University of Iowa Hospitals and Clinics, and John Kuder and Samuel Levey of the Graduate Program in Hospital and Health Administration of The University of Iowa in the preparation of this paper.

*By agreement between the editors and Mr. Colloton, his paper appears as he submitted it to the Sixth Private Sector Conference.

131

Proponents view increased competition in the health care marketplace as a means of reform by which to provide incentives to both consumers and providers to modify their behavior in a manner designed to encourage cost consciousness, reduce demand for services, and trigger other changes in the delivery system. Health insurance plans and health maintenace organizations (HMOs) would be encouraged to compete for enrollees, primarily on the basis of premium rates, but also on the benefits or services they offer. These competitive plans would serve as the foundation of an altered health care system for the nation. The proposals for competition, offered as alternatives to the present financing of the health care system, would initiate changes such as tax reform and the requirement that employers offer multiple health plan choices to their employees. One prominent proposal is the consumer choice health plan (CCHP), developed by Enthoven, which is designed to adjust consumer and provider behavior, primarily through financial incentives and rewards. The focus of competition proposals on the service demand issues underlying health care expenditures is attractive because of the potential for cost containment without further regulation. While acknowledging these positive features of the competition approaches, this paper concentrates on other aspects that have not yet received sufficient attention.

The evolution of these competition proposals has caused a great deal of concern among teaching hospitals because of the potential adverse impact of competition on their multiple responsibilities. Enthoven acknowledged the validity of these concerns when he stated, "For them to be able to compete, the teaching and research costs of university medical centers would need to be separately identified and subsidized on their own merits."[1] The theoretical approach to financing teaching hospitals under competition is set forth as one option to encourage further discussion regarding the implications and practicality of this concept.

This paper describes the characteristics of health care competition; raises questions concerning some of the assumptions underlying the proposals, including the likelihood of competition being accompanied by increased regulation; presents the basis for teaching hospitals' concerns with competition, including the risks to their multiple contributions to society; examines one theoretical approach for recognizing the unique needs of teaching hospitals within a competitive system; and, finally, reviews some of the related future challenges for teaching hospitals.

CHARACTERISTICS OF HEALTH CARE COMPETITION

The procompetition bills have various combinations of at least six objectives, some of which are in conflict, as is usually the case with complex legislation. A primary objective is control of federal expenditures through removal of open-ended commitments to Medicare and Medicaid and to income tax deductions for health care expenditures. The second objective is to assure a politically acceptable minimum level of services at a controlled level of expenditure. A third objective is to preserve the right of individuals, private industry, and state and local governments to allocate more resources to health, while removing all federal incentives for them to do so. Another objective is to discourage exercise of the freedom provided under the third objective by promoting cost consciousness in an effort to preserve more resources to satisfy other societal needs. The fifth objective is to reduce the regulatory burden of federal and other governmental agencies that has contributed significantly to the health cost increase.[2] The last objective is to promote flexibility in delivery systems.

In attempting to meet the last two objectives, some of the most serious contradictions arise. From one perspective, removal of such constraints as health planning, rate setting, and restrictions on the corporate practice of medicine may reduce governmental barriers to delivery of health care by qualified individuals and institutions. Others view deregulation as an opportunity to restrict the controls by state government of qualifications for licensure, thus permitting nonphysicians to perform many of the tasks now limited to physicians and permitting technicians to perform many of the functions presently limited to professional nurses. Some proponents also perceive deregulation as an opportunity to eliminate state and federal regulations requiring institutional peer review. There is a danger that deregulation of the health care system will be viewed as an opportunity to remove all governmental control of professional licensure so that some of the demand for health care can be satisfied by the unproven and possibly the unqualified.

The promotion of competition is advocated for two distinct markets related to health care. The first is the health care insurance market. Competition would be promoted in several of the proposals by mandating that each consumer be offered a choice among several competitive plans, each with various levels of benefits or out-of-pocket expenses. It is theorized that individuals will opt for low-cost plans in making their selection. Several of the proposals offer an incentive for each individual to select a low-cost plan, even when the plan is purchased by employers or government, by providing the individual a cash rebate of a portion of the cost savings.

Second is the health care service market, which would be affected through both competitive plans and direct participation of patients in payment. Most proposals are based on the assumption that increased competition in the insurance market will lead insurers to shop for the least expensive providers and limit their purchase of services to these providers. Some plans, as in the case of many HMOs, would actually become providers by operating their own facilities, directly employing professionals, and providing services. Some proposals also seek to promote cost consciousness by the patient when a health care provider or services are sought by increasing the use of out-of-pocket payments. With both health plans and patients exhibiting greater cost consciousness, it is expected that physicians, hospitals, and other providers would also become more concerned with costs, leading to direct price competition among providers in some market areas. However, the degree of this competition is likely to vary from area to area depending on factors such as distance between providers, size of the market, and perceived quality of care.

The advocates of broadened competition have introduced several bills in Congress which generally embrace the following principles based on the work of Enthoven, Ellwood, McClure, and others:

- First, each individual would be allocated a fixed sum of dollars by the employer or by government so that the individual could choose among competitive plans. Indigent individuals or families would be provided a governmental voucher to purchase an approved plan of their choice.
- Second, individuals would select one of the competitive plans, but could choose between health insurance plans with comprehensive or lesser coverage or an HMO-type plan. Plans could also vary in the extent of out-of-pocket expenses imposed, but most proposals require a ceiling on patient or family payments to protect against the financial burden of catastrophic illness or injury. In most approaches, only those plans approved by the federal government would be allowed to compete.

- Third, individuals who choose a plan that provides services at a cost lower than the amount allocated by the employer or the government would receive some or all of the difference as non-taxable income—a reward for diligence in the medical market-place.

Competition proposals present the framework for major change in the financing, organization, and delivery of health services in this country. Some of the possible outcomes of the enactment of a bill to promote competition include the following:

1. It will lead toward the evolution of a health care financing system made up predominantly of competing plans, encouraging physicians and hospitals to compete on the basis of price or to convince patients and plans that higher charges and fees are justified by either quality or service characteristics.
2. Some proposals would limit total governmental investment in health care to a federally determined per capita allotment, terminating the open-ended commitment to Medicare and Medicaid and to tax deductions for health care benefits. Arbitrary limits on aggregate health expenditures are avoided by permitting individuals to spend after-tax dollars for additional health care insurance or services. Thus, government would control its expenditures without mandating reduced services for all.
3. Government would discourage employers from exceeding set maximums for health care expenditures by limiting corporate and personal income tax deductions for health benefits to that maximum.
4. Procompetition legislation could temporarily slow the rate of growth of total expenditures for health care in the United States.[3]
5. Constraints on physician fees and hospital costs would evolve as competitive plans seek to include fee schedules and hospital rates in their agreements to refer patients and pay for resulting care.
6. Services available to some individuals may decline as they choose less comprehensive plans and as competitive plans and providers are motivated to reduce the scope, timeliness, and quality of their coverage and services in response to financial incentives and constraints. It is possible that competition may move providers too far from the focus on providing an adequate

level and quality of service, especially for patients afflicted with complex diseases. If this shift in focus occurs, increased regulation of the availability and quality of care may be anticipated to offset economic disincentives embodied in various plans. Competition would serve primarily as a substitute for price and cost regulation; it would not be a substitute for regulation of availability and quality of health care.

7. Competition proposals risk the reversal of the trend of the post-Medicare era away from a two-class system of access to care. Although these risks are mitigated in some of the proposals by requiring all qualified plans to cover a minimum acceptable mix of benefits, price competition may result in one system for those who can afford services above the benefit level of the competitive plan and another for those who cannot. To the degree that government alleviates this problem by providing vouchers in an amount closer to the comprehensive level, the objectives of constraint of costs and services would be compromised.

8. Disruption may occur in the administration and delivery of health care when 150 million Americans are thrust into an altered medical marketplace personally seeking to understand, choose, and bind themselves to a particular plan for the delivery and payment of services. This experience should be of special concern because differences in health products are often technical, and price and quality information is difficult to obtain and assess.

9. Competition proposals could significantly weaken the ability of teaching hospitals to meet their broad responsibilities of service, education, and research for the entire health system.

These characteristics and possible outcomes of competition proposals are based on the theory that marketplace competition will effect change in the health care system. Careful review of these proposals reveals a number of questionable assumptions and unresolved issues which must be addressed in the consideration of a competitive system of health care for the nation.

QUESTIONABLE ASSUMPTIONS AND UNRESOLVED ISSUES OF COMPETITION PROPOSALS

Competition should not be viewed as a panacea for the complex problems associated with constraining health care costs. First, competition would not completely substitute for regulation. For example, the National Health Care Reform Act of 1980, introduced by Representatives Richard Gephardt and David Stockman, specifies over fifty identifiable elements of governmental regulation by five regulatory agencies, including one new agency, the Health Benefits Assurance Corporation.[4] Second, competition may not produce the type of effective price competition that would, in the long run, significantly lower hospital costs. Third, many unintended consequences could result from the proposed competitive system, including the erosion of national resources embodied in teaching hospitals. These conclusions are drawn from an analysis of three of the questionable assumptions of the competition proposals.

The first assumption is: If consumers are given an incentive to save money on health insurance expenditures, they will have the expertise and desire to choose policies which provide maximum coverage for care needed in the future (and minimum coverage for care not needed), at a minimum total cost and at an appropriate level of quality. The current public policy regarding health insurance is based on the contrary assumption that individuals often lack the future-mindedness and the ability to predict their families' health needs, and are generally unable to decipher subtle variations in health insurance policies.[5] The poor and elderly are particularly at risk of being sold high-priced and low-benefit policies. Rather than reduce the need for regulation of insurance policy sales and quality of medical care, the competitive system may require more direct regulation of this type because the incentive would be to provide fewer services of lower quality.

The second assumption is: Consumers will purchase insurance in a truly competitive market. Insurance providers will compete on both price and product characteristics (including quality) of insurance plans. In such a market, consumers will have real choices from a variety of suppliers. The health insurance industry currently does not provide the type of competitive market atmosphere conducive to rigorous price competition. Several causes of this are apparent, including: state and federal regulations designed to protect consumers against insurance company failures; the presence of large economies of scale, particularly evident in the cost of administration for group health policies;[6] and the historical dominance of some market regions by nonprofit providers. With reductions in insurance regulation, many regional health insurance markets still may not become rigorously price competitive while the potential for bankruptcy of health insurance plans may increase. Continuation of this current limited competition is particularly likely in rural areas where population densities are low and the extent of the market is small. It will be very difficult for HMOs to attain strong market positions within these areas.[7] Many regional health insurance markets do not appear to be conducive to the development of rigorous price competition among large numbers of insurance providers. In such markets, rival health insurance companies may compete primarily on minor differences in benefit packages, service, and advertising activities but not engage in broader price competition.

The third assumption is: Under the competition proposals, competition among health service providers will force greater market control over the costs of care. Enthoven has stated, "competition among insurers does not create competition among providers and only the latter offers hope of bringing about changes toward less costly styles of care."[8] Such competition among providers seems to depend on the ability of competitive plans to bargain and contract with hospitals, physicians and other providers to lower charges and change the style of professional practice. Implicitly, the assumption seems to be that competitive plans, including HMOs and independent practice associations (IPAs), would be able to successfully bargain with providers to secure services at a lower cost, passing the savings on to their membership.[9] Existing evidence is not convincing that competitive plans will be successful in bargaining with providers to bring about the perceived need for change in style of practice and control of costs. Illustrative of this fact is that HMOs, even with significant subsidies, have experienced quite limited success in establishing advantageous financial arrangements with providers and expanding enrollment. While the first HMO was developed in the United States in the late 1920s, only 4 percent of the general population is currently enrolled in these plans.[10] In the Federal Employees Health Benefits Program, which has been a model for the consumer choice health plan, there was only a 9 percent enrollment in HMO-type plans during 1980, after twenty years of operation.[11]

Even in a scenario in which competitive plans make significant inroads in the insurance market, it is possible that long-run savings in cost would not occur. There is a demonstrated lower cost for HMO enrollees than for patients with other comparable insurance, but the source of this saving is elusive.[12] The cost savings appear to be the result of lower hospital admission rates for HMO enrollees.[13] This lower hospital utilization is for all inpatient hospital services, not merely discretionary inpatient days.[14] Therefore, increased enrollment in HMOs may not duplicate these initial savings, and this matter deserves additional investigation. Additionally, the actual rate of inflation in costs for HMO services has been the same as the rate for the remainder of the health provider system.[15] Published studies have not reported cost savings for IPA prepaid organizations, suggesting that this type of arrangement for care has substantially less impact on costs.[16]

The competition proposals also present some unresolved issues. First, how would society be assured that competing plans would not set up barriers to avoid selection of enrollees with poor health status in order to keep premium levels low, and enhance their competitive position in the marketplace? Open enrollment alone as a mechanism for guaranteeing the enrollment of individuals with poor health status is not likely to assure the coverage of health benefits for such individuals. Other barriers to enrollment, such as location of facilities and control of market information, could be used by competitive health plans to discourage the enrollment of high-risk individuals. Community rating would also not solve the problem because it could defeat the underlying purpose of competition by reducing a plan's ability to negotiate a favored position with providers. This issue must be resolved to protect the poor, aged, and infirm from vulnerability in a competitive system.

A second major unresolved question is the extent to which the American people would be willing to force individuals to live with decisions made in the marketplace. If health care is viewed as a right in this country, then the competitive system creates a dilemma. As Kinzer has indicated:

> When you think about it, is it really conceivable that the American people will accept as public policy the idea that the consumer of health care can really be put "at risk," starting with the example of the person who chooses a coverage option that excludes dialysis and then develops kidney failure? . . . You either believe that a person should get all the care that professional judgment dictates he needs, or you don't.[17]

This problem could be averted by requiring a sufficiently comprehensive minimum package, but it would be exacerbated if health plans are permitted to exclude specific diseases or therapeutic modalities from coverage. Today, individuals who are ill or injured expect access to at least one hospital, where they receive care and work out financial arrangements later. Hospitals now accepting patients on this basis would be forced to take steps to compete in the marketplace with hospitals that have more "economically prudent" admission policies.

Finally, it should be recognized that most hospitals are viewed as public service institutions. This raises the question McNerney has posed, "How does a provider institution work with its neighbors in the spirit of serving the overall community need while trying to put them out of business?"[18] Furthermore, it is questionable whether many communities will accept what Kinzer has called "the survival of the fittest approach to future hospital development" when it begins to threaten *their* hospital.[19] An indication of this public support is voters' historical willingness to accept substantial public bonded indebtedness and other tax levies in support of their community hospitals. Survival of the fittest could be accepted in some communities that have excess hospital capacity, but only until the number has been reduced to the level perceived as needed by the community.

TEACHING HOSPITAL CONCERNS WITH THE COMPETITIVE HEALTH SYSTEM

In contrast with traditional beliefs regarding the incompatibility of the health system and marketplace economics, some academic and congressional authorities now hold opinions that the delivery of health services is not "unique" and the features of supply, demand, investment, choice, and efficiency can be made to apply to health care. These proponents urge that payment to hospitals be converted from cost-based reimbursement to payment based on competitive pricing. Teaching hospitals should have little to fear in a purely competitive environment for health services because of their vast array of human, technological, and physical resources. Accordingly, it would be reasonable to expect that they would presumably not be concerned with true price competition within a free marketplace.

However, underlying the competition proposals is the implicit assumption that hospitals provide a relatively standardized product which is identifiable in terms of both cost and quality. This raises several concerns for the nation's teaching hospitals which, in concert with medical and other health science colleges, have multiple products benefiting not only the individual patient, but society as a whole. Because generation of these products results in higher costs, presently financed primarily through patient care revenues, price competition could seriously jeopardize the future capacity of teaching hospitals to make these essential contributions to society. These contributions include graduate medical and other health science education, new technology testing, clinical research, substantial amounts of charity care, highly specialized services, and extensive ambulatory care programs operating on a subsidized basis. Because of these unique characteristics and responsibilities, teaching hospitals must secure specific attention and consideration in any program of health care financing based on price competition.

While the potential reduction in patient care revenues from competition would present all providers with difficulties, teaching hospitals are at special risk. This risk arises because many of their societal contributions are dependent on the cash flow from patient service programs and also because their programs are highly dependent on patient referrals by primary- and secondary-level providers. It is important to recognize that these multiple responsibilities are highly interdependent in that they bring together the critical mass of clinical skills, educational and research initiatives, and technological resources essential to the advancement of the total health care system. The strength of academic medical centers and their contributions to society result from the synergism of these multiple functions. The capacity of these institutions to meet future societal needs is contingent on the continued presence of these integrated programs in the locus of the teaching hospital.

In this paper, the multiple products of teaching hospitals will be called "societal contributions." Compensated primary- and secondary-level patient care services provided in teaching hospitals are also contributions to society, but the term "societal contributions" will exclude them so that it can signify the functions of teaching hospitals that are at particular risk under competition proposals. These societal contributions are essential to the entire health care system, making their continuance under a competitive system a vital societal concern.

The 332 nonfederal short-term teaching hospitals comprising the Council of Teaching Hospitals (COTH) of the Association of American Medical Colleges (AAMC) constitute only 5 percent[20] of all hospitals in the United States, but they:

- Admit approximately 20 percent of patients hospitalized in the United States[21]
- Diagnose and treat 31 percent of hospital ambulatory patients[22]
- Operate more than half of the burn care units of our nation[23]
- Supply 44 percent of organ transplant services[24]
- Provide 40 percent of open-heart surgical services[25]
- Operate more than one-third of the nation's newborn intensive care units[26]

Health science educational programs dependent on these and other affiliated teaching hospitals involve more than 600 health science colleges providing instruction to more than 215,000 students in medicine, dentistry, nursing, pharmacy, and public health; 66,000 resident physicians and dentists and an estimated 15,000 clinical fellows in specialty training; and, a broad array of allied health trainees.[27]

The bulk of these educational programs are critically dependent on 270 nonfederal teaching hospitals which are the major affiliates of medical colleges and members of the COTH. One component of the support of these programs is provided by the estimated $18.6 billion in total operating expenses of these hospitals in fiscal year 1981.[28] An estimated 90 percent of these expenditures are paid from earnings generated by hospital charges for patient care services.[29] There is no centralized reporting of the cash flow from fees of teaching physicians for medical services, so it is impossible to develop an accurate estimate of the aggregate professional fees of faculty physicians functioning in teaching hospitals. The estimated $18.6 billion total expenditure by these teaching hospitals constitutes approximately 18 percent of the current annual national hospital expenditures.[30]

A risk under competition is that society may suffer severe losses in its health system if the vital contributions of teaching hospitals are not recognized and preserved. McNerney recently described the problem this way: "How do we avoid the virtual exclusion from the market of the academic medical centers offering the best—and most expensive—care?"[31] Ginsberg further underscored this issue when he stated, "But I see nothing but trouble ahead if the nation's teaching hospitals are forced to compete with community hospitals in providing routine services, since the former's per diem costs are 1.5 to 2 times as high as the latter's as a result of their diverse output, which goes far beyond performing an appendectomy or hysterectomy and involves such critically important societal goals as training the next generation of physicians and adding to the pool of knowledge and technique."[32] This and other elements of risk confronting teaching hospitals are described in the following section.

TEACHING HOSPITAL SOCIETAL CONTRIBUTIONS AT RISK

The quality of the nation's health care system is anchored by its "core" tertiary teaching hospitals that support the entire system by delivering highly specialized patient care. The teaching hospitals in university academic health centers also serve as the prime clinical base for the discovery, delivery, and dissemination of new knowledge and services; initial preparation and replenishment of community-based health professionals; and provision of a conducive environment for extensive continuing education that enables practicing professionals to maintain "state-of-the-art" knowledge. A reduction in the ability of teaching hospitals to finance and maintain these societal contributions could erode the quality of the entire system of health care.

The competition proposals present concerns for teaching hospital's contributions in three primary areas: patient referral patterns, financing, and retention of quality patient care throughout the system. Deterioration in any of these areas would detract from the sophisticated educational setting necessary to prepare the physicians and other health professionals of tomorrow. It is essential that the issues described below be addressed *now* while competition proposals are at an early stage of consideration.

Disruption of Patient Referral Patterns

Most teaching hospitals depend on the continuing flow of referred patients in order to provide specialized patient services economically, provide the clinical base for broad-scale teaching and research programs, and remain attractive to health science faculty. Deterioration of referral arrangements would reduce the critical mass of patients, comprehensive support services, and faculty and staff necessary to preserve high-quality specialty services, education, and research programs now based in the nation's academic health centers. Historically, the ability of specialists to attract referrals from primary care providers has been through assuring that both patients and referring physicians are satisfied with the quality and timeliness of services. While primary care providers are becoming more aware of costs to their patients and this awareness is influencing their referral decisions, such decisions continue to be largely based on the ultimate welfare of the patient, not the price of the service. Teaching hospitals must be concerned with the implications of competition proposals with financial incentives, which discourage community physicians from continuing referral relationships with tertiary care centers.

There is significant risk that competitive plans, which contract with community physicians and hospitals, would not be willing to establish appropriate referral arrangements with high-cost, specialized tertiary care centers for their enrollees. As a result, patients could be inappropriately retained in the home community or referred to non-teaching hospitals for specialty care. In making this statement, it is recognized that "super" tertiary patients, such as those requiring burn care or organ transplants, would likely continue to be referred to tertiary teaching hospitals (if plan benefits are available) because such services are not offered elsewhere.

The central question is whether patients with other complex problems would continue to be referred to tertiary-level teaching hospitals, or would they be shifted to secondary-level hospitals or investor-owned institutions that are less expensive because they avoid many of the additional costs intrinsic to tertiary teaching hospitals. Hospitals that concentrate on the high-volume, less complicated specialty services would obviously have a significant price advantage over teaching hospitals.

This patient referral constraint may point to the need for implementing associated regulatory controls. As Heyssel has stated: "In short, we will need additional mechanisms to assure that price does not limit the quality by withholding services, just as PSRO [professional standards review organizations] and utilization review were put in place to make sure that the lack of competitive price constraints did not result in unnecessary procedures and hospitalization."[33] Competition proposals could minimize this concern by prohibiting contractual provisions that place community physicians at financial risk when making a clinical judgment regardng the need for consultative referral to a tertiary care center. Optimally, such decisions should be made in a purely clinical context.

Financing the Societal Contributions of
Teaching Hospitals

The financial dilemma is a direct result of the underlying objective of the competition proposals—to constrict the amount of payment to hospitals and physicians to free resources to meet other national needs. The following comments and questions are raised to further explore some of the major financial issues influencing the societal contributions of teaching hospitals under a competitive system.

Educational Costs of Teaching Hospitals. One of the most significant issues is the continued financing of educational costs of teaching hospitals. The costs of medical and dental residency and fellowship training programs in teaching hospitals are now primarily financed through teaching hospital operating revenues. The total cost of these programs in teaching hospitals during fiscal year 1981, including instruction, is estimated to be $2.3 billion. Of this total approximately $1.8 billion is financed from revenues of nonfederal teaching hospitals, of which $1.2 billion is funded by the 270 COTH members that are the major affiliates of colleges of medicine.[34] In a competitive environment, these costs would obviously put teaching hospitals at a considerable price disadvantage.

The scope of educational programs in affiliated community hospitals would also be threatened. These programs assist in providing the clinical experience essential to a well-balanced health educational system. The number of community hospitals affiliated with medical schools grew from 517 in 1966 to 1,168 in 1976[35] and further increases are desirable to provide students and trainees the necessary exposure to primary and secondary levels of care. However, expanded competition in health care could discourage future growth in affiliations, as well as threaten existing agreements. If competition forces community hospitals to disengage from participation in medical education, tertiary teaching hospitals would not have the patient base and other resources to provide the necessary educational experience for all students, physicians, and dentists currently in training.

Several theoretical alternatives for financing graduate medical education were explored by the "Task Force on Graduate Medical Education" of the Association of American Medical Colleges (AAMC) in 1980. The report concluded that no alternative is likely to effectively replace funding through teaching hospital reimbursement.[36] The alternatives explored included the following:

- To finance graduate medical education from a separate governmental, tax-supported fund. The magnitude of such a fund, the complexities of its management and disbursements, and recent experience with capitation support of medical schools make this alternative a questionable option for long-term financing.
- To transfer the obligation for financing graduate medical education to medical schools. Since medical schools would be able to finance such education only through appropriated tax dollars or philanthropy (without relying on professional fee income), this alternative would severely tax their already tight budgetary situation.
- To utilize revenue generated by teaching physicians from professional fees. Reliance on professional fees could discourage patient admissions by some private practitioners who hold appointments on the staffs of teaching hospitals and could promote fee increases necessary to offset the costs of graduate medical education. Additionally, as a practical matter, the mix of income sources for most teaching hospital staffs would make implementation impossible.
- To have residents pay for their own graduate medical education. Such a policy would directly conflict with efforts to encourage students without financial means to enter medicine, by increasing the burden of indebtedness that must be repaid following completion of residency training. It could also reduce the quality of future practice as physicians who cannot afford to finish residency training opt to begin their practices earlier.

In summary, the AAMC study concluded that there was no practical alternative to the present practice of supporting residency training through teaching hospital revenues. Nor, in the opinion of the Association, was there any good reason to look for other alternatives because the present approach does, in fact, spread the burden equitably across the population. The report stated this conclusion as follows:

> Patients benefit from the services they receive as residents participate in their care in teaching hospitals, and 94% of all hospital revenues are now derived from third-party insurers. These insurers . . . diffuse the educational costs throughout the population through their premium charges

or taxation. These insurers have a social obligation to support graduate medical education, for the education and training of future practitioners is an essential investment by the public provided through private health insurance and government programs. This investment ensures that the medical care needs of future generations are met.[37]

While graduate medical and dental education has been the teaching hospital's largest educational expense, other educational programs conducted by and in teaching hospitals generate additional costs—directly through some support of stipends and instructor salaries and, to a larger extent, indirectly through additional spatial and environmental requirements and productivity losses in patient service associated with teaching. These educational programs include undergraduate training in medicine, nursing, dentistry, pharmacy, and an array of other health professional and technical fields. Teaching hosptials' financing of this broad range of socially essential educational programs is also at risk in a competitive health system.

Ambulatory Care Program Deficits. A second financial issue is whether specialized large-scale ambulatory care programs could continue to be provided in teaching hospitals. To evaluate the impact of a competitive system on the financing of ambulatory care programs and other responsibilities of teaching hospitals, The University of Iowa Hospitals and Clinics recently surveyed twenty university-owned teaching hospital members of the Council of Teaching Hospitals (Iowa survey). Based on an extrapolation of the data provided by the sample hospitals to the volume of ambulatory services provided by the 270 COTH members with major college of medicine affiliations, preliminary estimates of aggregate ambulatory care deficits in fiscal year 1981 were made and are reflected in Tables 5-1, 5-2, and 5-3. The aggregate deficit for ambulatory care in fiscal year 1981 was estimated to be $820 million. Of this total ambulatory care deficit, it was estimated that the charity and bad-debt component was $341 million. Costs of educational programs based in these ambulatory care settings amounted to $484 million. When these educational costs were removed from the $820 million estimated total deficit for ambulatory care in these hospitals, the remaining deficit was $336 million.[38]

These deficits arise in part from inappropriate methodologies for cost allocations that are required by governmental and other third-party payers. At the present time, space-related hospital costs must

Table 5-1. Ambulatory Care Program Financial Survey of Twenty University-owned Teaching Hospitals by the University of Iowa Hospitals and Clinics.

Hospital	Total Clinic Visits[a]	Gross Ambulatory Revenue[b]	Charity/Coll. Loss Allowances[c]	Contractual/Other Allowances[d]	Net Ambulatory Revenue[e]	Total Ambulatory Operating Expense[f]	Net Operating Surplus (Deficit)[g]	Educational Program Costs[h]
				Ambulatory Care Program Data—1979-80				
1.	318,056	$ 14,410,000	$ 417,042	$ 706,958	$ 13,286,000	$ 19,108,200	$ (5,822,200)	$ 3,053,114
2.	280,475	8,616,307	865,296	56,934	7,694,077	10,918,578	(3,224,501)	332,717
3.	219,921	14,337,445	1,546,112	645,367	12,145,966	20,174,172	(8,028,206)	4,066,089
4.	201,806	19,620,696	4,543,521	2,150,647	12,926,528	13,935,751	(1,009,223)	4,385,903
5.	200,792	14,333,461	129,748	—	14,203,713	15,976,617	(1,772,904)	1,055,901
6.	185,486	27,553,762	3,306,844	1,494,328	22,752,590	22,920,601	168,011	1,360,733
7.	182,008	10,654,415	1,065,442	(604,226)	10,193,199	13,791,697	3,598,498	1,588,990
8.	174,744	9,359,629	300,616	229,941	8,829,072	9,256,675	427,603	219,416
9.	168,823	6,201,515	1,089,367	497,845	4,614,303	8,575,578	3,961,275	1,168,489
10.	159,455	7,914,102	595,976	537,285	6,780,841	7,566,580	785,739	1,728,188
11.	157,756	5,250,782	765,466	555,350	3,929,966	4,899,238	969,272	401,897
12.	146,112	15,593,778	1,179,644	4,437,707	9,976,427	17,915,531	7,939,104	4,491,014
13.	140,762	5,770,959	917,670	(260,890)	5,114,179	7,346,886	2,232,707	973,211
14.	122,714	4,364,496	1,439,454	437,279	2,487,763	5,670,302	3,182,539	837,146
15.	100,255	5,127,294	1,673,184	147,134	3,306,976	4,705,017	1,398,041	867,128
16.	100,177	9,922,547	733,098	1,447,188	7,742,261	13,103,492	5,361,231	2,835,094
17.	96,062	3,510,436	837,642	258,255	2,414,539	6,404,743	3,990,204	1,967,944
18.	82,250	7,812,653	726,908	(435,315)	7,521,060	9,246,965	1,725,905	1,543,243

19.	37,876	7,021,578	503,482	841,440	5,676,656	5,969,332	(292,676)	201,410
20.	37,355	4,256,617	1,022,748	306,730	2,927,139	3,981,353	(1,054,214)	553,832
Totals	3,112,885	$201,632,472	$23,659,260	$13,449,957	$164,523,255	$221,467,308	$(56,944,053)	$33,631,459
Totals Adjusted to 1980–81[i]	3,112,885	$228,046,000	$26,758,000	$15,212,000	$186,076,000	$250,480,000	$(64,404,000)	$38,037,000

[a]Includes all clinic and emergency visits.

[b]Includes gross ambulatory, clinic, emergency, and ancillary service revenues related to ambulatory patients.

[c]Charity allowances represent the uncompensated dollar value of services provided to patients who at the time of their clinic visit are determined to be unable to pay costs of their care, while collection losses represent the revenue from patient accounts which the hospitals were unable to collect.

[d]Contractual and other allowances represents the difference between gross revenue from services rendered and amounts received from patients and third party payors.

[e]Net Ambulatory Revenue represents Gross Ambulatory Revenue less Charity/Collection Loss Allowances and Contractual and Other Allowances.

[f]Total Ambulatory Operating Expense includes direct and indirect expenses for clinic, emergency, and ancillary services related to ambulatory patients.

[g]Net Operating Surplus (Deficit) represents Net Ambulatory Revenue less Total Ambulatory Operating expense.

[h]Educational Program Costs include all measureable ambulatory clinic, emergency, and ancillary service educational costs. These costs are defined as those borne by the hospital relating to health science educational programs, as well as medical and dental residency programs including payments for stipends; supervisory physicians and dentists; professional liability insurance; house staff health insurance; uniforms; subsidized cafeteria services and other educational overhead costs as defined by Medicare cost reimbursement principles.

[i]Department of Labor, Bureau of Labor Statistics. This reflects a 13.1 percent increase in the Consumer Price Index change for Hospital "Room" Component of "Other Medical Care Services" component from July, 1979–July, 1980.

Table 5-2. A. Estimation of Total Ambulatory Care Program Deficit in 270 COTH Teaching Hospitals with Major College of Medicine Affiliations.

1979–80

1. Total Ambulatory Care Program Deficit in 20 Sample Teaching Hospitals	$ 56,944,053
2. Total Clinic Visits in 20 Sample Teaching Hospitals	3,112,885
3. Average Ambulatory Care Program Deficit Per Clinic Visit in 20 Sample Teaching Hospitals	$ 18.29
4. Total Clinic Visits in all 270 COTH Teaching Hospitals with Major College of Medicine Affiliations[a]	39,630,854
5. Total Estimated Ambulatory Care Program Deficit in 270 COTH Teaching Hospitals with Major College of Medicine Affiliations (39,630,854 Visits X $18.29)	$724,848,320

1980–81

1. Total Estimated Ambulatory Care Program Deficit in 270 COTH Teaching Hospitals with Major College of Medicine Affiliations ($724,848,320 x 1.131[b])	$819,803,000

B. Estimation of Ambulatory Care Program Deficit Exclusive of Charity/Collection Loss Allowance Costs in 270 COTH Teaching Hospitals with Major College of Medicine Affiliations.

1979-1980

1. Total Ambulatory Care Program Deficit ($56,944,053) *Less* Charity/Collection Loss Allowance Costs in 20 Sample Teaching Hospitals ($23,659,260) $ 33,284,793
2. Total Clinic Visits in 20 Sample Teaching Hospitals 3,112,885
3. Average Ambulatory Care Program Deficit Exclusive of Charity/Collection Loss Allowance Costs in 20 Sample Teaching Hospitals Per Patient Visit $ 10.69
4. Total Clinic Visits in 270 COTH Teaching Hospitals with Major College of Medicine Affiliations[a] 39,630,854
5. Total Estimated Ambulatory Care Program Deficit *Less* Charity/Collection Loss Allowance Costs for 270 COTH Teaching Hospitals with Major College of Medicine Affiliations (39,630,854 Visits x $10.69) $423,653,829

1980–81

1. Total Estimated Ambulatory Care Program Deficit *Less* Charity/Collection Loss Allowance Costs for 270 COTH Teaching Hospitals with Major College of Medicine Affiliations ($423,653,829 x 1.131[b]) $479,152,000

---

[a]Council of Teaching Hospitals, Associations of American Medical Colleges, *Committee Structure and Membership Directory, 1980*, Washington, D.C., 1980.

[b]Department of Labor, Bureau of Labor Statistics. This reflects a 13.1 percent increase in the Consumer Price Index change for Hospital "Room" Component of "Other Medical Care Services" Component from July, 1979, to July, 1980.

Table 5-3. A. Estimation of Charity/Collection Loss Allowance Costs Included in Ambulatory Care Program Deficits of 270 COTH Teaching Hospitals with Major College of Medicine Affiliations.

1979–80

1. Total Estimated Ambulatory Care Program Deficit in 270 COTH Teaching Hospitals with Major College of Medicine Affiliations — $724,848,320
2. Total Estimated Ambulatory Care Program Deficit *Less* Charity/Collection Loss Allowance Costs — $423,653,829
3. Total Estimated Charity/Collection Loss Allowance Costs Included in Ambulatory Care Program Deficits of 270 COTH Teaching Hospitals with Major College of Medicine Affiliations ($724,848,320 − $423,653,829) — $301,194,491

1980–81

1. Total Estimated Charity/Collection Loss Allowance Costs Included in Ambulatory Care Program Deficits of 270 COTH Teaching Hospitals with Major College of Medicine Affiliations ($301,194,491 x 1.131[a]) — $340,651,000

B. Estimation of Educational Costs Included in Ambulatory Care Program Deficits of 270 COTH Teaching Hospials with Major College of Medicine Affiliations

1979–80

1.	Educational Costs Included in Ambulatory Care Program Deficits in 20 Sample Teaching Hospitals	$ 33,631,459
2.	Total Clinic Visits in 20 Sample Teaching Hospitals	3,112,885
3.	Average Educational Cost Per Clinic Visit in 20 Sample Teaching Hospitals	$ 10.80
4.	Total Clinic Visits in 270 COTH Teaching Hospitals with Major College of Medicine Affiliations[b]	39,630,854
5.	Total Estimated Educational Costs in Ambulatory Care Program Deficits of 270 COTH Teaching Hospitals with Major College of Medicine Affiliations (39,630,854 x $10.80)	$428,013,223

1980–81

1.	Total Estimated Educational Costs in Ambulatory Care Program Deficits of 270 COTH Teaching Hospitals with Major College of Medicine Affiliations ($428,013,223 x 1.131[a])	$484,083,000

[a]Department of Labor, Bureau of Labor Statistics. This reflects a 13.1 percent increase in the Consumer Price Index change for Hospital "Room" Component of "Other Medical Care Services" Component from July, 1979, to July, 1980.

[b]Council of Teaching Hospitals, Association of American Medical Colleges, *Committee Structure and Membership Directory, 1980,* Washington, D.C., 1980.

often be allocated to ambulatory clinics on the basis of unweighted square feet, although it costs substantially less to construct, maintain, and heat a square foot of clinic space than other patient care units of the hospital. Additionally, educational costs must be allocated to clinics on the basis of assigned time of trainees in the clinic. The number of students, and to some degree residents, assigned to a clinic is often a function of the number of students needing training in ambulatory care and not necessarily a function of patient care needs in the clinic. Educational costs could be more appropriately allocated to revenue centers on a "general burden" concept recognizing that all hospital revenue centers and all hospital charges to the patient should contain a proportionate factor to support educational programs of teaching hospitals, whether or not a given revenue center is directly involved in an educational effort.

Also significantly affecting ambulatory care deficits are the increased spatial and other resources needed for clinic educational programs. Examination and treatment rooms in clinics, as well as inpatient rooms and other ostensibly noneducational space, require larger dimensions to accommodate students and teaching activities. Additional space and time is also required because the complexity of patient disease and related social condition requires a greater involvement of social workers, counselors, psychologists, therapists, dieticians, and other professional staff. Also, efficiency or "productivity" in providing ambulatory patient care is substantially reduced with the integration of clinic-based educational programs. Charges for ambulatory care services, which are largely uninsured, cannot reasonably be structured to cover the high overhead cost per patient visit that results from these educational requirements, even in a noncompetitive market.

It is not clear how clinic-based ambulatory care and the associated educational programs could continue if teaching hospitals are forced into direct price competition with hospitals that do not provide these programs requiring large subsidies from inpatient revenues or other sources. It should also be recognized that the ambulatory care setting has become increasingly important in meeting educational objectives related to the goal of training physicians and other health professionals in the methods of providing diagnostic and therapeutic care without expensive inpatient hospitalization.

Charity Care of Patients.   Most teaching hospitals provide substantial amounts of uncompensated care and will attempt to continue to care for patients "falling between the cracks" of health insurance coverage. Given the dearth of endowments and other philanthropic funds available for this purpose, it is not clear how this charity care could be maintained when institutions that avoid such care would be at a competitive advantage. Some hospitals may be required to continue charity care under federal, state, and local mandates, thus reducing their viability in the competitive marketplace.

To obtain an indication of the magnitude of the costs of charity care, the Iowa survey also collected data on uncompensated charity care and collection losses on the inpatient and ambulatory care services of the surveyed hospitals.[39] Among the twenty university-owned teaching hospitals surveyed, total charity and collection loss allowances ranged from $1.2 to $17.8 million, averaging 9 percent of gross patient revenue (Table 5-4). This includes *ambulatory* charity/collection losses ranging from $130 thousand to $4.5 million, averaging 11.7 percent of gross revenues from ambulatory care (Table 5-1). Projecting for the 270 COTH members with major college of medicine affiliations, total charity/collection losses were estimated at $2.0 billion in fiscal year 1981, of which $0.3 billion arises from ambulatory patient care programs (Table 5-3 and 5-5). The above figures would, obviously, be increased if all 332 nonfederal COTH hospitals were included.

Teaching hospitals are the primary source of health care services for millions of this nation's needy. These services will be difficult, if not impossible, to maintain if tertiary care centers are required to compete on the basis of price. The resultant erosion in the quality and accessibility of care for millions of patients should be of great concern to all.

Features of some competition bills might reduce the charity care burden for all hospitals. Bills that mandate universal coverage would minimize the need for charity care for those services covered. To the extent select services were not covered due to the economic incentive to opt for less comprehensive plans, there would be increased need for the excluded services to be provided as charity care. However, most of the bills do not mandate universal coverage. An alternative approach to the charity care issue is taken by the Gephardt-Stockman bill. It proposes to pay hospitals 50 percent of their charges in the case of services to nonmembers of approved plans who do not pay hospital accounts after reasonable collection efforts.[40] This would be beneficial for hospitals, but it would be a solution to the problem

Table 5-4. Total Inpatient and Outpatient Data for Twenty University-Owned Teaching Hospitals—1979–1980.

Hospital	Total Patient Days a	Gross Patient Revenue b	Charity/Collection Loss Allowances c	Contractual/Other Allowances d	Other Operating Revenue e	Total Operating Revenue f	Total Operating Expense g	Net Operating Surplus (Deficit) h	Educational Program Costs i
1.	313,009	$ 117,054,402	$ 4,700,779	$ 4,552,023	$ 6,237,319	$ 114,038,919	$ 101,243,193	$ 12,795,726	$ 8,362,600
2.	59,939	28,596,224	1,583,114	188,963	1,925,088	28,749,235	32,288,974	(3,539,739)	1,298,307
3.	218,674	106,625,233	11,494,865	4,798,135	3,278,378	93,610,611	104,561,982	(10,951,371)	12,768,210
4.	159,017	82,788,641	17,828,528	10,082,332	26,886,987	81,764,768	77,420,841	4,343,927	4,385,903
5.	203,393	99,182,037	1,249,590	3,165,240	10,771,969	105,539,176	106,408,560	(869,384)	11,767,841
6.	183,896	137,163,155	6,347,110	7,639,046	8,982,901	132,159,900	130,122,933	2,036,967	7,828,665
7.	149,682	66,163,083	3,268,339	474,954	5,056,091	67,475,881	64,735,783	2,740,098	5,000,000
8.	105,112	44,672,332	1,434,803	1,097,481	6,093,554	48,233,602	45,739,755	2,493,847	952,017
9.	80,204	36,301,345	4,091,265	2,988,372	5,286,104	34,507,812	35,392,226	(884,414)	3,633,377
10.	126,816	56,979,436	4,290,221	3,868,723	2,011,859	50,832,351	45,079,517	5,752,834	3,111,610
11.	129,195	41,261,594	3,155,589	4,669,041	215,973	33,662,937	32,433,325	1,229,612	2,580,990
12.	162,846	76,768,655	10,446,000	17,212,056	24,787,727	73,898,326	73,446,385	451,941	9,073,084
13.	243,373	84,095,592	4,346,171	1,803,681	1,810,739	79,756,479	81,892,078	(2,135,599)	4,986,083
14.	177,687	54,075,846	13,644,504	4,144,928	11,831,663	48,118,077	45,613,957	2,504,120	3,386,539
15.	118,081	44,605,757	13,567,976	6,368,723	8,098,225	32,767,283	30,362,434	2,404,849	3,272,905
16.	103,844	46,396,984	3,878,089	7,655,623	283,725	35,146,997	51,630,130	(16,483,133)	4,444,395
17.	106,171	30,737,477	7,244,632	2,234,042	—	21,258,803	34,473,650	(13,214,847)	6,541,243
18.	170,905	73,446,282	7,126,966	5,743,300	1,275,122	61,851,138	60,551,156	1,299,982	3,942,523

19.	221,023	1,429,611	25,326,895	2,016,281	88,448,224	87,409,616	1,038,608	5,899,123
20.	96,334	3,455,711	2,757,261	—	41,956,068	38,975,870	2,980,198	2,010,203
Totals	3,129,201 $1,388,271,564	$124,583,863	$116,760,819	$126,849,705	$1,273,776,587	$1,279,782,365	$(6,005,778)	$105,245,618
Totals Adjusted to 1980-81[j]	3,129,201 $1,570,135,000	$140,904,000	$132,057,000	$143,467,000	$1,440,641,000	$1,447,434,000	$(6,793,000)	$119,033,000

[a] Includes newborn patient days.

[b] Includes all patient service revenues.

[c] Charity allowances represent the uncompensated dollar value of services provided to patients who at the time of admission (or clinic visit) or during their stay are determined to be unable to pay costs of their care, while collection losses represent the revenue from patient accounts which the hospitals were unable to collect.

[d] Contractual and other allowances represent the difference between gross revenue from services rendered and amounts received from patients or third-party payors.

[e] Includes other revenues not identifiable with patient services.

[f] Total operating revenue represents gross patient revenue less charity/collection loss allowance and contractual/other allowance plus other operating revenue.

[g] Total operating expense includes salaries and fringe benefits, supplies and services, interest expense, and depreciation.

[h] Net operating surplus (deficit) represents total operating revenue less total operating expense.

[i] Educational program costs include all measurable direct and indirect educational costs. These costs are defined as those borne by the hospital relating to health science educational programs, as well as medical and dental residency programs including payments for stipends; supervisory physicians and dentists; professional liability insurance; house staff health insurance; uniforms; subsidized cafeteria services and other educational overhead costs as defined by Medicare cost reimbursement principles.

[j] Department of Labor, Bureau of Labor Statistics. This reflects a 13.1 percent increase in the Consumer Price Index change for Hospital "Room" Component of "Other Medical Care Services" component from July, 1979-July, 1980.

Table 5-5. A. Estimation of Total Inpatient and Outpatient Charity/Collection Loss Allowance Costs for 270 COTH Teaching Hospitals with Major College of Medicine Affiliations.

1979-80

1. Total Charity/Collection Loss Allowance for 20 Sample Teaching Hospital — $ 124,583,863
2. Total Adjusted Patient Days for 20 Sample Teaching Hospitals[a] — 3,660,882
3. Average Total Charity/Collection Loss Allowance Per Adjusted Patient Day for 20 Sample Teaching Hospitals — $ 34.03
4. Total Adjusted Patient Days for 270 COTH Teaching Hospitals with Major College of Medicine Affiliations[b] — 52,403,477
5. Total Estimated Charity/Collection Loss Allowance for 270 COTH Teaching Hospitals with Major College of Medicine Affiliations (52,403,477 Adjusted Patient Days x $34.03) — $1,783,290,322

1980-81

1. Total Estimated Charity/Collection Loss Allowance for 270 COTH Teaching Hospitals with Major College of Medicine Affiliations ($1,783,290,322 x 1.131[c]) — $2,016,901,000

B. Estimation of *Inpatient* Charity/Collection Loss Allowance Costs for 270 COTH Teaching Hospitals with Major College of Medicine Affiliations

1979-80

1. Total Estimated Charity/Collection Loss Allowance for 270 COTH Teaching Hospitals with Major College of Medicine Affiliations — $1,783,290,322

2. Total Estimated *Ambulatory* Charity/Collection Loss Allowance for 270 COTH Teaching Hospitals with Major College of Medicine Affiliations (Table 5-3). — $ 301,194,491

3. Total Estimated *Inpatient* Charity/Collection Loss Allowance for 270 COTH Teaching Hospitals with Major College of Medicine Affiliations ($1,783,290,322 − $301,194,491) — $1,482,095,831

1980-81

1. Total Estimated *Inpatient* Charity/Collection Loss Allowance for 270 COTH Teaching Hospitals with Major College of Medicine Affiliations ($1,482,095,831 x 1.131[c]) — $1,676,250,000

[a]"Adjusted patient days" is an aggregate figure reflecting the number of inpatient days of care rendered by the 20 sample teaching hospitals (3,129,201), plus (531,681) equivalent patient days extrapolated for outpatient services. The extrapolation was made after determining for the 20 hospitals the ratio of their average revenue per clinic visit ($64.77) to their average revenue per inpatient day ($379.21) which yields (.1708 clinic visits to 1 patient day). The total clinic visits for the 20 hospitals (3,112,885) was then multiplied by .1708 to determine the 531,681 equivalent patient days.

[b]"Adjusted patient days" for the 270 COTH teaching hospitals was derived using the same ratio of revenue per clinic visit to revenue per inpatient day (.1708 clinic visits to 1 patient day) as for the 20 sample hospitals. On this basis, the clinic visits for the 270 hospitals (39,630,854) were multiplied by (.1708) to yield 6,768,950 equivalent patient days. When this figure is added to total patient days (45,634,527) for the 270 hospitals, the total adjusted patient days is 52,403,477.

[c]Department of Labor, Bureau of Labor Statistics. This reflects a 13.1 percent increase in the Consumer Price Index change for Hospital "Room" Component of "Other Medical Care Services" Component from July, 1979–July, 1980.

only for those hospitals whose charity care is a small percentage of total care provided, not for hospitals with a large volume of uncompensated services.

Fostering of Advances in Health Care: New Technology Development. Another financial implication involves the cost of developing and implementing innovative procedures and technological advances designed to enhance patient care throughout the system. Some current hospital reimbursement formulas provide an increment for "growth and development" to encourage innovation, while others absorb such costs as a routine element of aggregate operating costs and charges. Recent and exciting breakthroughs in molecular and cellular biological research point to an expanded need for clinical research and technological development activities within teaching hospitals during the period immediately ahead. Therefore, these increments may be increasingly necessary. It is not clear how funding for this crucial development could be generated under a competitive system. In addition, it is not evident how compensation for services employing innovative technology would be generated during the initial testing phase when competitive plans would be motivated to exclude such procedures from coverage in their efforts to minimize costs. Unfortunately, no studies have been conducted to estimate the aggregate cost of these frontier-cutting responsibilities of teaching hospitals.

Clinical Research Support. The future of some biomedical research, essential to the vitality of academic health centers and to the improvement of health care, is also at risk. One element of a teaching hospital's responsibility is the creation of an environment that encourages and nurtures biomedical research in order to sustain this vitality. In addition to problems arising from a shrinking patient base, the financial support of this research initiative could also be reduced. Professional fee earnings of the medical faculty and teaching hospital patient care revenues have been used to support many small research projects that, for a variety of reasons, do not lend themselves to external grant support. Revenues of teaching hospitals have supported research of this nature through occasional direct allocations and substantial indirect allocations of technical staff, diagnostic tests, space, and other hospital resources. It is probable that a portion of the higher staff-to-bed ratios of some teaching hospitals is due to staff time devoted to research endeavors with a patient care orientation.

The potential decline of the patient base due to changes in referral patterns is an even greater threat to biomedical research, because many types of clinical research are possible only with a large patient base. In the case of some rare diseases, even the largest teaching hospitals have not had a sufficient patient base and have moved to research protocols involving multiple institutions. This multicenter research is extremely expensive and difficult to conduct because of the problem in establishing sufficient consistency between the centers to assure valid results. Decentralization of the patient base would force increased use of these expensive multicenter studies, smaller study populations, or longer study periods. Smaller study populations would create difficulties in obtaining appropriate sample sizes for study, and longer study periods would make consistency and interest over the study period more difficult to maintain. This reduction in patient base, coupled with constrained financial resources, could significantly impair the scope and quality of biomedical research.

Provision of Highly Specialized Services.   Another financial issue is whether high-cost, low-volume services that have historically been centralized in tertiary hospitals could be maintained. The patient case mix in tertiary teaching hospitals, presenting a broad array of complex clinical problems of patients referred from primary and secondary providers, enables these hospitals to meet their service, education, and research missions. When negotiating with a competitive plan, teaching hospitals would be at a significant disadvantage in competing with the rates of community hospitals because the teaching hospital, to meet the needs of a complicated patient case mix, must have clinical resources far beyond those required in community hospitals. To meet these added responsibilities, staff-to-patient ratios must be higher due to severity of patient problems; around-the-clock physician presence in major specialties is essential; breadth and depth of laboratory, radiology, and other ancillary services are greater; technological investments are substantial; and spatial requirements are greater due to educational programs, faculty offices, and the broad gamut of support services required. The funding necessary to support the extensive teaching hospital resources essential to diagnose and treat tertiary-level patients must be provided so such services can be maintained.

It is unlikely that competitors of teaching hosptials would either have the capacity or the desire to provide these services. There is also a question whether teaching hospitals would be able to continue to provide them under a price competitive system.

To make the introduction of highly expensive services within teaching hospitals more publicly acceptable, it is now common practice to partially underwrite the cost of these services with revenues from other patient earnings. Higher prices resulting from elimination of this practice could lead competitive plans to exclude such services from coverage, forcing teaching hospitals to either end the services, thereby depriving society of their availability, or develop a separate program to finance them.

Faculty Practice Plans: Reduced Support of Education.   In addition to problems associated with the continued financing of societal contributions, the competition proposals could also reduce the earnings derived from the professional fees of teaching physicians. This reduction could affect teaching physicians before private practitioners because of the relative ease with which fees emanating from physicians in teaching hospitals can be targeted by competitive plans. Because of the close association of teaching physicians and hospitals, some competitive plans could attempt to treat their combined fees and charges as a single "package," leading to pressure for physicians to reduce their fees to make the package of hospital and medical services more price competitive with the nonteaching setting. Coupled with possible reductions in patient referrals, this financial loss could further jeopardize faculty practice plans that are now heavily relied upon to finance programs of medical education, support nonsponsored research, and meet physician income levels essential to retention of medical faculties of high quality.[41]

This differential impact on the teaching hospital environment would create incentives for physicians and dentists to leave academia in favor of private practice or to convert practice plans into more private practice-oriented models, thereby curtailing their availability for support of academic programs. Because medical service plan earnings have been the fastest growing segment of college of medicine budgets over the past decade, this risk is of great import to both collegiate deans and university presidents.[42] Unless reductions in earnings of practice plans were replaced through general appropriations, endowments, or other support, universities would be confronted with the difficult, if not impossible, job of reallocating already depleted general university dollars to the extent they decide to sustain health science education programs at present levels.

It is important to recognize that the multiple functions of teaching hospitals are usually performed simultaneously and that the resulting costs of individual functions could ultimately be separated only on the basis of somewhat arbitrary criteria which have not yet been developed. The Iowa survey assessed three measurable societal contributions of teaching hospitals to estimate the financial magnitude of the problem. However, it is impossible to identify and quantify the costs for all societal contributions of teaching hospitals with sufficient accuracy on an institution-by-institution basis for categorical subsidy, even if other sources of funding could be identified. It is not simply a matter of altering current accounting procedures and transferring the costs to new, separately funded accounts.

System-Wide Quality of Care Erosion

The quality of care in the health system could be adversely affected by changes in patient referral patterns and by financial dilemmas resulting from competitive approaches. As discussed earlier, tertiary-level teaching hospitals anchor the nation's health care system by delivering highly specialized patient care, while serving as the clinical base for education, research, technology development, and continuing education. A decline in the ability of teaching hospitals to finance any of these societal contributions could erode the quality of health care at all levels. A reduction in the number and types of patients referred to teaching hospitals would intrinsically curtail the access of patients with complex and expensive diseases to the highest level of care.

A competitive system would also challenge the traditional emphasis on providing the best patient care possible by shifting the focus to cost. Health professionals and hospitals have already become increasingly sensitized to cost. There is, however, a danger that competition may move the system too far in the direction of cost consciousness, perhaps sacrificing the quality of care to patients.

Differences in quality are difficult to communicate to the typical person by either government or some other intermediary or agent, possibly causing disproportionate consideration to be given to the price of services. This facilitates the development of plans that are competitively priced, but that may not assure access to services of high quality. Additionally, if the services of teaching hospitals are either directly or indirectly excluded from competitive plans, a significant decline in the patient care function of teaching hospitals may be experienced. This would ultimately be reflected in the aggregate health status of the population.

The concentration on cost in any competitive financing structure could eventually lead to a counterbalancing focus on quality control. The public will demand service, and the government will expect a return on its investment in the form of improved health status. Unfortunately, this return is difficult to quantify with existing measures of quality and health status. Therefore, it is imperative for teaching hospitals to pursue a position of leadership in the evaluation and preservation of health services of high quality to patients, regardless of the future structure of the health system.

In addition, reductions in patient referrals would also limit opportunities for health science students to gain the broad clinical exposure necessary for quality health science education and future practice. Recently, there has been broad expansion in the use of affiliated community hospitals for attaining clinical experience, particularly in primary care. This may tempt some reformers to advocate further decentralization of health science education and, thus, bring about a narrowed role and need for teaching hospitals. While decentralization of selected portions of the educational experience may enrich overall training, it is essential that the bulk of medical education (all in some specialties) be conducted in a setting where a full-time faculty can provide essential knowledge and properly supervised clinical experience. The setting of teaching hospitals is necessary to insure that the student is challenged at the bedside and in regular conferences with the searching questions of academic clinicians actively engaged in the testing and discovery of new knowledge through current research. The case mix in tertiary teaching hospitals assures that all students and trainees are exposed to an appropriate range of challenging medical problems at each level of clinical education so that they can be trained systematically and efficiently. Since the entire professional staff of the teaching hospital is oriented to and encourages education, the requisite environment for learning and appropriate supervision can be maintained, despite the associated loss in "productivity" related to patient care. Educational opportunities in affiliated community hospitals are an important adjunct to the clinical education in teaching hospitals, but cannot serve as a substitute as long as society desires to maintain and enhance the present level of performance of its physicians and other health professionals.

A THEORETICAL APPROACH TO STRUCTURING OF THE COMPETITIVE SYSTEM TO RECOGNIZE THE UNIQUE SOCIETAL CONTRIBUTIONS OF TEACHING HOSPITALS

While the wisdom and likelihood of widescale implementation of expanded competition in the health field is still a matter of broad debate, it is a fact that the concept currently has significant support. One of the perplexing questions that remains is how the nation might alternatively finance the approximately $6.7 billion cost of societal contributions now financed through teaching hospital patient charges (Table 5-6, 5-7, 5-8, 5-9, 5-10, and 5-11). If any competitive system that may evolve is to fairly and effectively include teaching hospitals, a practical answer to this dilemma must be found. Some competition advocates have proposed that the "teaching and research costs" of teaching hospitals be supported from another source. However, none of the current competition proposals have explored in sufficient depth how this might be accomplished.

A theoretical approach is set forth here to stimulate further discussion regarding options for addressing this vital concern. Based on the broad range of complexities and assumptions involved in structuring this conceptual approach to reimbursement of societal contributions under competition, it would not be unreasonable to anticipate reservation, or even opposition, by teaching hospitals. Such concern would flow from the financial uncertainties involved in converting to a new, untried payment system for a broad range of their ongoing responsibilities. Nevertheless, a need to theoretically address the issue remains. If the movement toward expanded competition is to become a long-range reality, it is essential that the competitive proposals include some appropriate mechanism for preserving teaching hospital societal contributions.

Industries of all types finance "research and development" activities as an integral operating cost, recognizing that their future in the

Table 5-6. Measurability and Estimated Annual Cost of Societal Contributions for 270 COTH Teaching Hospitals with Major College of Medicine Affiliations. *(Graduate Medical and Dental Educational Costs Relate to All Nonfederal Teaching Hospitals).*

Societal Contribution	Measurable	Unmeasurable
1) GRADUATE MEDICAL & DENTAL EDUCATION:		
A. Direct	$1,570,000,000	—
B. Indirect (Measurable)	$ 238,000,000	—
C. Indirect (Unmeasurable)	—	$?
SUBTOTAL	($1,808,000,000)[a]	($?)
2) OTHER EDUCATIONAL PROGRAMS:		
A. Direct	$ 126,000,000	
B. Indirect (Measurable)	$ 22,000,000	
C. Indirect (Unmeasurable)	—	$?
SUBTOTAL	($ 148,000,000)[a]	($?)
3) AMBULATORY CARE PROGRAM DEFICITS:	$ 336,000,000 [b]	—
(Excludes all educational program costs included in items #1 and #2 above and includes ambulatory charity/collection loss costs)		
4) CHARITY CARE/COLLECTION LOSSES ARISING FROM *INPATIENT* CARE PROGRAMS FOR WHICH NO DIRECT COMPENSATION IS RECEIVED	$1,676,000,000 [c]	
5) NEW TECHNOLOGY TESTING:		
A. Direct	—	$?
B. Indirect	—	$?

6) CLINICAL RESEARCH:
   A. Direct — $?
   B. Indirect — $?

7) LOW VOLUME, HIGHLY SPECIALIZED SERVICES:
   A. Direct — $?
   B. Indirect — $?

8) INTENSIVE CASE MIX:
   A. Direct — $?
   B. Indirect — $?

TOTAL SOCIETAL CONTRIBUTIONS FOR 270 COTH TEACHING HOSPITALS
WITH MAJOR COLLEGE OF MEDICINE AFFILIATIONS $3,968,000,000 $2,725,000,000

GRAND TOTAL $6,693,000,000   (Estimated on Table 5-8.)

[a]Source: W. McNerney: "Control of Health-Care Costs in the 1980's" *New England Journal of Medicine* 303, no. 19 (November 6):1091.
[b]For calculation see Table 5-7.
[c]For calculation see Table 5-5.

Table 5-7. Measurability and Estimated Annual Cost of Societal Contributions for 270 COTH Teaching Hospitals with Major College of Medicine Affiliations (with Remarks). *(Graduate Medical and Dental Education Costs Relate to All Nonfederal Teaching Hospitals).*

Societal Contribution	1980–81		Remarks
	Measurable	Unmeasurable	
1) GRADUATE MEDICAL & DENTAL EDUCATION:			
A. Direct	$1,570,000,000	—	Direct costs of Graduate Medical and Dental Education could be derived directly from each teaching hospital's annual budget. The aggregate data reported here were derived from existing data and extrapolations of data from COTH, Institute of Medicine and GMENAC sources, adjusted for inflation.
B. Indirect (Measurable)	$ 238,000,000	—	Measurable indirect costs could be derived directly from each teaching hospital's cost finding report. These include depreciation on space and associated overhead costs (e.g. housekeeping, building maintenance, equipment depreciation, interest on capital borrowing) for clinical faculty and associated academic support personnel offices, call quarters, conference rooms, library and classrooms; and, subsidized cafeterias, housing services, uniforms, house staff affairs

office functions and other general supporting services. The aggregate measurable data reported here for indirect costs were derived from existing data and extrapolations from the sources indicated above.

Numerous unmeasurable indirect costs are also associated with graduate medical and dental education programs. These include the costs of staff other than teaching physicians who provide support to house staff in their learning process, additional space included in patient accommodations and other supporting facilities to meet educational program needs, and an undetermined proportion of diagnostic testing which may be utilized for educational purposes. However, no estimates exist or can be developed at this time which would provide these costs.

Actual cost figures could be derived for direct and measurable indirect costs of Other Educational Programs from operating budgets and cost finding reports of each teaching hospital.

C. Indirect (Unmeasurable)	— $?
SUBTOTAL	($1,808,000,000) ($?)
2) OTHER EDUCATIONAL PROGRAMS:	
A. Direct	$ 126,000,000
B. Indirect (Measurable)	$ 22,000,000

Table 5-7. continued

Societal Contribution	1980–81		Remarks
	Measurable	Unmeasurable	
			The estimates provided here were derived by using 1978 COTH data to determine the relationship between graduate medical and dental education costs and other health science educational program costs for 58 university owned teaching hospitals and applying this relationship to the total graduate medical and dental education costs of the 270 teaching hospitals with major college of medicine affiliations. This estimate of total Other Educational Program cost was then segregated into direct and indirect measurable costs on the basis of the direct – indirect cost relationship for Graduate Medical and Dental Education set forth above.
C. Indirect (Unmeasurable)	—	$?	Unmeasurable indirect costs also exist as they do for graduate medical and dental education, and no means is available for measuring them.
SUBTOTAL	($ 148,000,000)	($?)	

3) AMBULATORY CARE PROGRAM DEFICITS: (Excludes all educational program costs included in items #1 and #2 above and includes ambulatory charity/collection loss costs.)

$ 336,000,000

—

Figures for total Ambulatory Care Program Deficits could be measured for each teaching hospital from existing accounting records. The figure specified here was derived by extrapolating data from 20 university owned teaching hospitals on their clinic, emergency and ancillary ambulatory program deficits to the volume of ambulatory services provided by the 270 COTH teaching hospitals. See Exhibit I – 2 & 3: Total estimated ambulatory care program deficit in the 270 COTH teaching hospitals ($819,803,000) less total estimated educational costs in ambulatory care program deficits ($484,083,000) = $335,720,000.

4) CHARITY CARE/COLLECTION LOSSES ARISING FROM *INPATIENT* CARE PROGRAMS FOR WHICH NO DIRECT COMPENSATION IS RECEIVED

$1,676,000,000

—

This figure could be derived from existing accounting records in teaching hospitals. The estimate provided here was derived by extrapolating data obtained from 20 university owned teaching hospitals on uncompensated charity care and collection losses to the 270 COTH teaching hospitals.

Table 5-7. continued

Societal Contribution	Measurable	1980–81 Unmeasurable	Remarks
5) NEW TECHNOLOGY TESTING:			New Technology Testing encompasses all activities which teaching hospitals undertake to test and develop new equipment and procedures used for patient diagnosis and treatment. No means exist for measuring the direct and indirect costs of new technology testing and innovation, but it is generally recognized that the cost of this societal contribution is significant. At the University of Iowa Hospitals and Clinics alone, some 250 new procedures and tests were introduced for patient care and diagnosis in the period from 1973 to 1978.
A. Direct	—	$?	
B. Indirect	—	$?	
6) CLINICAL RESEARCH:			While the bulk of Clinical Research conducted in teaching hospitals is supported by grants and other separate funding awarded for research purposes, some clinical research is directly or indirectly supported through patient care earnings. There are no studies which have been con-
A. Direct	—	$?	
B. Indirect	—	$?	

7) LOW VOLUME, HIGHLY SPECIALIZED SERVICES:

A. Direct	—	$?
B. Indirect	—	$?

ducted to determine the aggregate costs of clinical research support provided directly by teaching hospitals.

No estimates of the cost of Low Volume, Highly Specialized Services are available and no methodology has been developed for deriving such estimates.

8) INTENSIVE CARE MIX:

A. Direct	—	$?
B. Indirect	—	$?

No studies have been conducted to determine the costs which the 270 teaching hospitals incur in providing Intensive Case Mix Services and no reliable methodology has yet been developed to provide such costs.

TOTAL SOCIETAL CONTRIBUTIONS FOR 270 COTH TEACHING HOSPITALS WITH MAJOR COLLEGE OF MEDICINE AFFILIATIONS	$3,968,000,000[a]	$2,725,000,000

(See Table 5-8 for calculation of this unmeasurable figure.)

Grand TOTAL	$6,693,000,000

[a]The above figure would be increased if all 332 nonfederal COTH teaching hospitals were included. However, inclusion of all 332, for other than Graduate Medical and Dental Education, was not felt warranted because the preponderance of societal contributions are generated in teaching hospitals with major college of medicine affiliations.

Table 5-8. Estimation of Unmeasurable Societal Contributions for 270 COTH Teaching Hospitals with Major College of Medicine Affiliations.

1. Estimated Average Charge Per Inpatient Day for 270 COTH Teaching Hospitals with Major College of Medicine Affiliations[a]	$	414
2. Estimated Average Charge Per Inpatient Day for All U.S. Nonfederal Short-Term General and Other Special Hospitals Excluding 270 COTH Teaching Hospitals[b]	$	297
3. Average Cost Per Inpatient Day of Societal Contributions of Teaching Hospitals ($414 – 297)	$	117
4. Average Cost Per Adjusted Patient Day of Measurable Societal Contributions for 270 COTH Teaching Hospitals (3.397 Billion[c]) 52,403,477[d] adjusted patient days)	$	65
5. Average Cost per Adjusted Patient Day of Unmeasurable Societal Contributions ($117 – $65)	$	52
6. Total Annual Cost of Unmeasurable Societal Contributions ($52 x 52,403,477 adjusted patient days[d])	$2,725,000,000[e]	

[a]See Table 5-9 for derivation.

[b]See Table 5-10 for derivation.

[c]See Table 5-11 for derivation.

[d]"Adjusted Patient Days" is an aggregate figure reflecting the number of inpatient days of care rendered by the 270 COTH teaching hospitals (45,634,527) plus (6,768,950) equivalent patient days extrapolated for outpatient services. The extrapolation was made by multiplying the ratio of revenue per clinic visit to revenue per inpatient day for the 20 sample hospitals (.1708 clinic visits to 1 patient day) by the 20 hospitals' total clinic visits (39,630,854) to determine the equivalent patient days (6,768,950). (Source for 270 COTH Teaching Hospital patient days and clinic visits—Council of Teaching Hospitals, Association of American Medical Colleges, *Committee Structure and Membership Directory, 1980,* Washington, D.C., 1980).

[e]The above figure would be increased if all 332 nonfederal COTH teaching hospitals were included. However, calculation of the additional increase by extrapolation to them is probably not warranted because the preponderance of these societal contributions is in the 270 COTH members with major College of Medicine affiliations.

Table 5-9. Estimation of Average Charge per Inpatient Day in 270 COTH Teaching Hospitals with Major College of Medicine Affiliations 1980–81.

I. ESTIMATION OF RELATIONSHIP OF INPATIENT COST TO INPATIENT REVENUE IN 20 SAMPLE TEACHING HOSPITALS

A. Gross 1980-81 Inpatient Revenue in 20 Sample Teaching Hospitals [Weighted Average Charge Per Inpatient Day Reported by 20 Sample Teaching Hospitals ($388)[a] x 1.131[b] x Total Patient Days (3,129,201)] $ 1,373,181,000

B. Total Inpatient Expense in 20 Sample Teaching Hospitals [Total Operating Expense ($1,447,434,000) less Total Ambulatory Operating Expense ($250,480,000) less Expense Allocated to Other Operating Revenues[c] ($144,743,000)] $ 1,052,211,000

C. Relationship of Inpatient Costs to Inpatient Charges in 20 Sample Teaching Hospitals ($1,052,211,000 ÷ $1,373,181,000)   77%

II. ESTIMATION OF AVERAGE COST PER INPATIENT DAY IN 270 NONFEDERAL COTH TEACHING HOSPITALS WITH MAJOR COLLEGE OF MEDICINE AFFILIATIONS

A. Total Inpatient and Ambulatory Care Operating Expense for 270 Nonfederal COTH Teaching Hospitals with Major College of Medicine Affiliations [1978–79 Total Operating Expense ($14,744,786,000[d] x 1.259[b] = $18,563,686,000) Less Expense Allocable to Other Operating Revenue ($18,563,686,000 x the Ratio of Other Operating Revenue to Total Operating Revenue for 20 Sample Teaching Hospitals, .10 = $1,856,369,000)] $16,707,317,000

B. Total Adjusted Patient Days for 270 Nonfederal COTH Teaching Hospitals with Major College of Medicine Affiliations[e]   52,403,477

C. Estimated Average Cost Per Inpatient Day for 270 Nonfederal COTH Teaching Hospitals with Major College of Medicine Affiliations ($16,707,317,000 ÷ 52,403,477 Adjusted Patient Days) $ 319

Table 5-9. continued

III. ESTIMATION OF AVERAGE *CHARGE* PER INPATIENT DAY IN 270 NONFEDERAL COTH TEACHING HOSPITALS WITH MAJOR COLLEGE OF MEDICINE AFFILIATIONS

   A.   Estimated Average Cost Per Inpatient Day for 270 Nonfederal COTH Teaching Hospitals with Major College of Medicine Affiliations $ <u>319</u>

   B.   Relationship of Average Estimated Cost Per Inpatient Day to Average Estimated Charge Per Inpatient Day in 20 Sample Teaching Hospitals   77%

   C.   Estimated Average *Charge* Per Inpatient Day in 270 Nonfederal COTH Teaching Hospitals with Major College of Medicine Affiliations ($319 ÷ 77%)   <u>414</u>

[a]Calculated by multiplying the Gross Average Charge Per Inpatient Day Reported by Each of the 20 Sample Teaching Hospitals by their Individual Reported Patient Days and Dividing by Total Patient Days for all 20 Hospitals.

[b]Department of Labor, Bureau of Labor Statistics. This reflects a 13.1 and 25.9 percent increase in the Consumer Price Index for Hospital "Room" Component of "Other Medical Care Services" Component from July, 1979 – July 1980, and July, 1978 – July 1980, respectively.

[c]Derived by relating Other Operating Revenue for the 20 Sample Teaching Hospitals ($143,467,000) to Total Operating Revenue ($1,440,641,000) and applying this relationship (.10 to 1) to Total Operating expense ($1,447,434,000).

[d]Council of Teaching Hospitals, Association of American Medical Colleges, *Committee Structure and Membership Directory, 1980,* Washington, D.C., 1980; and American Hospital Association, *Guide to the Health Care Field, 1980,* (Chicago: American Hospital Association, 1980).

[e]"Adjusted Patient Days" for the 270 COTH Teaching Hospitals was derived using the ratio of revenue per clinic visit to revenue per inpatient day (.1708 clinic visits to 1 patient day) for the 20 sample hospitals. On this basis, the clinic visits for the 270 COTH hospitals (39,630,854) were multiplied by (.1708) to yield 6,768,950 equivalent patient days. When this figure is added to total patient days (45,634,527) for the 270 COTH hospitals, the total is 52,403,477.

Table 5–10 Estimation of the Average Charge Per Inpatient Day for U.S. Nonfederal, Short-Term General and Other Special Hospitals Excluding 270 COTH Teaching Hospitals with Major College of Medicine Affiliations.

	Gross Inpatient Revenue	Inpatient Days of Care	Average Charge (Revenue) Per Inpatient Day
1. 1978-79 Inpatient Revenue, Inpatient Days of Care and Average Charge (Revenue) Per Inpatient Day for 5,842 Nonfederal, Short-Term General and Other Special Hospitals	$66,821,103,000[a]	265,205,203[b]	$251.96[a]
2. 1980-81 Inpatient Revenue, Inpatient Days of Care and Average Charge (Revenue) Per Patient Day for 5,842 Nonfederal, Short-Term General and Other Special Hospitals	$84,127,768,677[c]	265,205,203[d]	$317.00[c]
3. 1980-81 Inpatient Revenue, Inpatient Days of Care, and Average Charge (Revenue) Per Inpatient Day for 270 COTH Teaching Hospitals with Major College of Medicine Affiliations	$18,892,694,178[e]	45,634,527[f]	$414.00[g]
4. Estimation of Gross Inpatient Revenue and Inpatient Days of Care for U.S. Nonfederal, Short-Term General and Other Special Hospitals Excluding 270 COTH Teaching Hospitals			
a. Gross Inpatient Revenue (84,127,768,677 − $18,892,694,178)	$65,235,074,499[h]		
b. Inpatient Days of Care (265,205,203 − 45,634,527)	219,570,676[h]		

Table 5-10 continued

Gross Inpatient Revenue	Inpatient Days of Care	Average Charge (Revenue) Per Inpatient Day
		$297.10 = $297

5. Estimation of Average Charge Per Inpatient Day for U.S. Nonfederal, Short-Term, General and Other Special Hospitals Excluding 270 COTH Teaching Hospitals with Major College of Medicine Affiliations [Gross Patient Revenue ($65,235,074,499) ÷ Inpatient Days of Care (219,570,676)]

[a] American Hospital Association, *Hospital Statistics* (Chicago: American Hospital Association, 1980), p. 186.

[b] Gross Inpatient Revenue ($66,821,103,000) ÷ Average Charge (Revenue) Per Inpatient Day ($251.96) = 265,205,203 Inpatient Days of Care.

[c] These figures were obtained by multiplying 1978-79 Gross Inpatient Revenue ($66,821,103,000) and Average Charge (Revenue) Per Inpatient Day ($251.96) by 1.259. The 1.259 reflects a 25.9 percent increase in the Consumer Price Index for the Hospital "Room" Component of the "Other Medical Services" Component from July, 1978 - July, 1980, per Department of Labor, Bureau of Labor Statistics.

[d] It is assumed that Inpatient Days of Care remained constant between 1978-79 and 1980-81.

[e] This figure is determined by multiplying Total Inpatient Days of Care for 270 COTH Teaching Hospitals with Major College of Medicine Affiliations (45,634,527) by the Average Charge (Revenue) Per Inpatient Day Estimated for the 270 COTH Teaching Hospitals ($414.00).

[f] Council of Teaching Hospitals, Association of American Medical Colleges, *Committee Structure and Membership Directory, 1980*, Washington, D.C., 1980.

[g] See Table 5-11 for derivation.

[h] It is assumed that all 270 COTH Teaching Hospitals are included in the 5,842 Nonfederal, Short-Term General and Other Special Hospitals in performing these calculations. This assumption is supported by the response rate to the American Hospital Association survey from which the 1978-79 Gross Revenue and Average Charge (Revenue) Per Inpatient Day data for the 5,842 Nonfederal, Short-Term General and Other Special Hospitals were drawn. All 270 COTH hospitals have over 100 beds and the response rate to the AHA survey for hospitals with over 100 beds exceeded 92 percent. See American Hospital Association, *Ibid.*, p. xxi.

Table 5-11.   Estimation of Total Measurable Societal Contribution Costs for 270 COTH Teaching Hospitals Only.

1980–81

I. ESTIMATION OF GRADUATE MEDICAL AND DENTAL EDUCATION COSTS FOR 270 COTH TEACHNG HOSPITALS WITH MAJOR COLLEGE OF MEDICINE AFFILIATIONS

1. Total Graduate Medical and Dental Education Costs for All Nonfederal Teaching Hospitals[a]	$1,808,000,000
2. Total *Medical* Residents[b] Engaged in Residency Training in All Teaching Hospitals[c]	64,615
3. Total *Medical* Residents[b] Engaged in Residency Training in 270 COTH Teaching Hospitals with Major College of Medicine Affiliations[d]	44,206
4. Relationship of 270 COTH Teaching Hospital Medical Residents to all Medical Residents (44,206 ÷ 64,615)	68.4%
5. Total Graduate Medical and Dental Education Costs for 270 COTH Teaching Hospitals with Major College of Medicine Affiliations ($1,808,000,000 x .684)	$1,237,000,000

II. TOTAL MEASURABLE SOCIETAL CONTRIBUTION COSTS FOR 270 COTH TEACHNG HOSPITALS ONLY

1. Graduate Medical and Dental Education[a]	$1,237,000,000
2. Other Educational Programs[a]	$ 148,000,000
3. Ambulatory Care Program Deficits Excluding Educational Costs Included in A and B but including Ambulatory Charity/Collection Loss Costs[a]	$ 336,000,000
4. Inpatient Charity Care/Collection Loss Costs[a]	$1,676,000,000
5. Total	$3,397,000,000

[a]See Table 5-7.

[b]Medical Residents only are used to estimate the proportion of total graduate Medical and Dental Education Costs funded from Hospital revenues which are attributable to the 270 COTH teaching hospitals with major College of Medicine affiliations because information is not available on the number of dental residents and clinical fellows in the individual teachng hospitals.

[c]American Medical Association, *80/81 Directory of Residency Training Programs Accredited by the Liaison Committee on Graduate Medical Education*, (Chicago: American Medical Association, 1980).

[d]Council of Teaching Hospitals, Association of American Medical Colleges, *Committee Structure and Membership Directory, 1980*, Washington, D.C., 1980; and *Ibid.*

market will be impaired by lack of knowledge or failure to innovate. In the past, the financial decisions of teaching hospitals to invest in education, research, and development have served the public well. Fragmentation or scaling down of the existing system whereby teaching hospitals effectively invest in the future of the nation's health care system would be unwise and short-sighted. Two of the theoretical options for avoiding this problem are for the competition proposals to include mechanisms for payment of the cost of teaching hospital societal contributions through grants for individual programs or through payments for institutional support.

One of the first competition promotion bills to recognize the need for such mechanisms was the Gephardt-Stockman bill. It proposed a program grant approach by providing for grants covering not more than 70 percent of the direct costs of educational programs "to the extent the Secretary [of Health and Human Services] finds such compensation is necessary to provide training for needed health care professionals."[43] As the authors of the bill recognize, this provision does not fully address the problems of teaching hospitals. It does not provide for any of the societal contributions other than education, and it implicitly assumes that teaching hospitals will be able to cover the remaining 30 percent of direct educational costs plus all of the indirect costs of these programs. However, the 1980 bill served its intended purpose because it has led to further discussion of this issue, assisting Representative Richard Gephardt's attempts to formulate a more comprehensive approach to the whole problem of funding teaching hospital societal contributions for inclusion in a modified bill he plans to introduce later in the Ninety-seventh Congress.

There are other difficulties with program grants which suggest that they are less practical than payments for institutional support. Program grants cannot provide the continuing commitment of resources to create the necessary stability within teaching hospitals because they are subject to frequent review and short-term decisionmaking. Program grants would also present virtually insurmountable administrative barriers in separating the costs of each societal contribution. They would not provide for the continuing allocation of these monies within each teaching hospital by knowledgeable executive and academic staff, essential to sustaining the proper balance of all functioning patient care and academic programs.

Institutional support payments could be viewed as more appropriate because they avoid many of these difficulties. The calculation of these institutional payments would still be based in whole or in part on the aggregate costs of programs within the institution, but the payments would not be tied to governmental program evaluations or to a mandated allocation among individual programs. However, the problem remains of maintaining a commitment over the long term. This problem could be mitigated, but not eliminated, by providing some insulation from short-term political decisions through an earmarked surcharge on premiums for all health plan coverage. The surcharge would be deposited in a trust fund and allocated to teaching hospitals under the guidance of an academically oriented Teaching Hospital Advisory Council. If this approach were adopted, the government could wisely forego the additional burden of the program grant alternative to meet these needs, as well as the annual appropriation process. This would continue the flexibility and stability necessary for sustaining the vital clinical and academic environment now fostering a broad spectrum of societal contributions within teaching hospitals.

The theoretical payment approach outlined here is predicated upon teaching hospitals continuing to generate a large portion of their financial requirements through charges to competitive health plans and patients for patient care services at competitive rates. Beyond this, the approach would create a Teaching Hospital Societal Contribution Fund generated from a surcharge on health plan premiums. Monies from the fund would be distributed to teaching hospitals to reimburse for societal contribution costs through two payment mechanisms:

1. The first mechanism would encompass prospective payments for measurable societal contributions, which include graduate medical and dental education, ambulatory care deficits, and charity care. The measurable cost of graduate medical and dental education for all nonfederal teaching hospitals is approximately $1.8 billion for 1980–81, of which $1.2 billion is incurred in the 270 COTH members with major college of medicine affiliations. The estimated additional costs for measurable societal contributions in these 270 teaching hospitals is $2.2 billion. Thus, the total estimated value of measurable societal contributions is approximately $4.0 billion for 1980–81 (Tables 5–6 through 5–11).

2. The second mechanism would be retrospective payment of the costs of unmeasurable societal contributions, which include all other educational programs, new technology testing, clinical

research, and care of a highly intense patient case mix. The estimated cost of unmeasurable societal contributions for the 270 COTH members is approximately \$2.7 billion for 1980–81 (Tables 5-6 through 5-11).

Payment Mechanism I: Separately identified and quantified analysis of each teaching hospital's measurable societal contributions for prospective funding. All teaching hospitals would receive payment under this mechanism for their measurable societal contributions. This could enhance the capability of a large number of teaching hospitals, including many large urban and specialized children's hospitals, to fairly compete in a competitive health care system because their costs of societal contributions are predominantly in three areas—graduate medical and dental education, ambulatory care deficits, and charity care—which are sufficiently identifiable for prospective quantification and payment. These hospitals would be able to avoid seeking payment under payment mechanism II with its attendant involvement in extensive financial analyses and reporting.

While the three societal contributions identified for prospective payment under Payment Mechanism I are reasonably measurable on a prospective basis, there are many contingencies, such as changes in the local or national economy, that could make prospectively calculated payments inequitable for some or all teaching hospitals in certain years. Thus, a means for teaching hospitals to apply for a retrospective adjustment of prospective payments would be necessary to preclude undue hardships.

Payment Mechanism II: Separate retrospective funding of the nation's comprehensive tertiary teaching hospitals' unmeasurable societal contributions. A second payment mechanism would be needed to accommodate the costs of the unmeasurable societal contributions of undergraduate education, new technology testing, clinical research, and the incremental cost of the highly intensive patient case mix common to most comprehensive tertiary care teaching hospitals. These contributions defy separate and accurate quantification under any accounting system because they are so inextricably interwoven with the patient care and graduate medical and dental education programs of teaching hospitals. Sufficiently refined analyses of case mix and related costing methodologies, now under intensive investigation by the Association of American Medical Colleges, the Health Care Financing Administration, and others, are probably several years away from a sound methodological basis. One might consider encompassing the unmeasurable costs within the first payment mechanism described above by applying a multiplier to the measurable costs to arrive at the total required payment for measurable and unmeasurable societal contributions for each teaching hospital. However, as described in the Appendix, when the measurable costs of the group of twenty surveyed university teaching hospitals were compared, it became clear that the costs predicted by the multiplier were not reasonable estimations of actual costs. While it is natural to hope for a simple methodology such as a multiplier or resident trainee capitation allowance, it should be recognized that complex problems frequently require complex solutions. The fact that the competition dialogue over the past several years has not resulted in a single comprehensive proposed solution to the societal contribution issue reflects the high level of complexity involved.

The second payment mechanism suggested would be used by those teaching hospitals with substantial involvement in unmeasurable societal contributions. Generally, these would be the comprehensive tertiary teaching hospitals that serve as principal teaching hospitals of the nation's medical schools. Such teaching hospitals would charge insurers, prepaid health plans, and self-pay patients for hospital services at competitive rates. They would receive prospective reimbursement of their measurable societal contributions through Payment Mechanism I. Unmeasurable societal contributions would be reimbursed through retrospective payments to these teaching hospitals of the difference between full financial requirements and the amounts received from direct patient care payments, Payment Mechanism I, and other sources of revenue, as certified by audited financial statements. As the Medicare and Medicaid programs have recognized, interim payments would be required with a retrospective settlement after the end of each year in order to maintain an operating cash flow within these hospitals.

Under this payment system, teaching hospitals would compete both on the basis of quality and price. They would be motivated to contain costs and prices by three forces. First, there would not be unlimited dollars available for societal contribution payments. In some years, the aggregate needs of teaching hospitals would exceed available funds, resulting in some hospitals receiving less than the full amount sought from the Fund. An equitable allocation system could be designed to assure that partial payments were made to the less efficient teaching hospitals, while full payment of the costs of societal contributions were preserved for the more efficient. This threat of potential nonpayment could motivate further cost containment and possible programmatic reduction efforts by teaching hopsitals. Second, the long-term viability of the Surcharge and Teaching Hospital Societal Contribution Fund would depend on their political acceptability. Because cost would be an important factor in this outcome, teaching hospitals would be motivated to contain costs to preserve the Surcharge and Fund. Finally, public opinion would have substantial impact because attention would be focused on the costs of providing highly expensive tertiary services and other societal contributions common to teaching hospitals. It is possible that some teaching hospitals could not respond to these forces immediately, but the system for allocation of the Fund would eventually require additional cost containment, except where other sources of revenue were developed on a local basis.

These payment mechanisms could substantially reduce one hazard in the competitive system. Because competitive plans would pay teaching hospitals at rates competitive with those paid to community hospitals, the disincentive to refer patients requiring expensive diagnostic and therapeutic care to the tertiary teaching hospital would be curtailed. Thus, teaching hospitals would be able to continue to serve as the referral centers for community hospitals without a substantial impediment related to price.

One practical difficulty in implementing Payment Mechanism II would be the identification of the comprehensive tertiary teaching hospitals for participation. One approach would be to focus participation in Payment Mechanism II on the teaching hospitals which have substantial involvement with the full array of societal contributions, where the payment is most needed. Consultation with the AAMC and other organizations in developing criteria to be used in identifying the appropriate hospitals for inclusion under the two payment mechanisms would be essential. Congress could place such criteria in the legislation or leave their development and promulgation to an administrative agency, after mandatory consultation with an appropriate academically related advisory group, such as the Teaching Hospital Advisory Council previously identified.

Both payment mechanisms would have the benefit of not interjecting any further governmental regulation of decisions regarding the numbers and types of residency training positions in teaching hospitals or the scope of other programs in teaching hospitals. The development of new technology and services would continue to be subject to substantial regulation by the Food and Drug Administration and selective monitoring by the National Center for Health Care Technology.

These payment mechanisms would involve reimbursement of hospital dollars only. It is essential that physicians and dentists practicing in teaching hospitals continue to have the opportunity to be paid for their services in the same manner as their colleagues in the community, so that academic medical centers are not put at a competitive disadvantage in attracting and retaining clinical faculty of high quality.

The Teaching Hospitals Societal Contribution Fund and Surcharge. The dual payment mechanisms would be predicated on the availability of a reliable continuing source of funding relatively insulated from short-term political decisions. It is suggested that a Health Manpower Replenishment and Health Service Development Surcharge on all health plan premiums could be such a source of funding. The Surcharge would not constitute new dollars to the health field or teaching hospitals and would not represent a new burden for patients. Rather, it would represent a "transfer payment" in order to continue the traditional practice of patients paying for the replenishment and advancement of their health care system while purchasing health insurance or hospital services.

The Surcharge could be collected from competitive plans and could be based on a percentage of their total premiums. If such a system were initiated on a national scale in fiscal year 1981, the Surcharge would be required to generate approximately $6.7 billion in teaching hospital societal contribution costs (Tables 5–6 to 5–11). In order to cover this cost, an estimated 8 percent surcharge on competitive plan premiums would be required.[44] A flow chart portraying the theoretical flow of dollars into the Fund and its subsequent distribution among societal contributions is reflected on Figure 5–1. The Fund would support approximately 30 percent of the total cash flow of the 270 COTH members with major college of medicine affiliations.

It should be recognized that inordinate inflation, the establishment of new programs in teaching hospitals, and other factors would result in insufficient dollars in the Teaching Hospital Societal Contribution Fund in some years. To accommodate this circumstance

Figure 5-1. A Theoretical Approach to Structuring the Competitive System to Recognize the Unique Societal Contributions of Teaching Hospitals (Dollars are 1980-81 estimates).

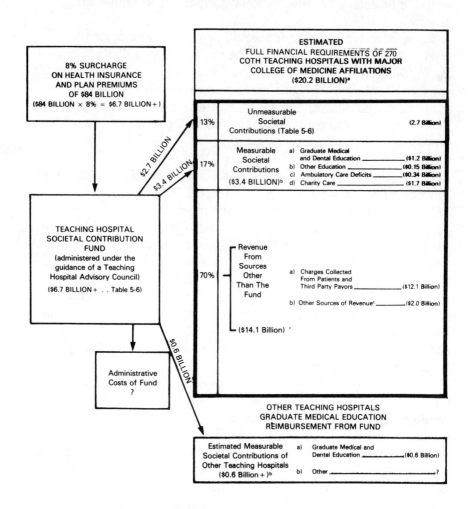

aFull financial requirements are total operating expenses ($18.6 billion - Footnote No. 27) increased to include an estimated eight percent margin to meet working capital and a portion of capital requirements. ($20.2 billion = $18.6 billion + .92).

b$3.4 billion + $.6 billion below = $4.0 billion total of measurable societal contributions (Table 5-6).

cSources of revenue other than changes and the societal contribution fund are estimated to be 10% of total requirements (Table 5-9, footnote c).

and to moderate the reasonableness of teaching hospital requests from the fund, reasonable standards and formulas for allocation of shortfalls would have to be developed by the Teaching Hospital Advisory Council previously described. As indicated, such standards and formulas could be used to create additional incentives for teaching hospitals to further contain costs and to be maximally competitive.

The Surcharge and resulting Teaching Hospital Societal Contribution Fund would serve as a safeguard for the entire health care system. The competition proposals have, as a prime feature, the minimization of regulation in the health field in exchange for hospitals' willingness to risk their survival in a free market. One of the anticipated outcomes is a shrinkage of the health system and resulting economy through closure of hospitals. Use of a free market for bringing this about represents a revolutionary change in the structure of this nation's health system, the outcome of which no one can accurately predict. Accordingly, discretion would require the establishment of certain safeguards in a system change as colossal as the one being proposed. One of these protections should be a device to sustain the vigor of our nation's teaching hospitals which underpin the quality of the entire health care system.

If the unique societal contributions of teaching hospitals were separately provided for in the manner outlined, the patient care functions of all hospitals theoretically could be encompassed in a competitive system. A provision for the protection of teaching hospital societal contributions is the prudent minimum which should be in place if the nation is to conduct a massive experiment with competition within its health care system. After several years of experience with a competitive system, it might be possible to alter these safeguards when such changes could be based on actual knowledge of the effects of competition on teaching hospitals and other health system components. Techniques for quantifying the costs of the now unmeasurable societal contributions (such as patient case mix methodologies) could also evolve, permitting the consolidation of the two mechanisms for payment of societal contributions into a single, simpler method.

The above discussion of a theoretical approach to financing the societal contributions of teaching hospitals under competition is intended to respond to the challenge to develop a framework for modified funding and examine its implications. It is not intended as support for the approach, but is presented as a contribution to the debate.

FUTURE CHALLENGES FOR TEACHING HOSPITALS

The competitive environment appears to be evolving, albeit slowly. To stay abreast of this trend, there are a number of initiatives that teaching hospitals should pursue with increasing vigor.

Teaching hospitals and health services researchers should undertake further studies of the resources committed to societal contributions and of possible alternative ways of securing support for these programs. If legislation promoting competition is not passed, teaching hospitals will require the results of such studies to support their submissions and their appeals to conventional funding agencies. If such legislation is passed, the research findings will be needed to justify reimbursement from the Teaching Hospital Societal Contributions Fund described earlier or some similar mechanism.

The agenda for teaching hospital self-study should include the following:

- Teaching hospital educational costs. Analyses of health personnel should be undertaken to quantify more precisely the extent to which the quality and output of educational programs are compatible with the needs of society at local and regional levels. Such studies could exert a positive impact upon the strategic planning processes of teaching hospitals, medical schools, and other health colleges.
- Ambulatory care program deficits. Teaching hospitals must continue to study their ambulatory care programs to determine whether they can be further restructured to reduce current operating deficits while preserving the essential educational experience for medical and other health science trainees.
- Highly specialized services. The AAMC has initiated a major study to evaluate the patient case mix of teaching hospitals, and, as previously mentioned, research and development experiments in this area are being conducted by HCFA and others. Teaching hospitals should participate in the voluntary evaluation of patient case mix, review their own internal data gathering and review systems, and support the future development of refined methodologies to evaluate the intensity of services required by their patient populations.
- Charity care of patients. Some teaching hospitals are already addressing a segment of the cost problem associated with charity

care through state and local governmental programs and development of new financing initiatives must be pursued if teaching hospitals are to continue to serve all patients without regard to financial means.

- Clinical research. Teaching hospitals should be reviewing the research being conducted within their facilities supported by hospital patient care dollars. While continued teaching hospital support for research is necessary, it should be done systematically, based on clearly articulated institutional priorities. Appropriate outside funding should be sought whenever possible, and ways should be explored to promote greater indirect support for such research by private philanthropy and government.

- Relationships within academic health centers. Teaching hospitals must more closely scrutinize their financial relationships with academic health centers. Some teaching hospitals have shouldered a much larger proportion of the cost of educational and research programs than others. The wide range of staff-to-occupied bed ratios and per diem costs now present in the nation's teaching hospitals may be due in part to variable patterns of supporting research and educational costs.

- Alternative delivery systems and multihospital systems. Teaching hospitals will also need to expand their efforts in exploring relationships with evolving multihospital systems and alternative delivery systems such as HMOs. Some teaching hospitals have found it beneficial to create such systems, others have developed relationships with existing systems, and the remainder have no relationships of this type. The experiences of teaching hospitals have varied on a continuum from success to disaster. Because teaching programs have generally been successful in alternative delivery settings only on a subsidied basis, such relationships must be carefully structured if teaching hospitals are to sustain their societal contributions.

CONCLUDING STATEMENT

It is clear that the United States system of health care financing and delivery must undergo change to reach a new balance between the demands of society and available resources. The extent of these changes and how they will be initiated and implemented is still an open question. A variety of approaches should be examined and tested prior to wide-scale adoption. The theory of competition with its concomitant deregulation represents an intriguing idea that appears to be in accord with the emerging national mood. It would be ill-advised, however, to rapidly convert a highly complex and pluralistic system of 7,000 hospitals and 440,000 physicians serving 225 million people to a new system unproved on a national scale—particularly when this nation's system of health care currently delivers the best medical care in the world. A more prudent approach would involve study of the effects of competition through evaluation of demonstration projects and other research. Areas for further research would include the sources and extent of cost savings, the effects on access and quality, and the impact of competition on education, research, and other societal contributions of teaching hospitals. Perhaps, government, industry, and labor could help create incentives in the voluntary development of new competitive systems through full integration in competitive experiments of Medicare, Medicaid, and other health care plans. If consistent, positive results begin to emerge, after full evaluation of the experiments, it is likely that competition will continue to expand on a voluntary basis. Further promotional steps could then be taken when there is solid evidence and confidence that a positive national outcome will be achieved.

Budget-conscious members of Congress may be attracted to some features of the competition proposals in order to establish control over federal expenditures for health care. As outlined earlier, current competition proposals have a complex mixture of objectives. The main attraction to Congress may be the possible containment of federal expenditures. Congress could choose to enact alterations in the federal income tax structure in order to limit governmental expenditures for health care, without including the full agenda of current competition proposals. In making this decision, Congress should be cognizant that it would risk reversal of the trend away from the two-class system of health care.

If this pragmatic view of controlled evolution of competition in the health care system does not prevail and Congress instead decides to promote competition on a national scale, it is crucial that safeguards be included to protect the essential societal contributions of teaching hospitals. Fortunately, teaching hospitals and those who understand their importance still have time in which to address these issues and influence the future direction of health policy. The analysis and ideas advanced in this paper are designed to generate thought and discussion of the important issues facing society as it shapes the health care system of the nation's future.

NOTES

1. A. Enthoven, "Shattuck Lecture: Cutting Cost without Cutting the Quality of Care," *New England Journal of Medicine* 298, no. 22 (June 1, 1978): 1236.
2. The added cost of the regulatory burden has been estimated in studies, such as the Hospital Association of New York State study discussed on pages 89-94 of the January 16, 1979, issue of *Hospitals*. While these studies do not give precise estimates due to methodological and definitional problems, they clearly establish that there is a substantial added cost. One example of an effort to reduce this burden is sections 302 and 306 of the "National Health Care Reform Act of 1980," H.R. 7527, introduced in 1980 by Representatives Gephardt and Stockman. The bill was reintroduced as the "National Health Care Reform Act of 1981," H.R. 850, on January 16, 1981.
3. H. Luft, "Trends in Medical Care Costs: Do HMOs Lower the Rate of Growth?" *Medical Care* 18, no. 1 (January 1980): 1-16.
4. U.S. Congress, House, "National Health Care Reform Act of 1980" (H.R. 7527, 96th Cong., 2nd sess., 1980).
5. O.D. Dickerson, "Regulation," in *Health Insurance* (Homewood, Ill.: Richard D. Irwin, 1968), 3rd ed., pp. 435-52.
6. R. Blair, J.R. Johnson, and R. Vogel, "Economies of Scale in the Administration of Health Insurance," *Review of Economics and Statistics* (May 1975): 185-89.
7. J.A. Lennie, "Economic Liability of Community-Operated Prepaid Health Plans," *Health Care Management Review* 1 (Summer 1976): 53-57.
8. A. Enthoven, "How Interested Groups Have Responded to a Proposal for Economic Competition in Health Services," *American Economic Review* 70, no. 2 (May 1980): 142-48.
9. *Ibid.*
10. *Group Health News* 22 (January 1981): 1, 4-5.
11. Telephone conversation with Ms. Monti Laughnan of the Office of Personnel Management on January 5, 1981. The 9 percent reflects HMO enrollment on April 22, 1980.
12. H. Luft, "How Do Health Maintenance Organizations Achieve Their 'Savings'? Rhetoric and Evidence," *New England Journal of Medicine* 298, no. 24 (June 15, 1978): 1336-43.

13. *Ibid.*
14. H. Luft, "Trends in Medical Care Costs, Do HMOs Lower the Rate of Growth?" *Medical Care* 18, no. 1 (January 1980): 1–16.
15. Ibid.
16. H. Luft, "HMO Performance: Current Knowledge and Questions for the 1980s," *The Group Health Journal* (Winter, 1980).
17. D.M. Kinzer, "The Future of Health Care in the United States and Canada" (Paper presented to the AHA-CHA Convention, Montreal, Canada, July 28, 1980), p. 11.
18. W. McNerney, "Control of Health-Care Costs in the 1980's," *New England Journal of Medicine* 303, no. 19 (November 6, 1980): 1091.
19. D.M. Kinzer, "The Future of Health Care in the United States and Canada" (Paper presented to the AHA-CHA Convention, Montreal, Canada, July 28, 1980), p. 11.
20. R. Knapp, "Toward a More Contemporary Public Understanding of the Teaching Hospital" (Paper prepared for the Council of Teaching Hospitals, AAMC, Spring Meeting, May 1979), p. 42.
21. *Ibid.*
22. *Ibid.*
23. J.W. Colloton and R. Knapp, "Testimony on the Health Incentives Reform Act, S. 1968" (Before the Subcommittee on Health, Committee on Finance, U.S. Senate, on behalf of the Association of American Medical Colleges, March 19, 1980), p. 3.
24. *Ibid.*, p. 4.
25. *Ibid.*
26. *Ibid.*
27. The 215,336 undergraduates include 63,533 medical students (*1980–81 AAMC Directory of American Medical Education*), 22,225 dental students (*Annual Report-Dental Education in 1979/80*, p. 15), 98,939 nursing students (*State-Approval Schools of Nursing-R.N. 1980*, pp. 82–83), 22,560 pharmacy students (*American Journal of Pharmaceutical Education* 44, no. 2 (May 1980): 177–81) and 8,079 public health students (telephone conversation with Mr. Steven Howard, Association of Schools of Public Health, January 6, 1981). The 66,252 residents in training include 64,615 resident physicians (*'80–'81 Directory of Residency Training Programs*, p. 51) and 1,637 resident dentists (telephone conversation with Alice Deforest, American Dental Association, January, 1981). The *Interim Report of the Graduate Medical Education National Advisory Committee* (DHEW Publication No. (HRA) 79–633, April 1979), p. 287, estimated that the 5,582 internal medicine fellows were 37.5 percent of the total, yielding a total of 14,885.

28.   The $18.6 billion estimate is derived from adding the total operating expenses for fiscal year 1978-79 of the 270 COTH teaching hospitals that are major affiliates of medical colleges (total: $14.74 billion), and increasing the total by the 25.9 percent increase in the consumer price index for the hospital "room" component of "other medical care services" from July, 1978 to June, 1980. The operating expense data is from the Council of Teaching Hospitals, *Committee Structure and Membership Directory, 1980,* and the American Hospital Association, *Guide to the Health Care Field, 1980.*

29.   The other operating revenue of the twenty surveyed teaching hospitals was 10 percent of total operating revenues (Table 5-9, note 3).

30.   The percentage estimate is based on the assumption that the present percentage is the same as the 1978-79 percentage. The $14.74 billion total teaching hospital expenses in 1978-79 (see note 28) were 18 percent of the total annual hospital expenditure level, $79.8 billion, for the same year reported in the American Hospital Association, *Guide to the Health Care Field,* (1980 ed.), p. A6.

31.   W. McNerney, "Control of Health-Care Costs in the 1980's," *New England Journal of Medicine* 303, no. 19 (November 6, 1980): 1091.

32.   E. Ginsberg, "Sounding Boards—The Competitive Solution: Two Views, Competition and Cost Containment," *New England Journal of Medicine* 303, no. 19 (November 6, 1980): 1115.

33.   R.M. Heyssel, "Competition and the Market Place Approach to Containing the Cost of Medical Care," p. 7. (Unpublished.)

34.   This includes estimates for the costs of resident and clinical fellow stipends and benefits supported by hospitals; measurable indirect costs for graduate medical education; and the costs of supervisory and teaching services of faculty physicians. In developing these estimates, the following sources were used: Richard M. Knapp and Peter W. Butler, "Financing Graduate Medical Education," *New England Journal of Medicine* 301 (October 4, 1979): 749; Letter, Richard M. Knapp to John W. Colloton, December 5, 1980, University of Iowa Hospitals and Clinics; *Interim Report of the Graduate Medical Education National Advisory Committee* (DHEW Publication No. (HRA) 79-633 April, 1979), pp. 285-88; *COTH Survey of House Staff Stipends, Benefits, and Funding, 1980* (Washington, D.C.: Department of Teaching Hospitals, Association of American Medical Colleges, November, 1980), pp. 7, 76; *COTH Survey of House Staff Policy and Related Issues, 1976* (Washington, D.C.: Council of Teaching Hospitals, Association of American Medical Colleges, 1976), p. 10; and U.S. Department of Labor, Bureau of Labor Statistics, "Consumer Price Index: U.S. City Average for July, 1973 and July, 1980."

35.   J.W. Colloton and R. Knapp, "Testimony on the Health Incentives Reform Act S.1968" (Submitted to the Subcommittee on Health, Committee on Finance, U.S. Senate, on behalf of the Association of American Medical Colleges, March 18, 1980), p. 9.

36.   Association of American Medical Colleges, Task Force on Graduate Medical Education, *Graduate Medical Education: Proposals for the Eighties* (Washington, D.C.: AAMC, 1980), pp. 115–53.

37.   *Ibid.,* p. 128.

38.   It is probable that the ambulatory care deficit estimate is low because reimbursement formulas and insurance coverage make it desirable to maximize allocation of costs to inpatient units and to minimize such allocations to outpatient ambulatory care programs. The figures in the text would also be increased if all 332 nonfederal COTH teaching hospitals were included. However, calculation of the increase by extrapolation to these hospitals is probably not warranted because the preponderance of these societal contributions is in teaching hospitals with major college of medicine affiliations.

39.   Charity care allowances represent the uncompensated dollar value of services provided to patients who, at the time of admission or during their stay, are determined to be unable to pay the costs of their care. Collection losses represent revenue lost by a hospital due to nonpayment for services by patients classified as paying. Uncompensated charity patient care cost and collection loss allowances have been aggregated because in many hospitals a clear distinction between these elements of cost is not made unless there is a formalized indigent care charity program with specified determination protocols for prospectively identifying eligible patients. Thus, accounts retrospectively written off as collection losses in one institution would have been prospectively classified as charity in another institution.

40.   U.S. Congress, House, "National Health Care Reform Act of 1980" (H.R. 7527, 96th Cong., 2nd sess., 1980), Section 223.

41.   *Des Moines Register* (December 21, 1980), p. 3C.

42.   D. Rogers, "On Preparing Academic Health Centers for the Very Different 1980s," *Journal of Medical Education* 55, no. 1 (January 1980): 1–12.

43.   U.S. Congress, House, "National Health Care Reform Act of 1980" (H.R. 7527, 96th Cong., 2nd sess., 1980), section 301.

44.   The surcharge percentage would depend on the fund size required and the total number of dollars to which the surcharge was applied. Since under many of the competition proposals governmental payments would be channeled through commercial premium payments, it is probably not accurate to extrapolate from historical premium payment totals. Thus, the base was estimated to be $84 billion, by adding

the $85.3 billion in aggregate hospital charges and $40.6 billion in physician fees in 1979 (HCFA estimates cited in *Hospitals* (September 16, 1980): 37) and deducting 33 percent for the approximate portion of payments which are out of pocket (*Health United States, 1979* (DHEW Publication No. (PHS) 80-1232), p. 191). The estimated amount needed in the fund, $6.7 billion (see Tables 5-6 to 5-11), is 8 percent of $84 billion.

APPENDIX 5A
USE OF AN AVERAGE MULTIPLIER TO ESTIMATE TOTAL SOCIETAL CONTRIBUTIONS OF TEACHING HOSPITALS AN IMPRACTICAL METHOD

In view of the current inability to separately identify the costs associated with the multiple societal contributions of teaching hospitals, an alternative procedure has been proposed by some individuals for determining reimbursement to a teaching hospital for *all* such costs. This alternative procedure would involve estimating the cost of unmeasurable societal contributions on a formula basis from known characteristics and financial data about teaching hospitals.

An approach that has been proposed for deriving this estimation would involve selection of one societal contribution of teaching hospitals for which cost data are available, for example, measurable educational costs, and then applying a multiplier to these costs to estimate the total amount of a teaching hospital's societal contributions. In an attempt to determine if such a method would be feasible, data were collected from a sample of twenty major teaching hospitals on the costs of three measurable societal contributions: education costs, charity care costs, and ambulatory care deficits.

A review of the data indicates that a dramatic difference exists among teaching hospitals both in the individual amounts of each societal contribution and in the relative proportion of the cost of individual measurable societal contributions to the aggregate costs of all measurable societal contributions. If the variation in unmeasurable societal contribution costs across teaching hospitals is as great as these measurable items, it is apparent that no simple estimating procedure would be satisfactory as a basis for reimbursement.

In order to dramatically demonstrate this point, the average ratio of educational costs to total measurable costs (defined here as the total of education costs, charity and collection loss, allowances, and ambulatory care deficits) was calculated for all twenty hospitals in the sample (see Table 5A-1) and for hospitals grouped according to total clinic visits and by bed size (see Table 5A-2). The relevant ratio (multiplier) was then multiplied by each hospital's educational costs to derive a predicted aggregate cost of education, charity and collection loss allowances, and ambulatory care program deficits. Comparisons of actual total measurable costs to predicted total measurable costs are presented in each of the tables. Table 5A-1 compares the actual total measurable costs to the multiplier predicted total measurable costs; Table 5A-2 compares total actual measurable costs to the distribution of the multiplier predicted total measurable costs for each of the hospital clinic-visit and bed-size groupings. As is readily apparent, with a few exceptions, the predictions were in gross error; and these results show that a simple technique for estimation of the societal contributions of teaching hospitals does not appear to be viable.

More elaborate and accurate estimating procedures have, as yet, eluded researchers investigating this issue. Therefore, prospective reimbursement programs have been faced with many difficulties in their attempts to devise a systematic method for dealing with teaching hospitals. Most of these programs have resorted to bilateral bargaining mechanisms rather than depending on strict formulas for estimating. While several promising research projects for investigating this issue are now underway, none appear to have an accurate and practical method that can be safely and equitably utilized in the near future.

RESPONSE
by *Alain C. Enthoven*

John Colloton summarizes the teaching hospital concerns over the competition strategy for health care financing and delivery system reform as follows:

> the nation's teaching hospitals . . . have multiple products benefiting not only the individual patient, but society as a whole. Because generation of these products results in higher costs, presently financed primarily through patient care revenues, price competition could seriously jeopardize the future capacity of teaching hospitals to make these essential

Table 5A-1. Comparison of the Actual and Average Multiplier Predicted Total Cost of Education, Charity/Collection Loss Allowances, and Ambulatory Care Deficits for a Sample of Twenty University-Owned Teaching Hospitals, 1979–80.

Hospital	Actual Cost of Education	Actual Total Cost of Education Charity/Collection Loss Allowances, and Ambulatory Patient Care Deficits	Predicted Total Cost of Education Charity/Collection Loss Allowances, Ambulatory Patient Care Deficits[a]	Error Between Actual and Average Multiplier Predicted Total Cost of Education, Charity/Collection Loss Allowances, and Ambulatory Patient Care Deficits	
				Monetary	Percentage
1.	$ 8,362,600	$ 15,832,465	$ 20,739,248	$ 4,906,783	31.0%
2.	1,298,307	5,773,205	3,219,801	(2,553,404)	(44.2)
3.	12,768,210	28,225,192	31,665,161	3,439,969	12.2
4.	4,385,903	18,837,751	10,877,039	(7,960,712)	(42.3)
5.	11,767,841	13,734,434	29,184,246	15,449,812	112.5
6.	7,828,665	12,983,053	19,415,089	6,432,036	49.5
7.	5,000,000	10,277,847	12,400,000	2,122,153	20.6
8.	952,017	2,151,943	2,361,002	209,059	9.7
9.	3,633,377	10,517,428	9,010,775	(1,506,653)	(14.3)
10.	3,111,610	7,469,260	7,716,793	247,533	3.3
11.	2,580,990	6,303,954	6,400,855	96,901	1.5
12.	9,073,084	22,967,174	22,501,248	(465,926)	(2.0)
13.	4,986,083	10,591,750	12,365,486	1,773,736	16.7
14.	3,386,539	19,376,436	8,398,617	(10,977,819)	(56.7)
15.	3,272,905	17,371,794	8,116,804	(9,254,990)	(53.3)
16.	4,444,395	10,848,621	11,022,100	173,479	1.6
17.	6,541,243	15,808,135	16,222,283	414,148	2.6
18.	3,942,523	18,590,549	9,777,457	(8,813,092)	(47.4)
19.	5,889,123	7,420,000	14,629,825	7,209,825	97.2
20.	2,010,203	5,966,296	4,985,303	(980,993)	(16.4)
Totals	$105,245,618	$261,047,287	$261,009,132		

[a]Average Multiplier Used in Calculation = $261,047,287 ÷ $105,245,618 = 2.48

Table 5A–2. Comparison of the Actual and Average Multiplier Predicted Total Costs of Education, Charity/Collection Loss Allowances, and Ambulatory Care Deficits for a Sample of Twenty University-Owned Teaching Hospitals According to Clinic Visit and Bed Size Groupings 1979–80.

Sample Hospital Grouping	Actual Average Cost of Education	Actual Average Total Cost of Three Societal Contributions	Multiplier Value	Distribution of the Ratio of Cost Estimated by Use of A Multiplier to Actual Hospital Costs for Three Societal Contributions (Number of Hospitals in the Ratio Ranges)					
				Under .50	.50–.75	.75–1.00	1–1.25	1.25–1.50	over 1.50
1. Distribution Based on Total CLINIC VISITS									
200,000 & Over	$7,716,572	$16,480,609	2.14	2		1	1		1
150,000 – 199,999	$3,851,110	$ 8,283,914	2.15		1	3	1	1	1
100,000 – 149,999	$5,032,601	$16,231,153	3.23		2			2	1
Under 100,000	$4,598,273	$11,946,245	2.60		1	1	1		1
2. Distribution Based on BED SIZE									
Over 750	$8,004,004	$15,517,349	1.94			2	1		1
600 – 750	$6,842,237	$16,232,919	2.37	1	1			1	1
400 – 599	$4,788,908	$14,112,673	2.95		2	2	4	1	
Under 400	$2,467,660	$ 7,051,498	2.86		1	2	1	1	

contributions to society. These contributions include graduate medical and other health science education, new technology testing, clinical research, substantial amounts of charity care, highly specialized services, and extensive ambulatory care programs operating on a subsidized basis. Because of these unique characteristics and responsibilities, teaching hospitals must secure specific attention and consideration in any program of health care financing based on price competition.

Some competition advocates have proposed that the 'teaching and research costs' of teaching hospitals be supported from another source. However, none of the current competition proposals have explored in sufficient depth how this might be accomplished.

Therefore, Colloton sets forth what he characterizes as "a theoretical approach to structuring of the competitive system to recognize the unique societal contributions of teaching hospitals" whose essentials are as follows:

1. There should be created a Teaching Hospital Societal Contribution Fund, the source of which would be a surcharge on the premiums of all health care financing and delivery plans.

2. Monies from the Fund would be distributed to teaching hospitals to reimburse expenditures for societal contribution costs through two payment mechanisms:

    a. Prospective payments for measurable societal contributions, which include graduate medical and dental education, ambulatory care deficits, and charity care. The educational costs are estimated at $1.8 billion in 1980–81; the other measurable costs are estimated at $2.2 billion for a total of $4 billion.

    b. Retrospective payment of the costs of unmeasurable societal contributions which include all other educational programs, new technology testing, clinical research, and care of a highly intense patient care mix. The estimated cost is $2.7 billion.

3. A means for teaching hospitals to apply for a retrospective adjustment of prospective payments would be necessary to preclude undue hardships.

4. Since the Fund would not be open-ended, "An equitable allocation system could be designed to assure that partial payments were made to the less efficient teaching hospitals, while full payment of the costs of societal contributions were preserved for the more efficient."

5. Allocation of the Fund's resources, including identification of the teaching hospitals eligible for participation, would be based on criteria developed in consultation with the Association of American Medical Colleges (AAMC) and other organizations, and would be administered "under the guidance of an academically oriented Teaching Hospital Advisory Council."

6. An important goal of the Fund and the Council would be to create "a reliable continuing source of funding relatively insulated from short-term political decisions."

I accept Colloton's concerns as valid: teaching hospitals do produce important contributions to society beyond patient care, and these need to be paid for. And the current competition proposals have not explored in much depth how this might be accomplished. So I welcome Colloton's thoughtful proposal, and I consider it to be a useful basis for further discussion. Because much of my discussion must point out negative aspects, I want to emphasize at the outset that I think that Colloton's proposal is constructive and that something broadly along the lines he proposes ought to be done. I hope that this discussion will lead to further development and refinement and that such a plan will eventually become a recognized part of the competition strategy.

I believe that a satisfactory plan must meet these criteria. First, it must be responsive to society's needs. For example, we cannot and should not expect the public and Congress to go on indefinitely subsidizing the overproduction of physicians in general or of certain specialists in oversupply. We need to be sure that the guidance system for allocation of the Fund is responsive to the numbers and types of physicians needed, and not to the continuation of well-entrenched residency and other educational programs.

Instead of an academically oriented Teaching Hospital Advisory Council, I would recommend that the central governance be more broadly based. It should include strong representation from the health care financing and delivery organizations because they are the ones best placed to assess future physician personnel requirements and because they have an interest in seeing an appropriate number and mix of physicians produced. Sole reliance on teaching hospitals is far too likely to produce nothing more than protection of the vested interests in the status quo.

Second, the method of payment ought to reward economy in the use of health care resources, as well as good financial planning and discipline. Payment should not be based on retrospective analyses of an institution's own costs. Industry averages or estimates of what things "should cost" ought to be used. And retrospective adjustments to bail out the bad planners are undesirable.

Third, the redistributive aspects of the program ought to be equitable. One trouble with proposals of the sort Colloton advances for public financing of undergraduate and postgraduate medical education is that they tax the ordinary citizen to pay for the education of physicians who will become high-income people. It is possible that there is a perfectly acceptable justification for this. But the proponents of public support for medical education should be willing to see such issues debated on their merits.

The surcharge that supports the fund should be broadly based. It should not draw only on private insurers and health maintenance organizations (HMOs), for example, while sparing employers who are "self-insuring." In the context of Gephardt-Stockman[1] or consumer-choice health plan,[2] a flat per capita tax on all qualified health plans would appear to be appropriate.

A tax-supported subsidy of $1.8 billion per year for graduate medical and dental education would be a very small price to pay to solve the problem of support for graduate medical education and to allow us to get on with the competition strategy. Indeed, as Colloton correctly notes, this would not be entirely an additional expenditure for government. Much of the cost of graduate medical education is already paid for through Medicare, Medicaid, and tax-subsidized private health insurance. So this proposal would be a "repackaging" of the same dollars in a way that would facilitate the development of competition and cost consciousness. The cost would come to about $27,000 per resident in training per year. Such a subsidy should be paid as a flat amount, not tied to the cost of a particular institution, so that the government would not have to engage in retrospective cost finding with all its complexities and perverse incentives. And the estimated cost should be reduced by the value of the services produced by residents. I would favor such a proposal as part of the competition strategy. (I accept Colloton's numerical estimates at face value for the sake of discussion. I am not endorsing any particular number of dollars.)

Colloton's position on this point appears contradictory. He refers with apparent approval to the 1980 report of the AAMC Task Force on Graduate Medical Education. On the idea of financing graduate medical education from a separate, governmental, tax-supported fund, Colloton summarizes the Task Force conclusion as follows: "The magnitude of such a fund, the complexities of its management and disbursements, and recent experience with capitation support of medical schools make this alternative a questionable option for long-term financing." And later: "The AAMC study concluded that there was no practical alternative to the present practice of supporting residency training through teaching hospital revenues."

If the "complexities" of a tax-supported fund are serious, that is a problem for Colloton's scheme. However, I think it would be possible to come up with a reasonable per capita amount. The answer produced by cost analysis might be uncertain within a factor of two (perhaps between $15,000 and $30,000 per year) but Congress can make a judgment based on the data. Precision is not necessary for a workable solution. The real difficulty would come in determining who gets the residencies, which hospitals and which specialties. I would expect to see a lot of politics in this game.

As for the demise of capitation, I believe that it can be attributed primarily to two factors. The first is the perception that we are now producing too many doctors. This is a problem that must be faced in any scheme. The second is that government financial support for teaching and research and a lot of other things has had to be cut back to pay for the enormous increases in Medicare and Medicaid. Those who are concerned with the financing of medical education and research should favor the competition strategy as the only effective means for getting the costs of patient care under control so that there will be some money left over for teaching and research. Recall that the increase in annual federal Medicare and Medicaid outlays from fiscal year 1980 to fiscal year 1982 is $16.3 billion dollars. Total direct federal spending for health research and education in FY 1980 was only $4.2 billion (not counting amounts hidden in patient care costs).

The next societal contribution that Colloton would finance with the Fund is the Ambulatory Care Program Deficits of the teaching hospitals. As Colloton explains, these deficits, estimated at $820 million, are made up of $341 million of charity and bad debts, and $484 of educational programs in ambulatory settings. "These deficits arise in part from inappropriate methodologies for cost allocations mandated by governmental and other third-party payers." The educational costs ought to be reflected in the per capita subsidies to education already discussed. The inappropriate cost allocation methodologies ought to be changed to methods that approximate true costs. And the charity care ought to be paid for by government.

Colloton notes that total charity and collection loss allowances averaged 9 percent of gross patient revenue for his sample of Iowa teaching hospitals. As he also notes: "Bills that mandate universal coverage would minimize the need for charity care for those services covered." He is, of course, referring to Gephardt-Stockman and Consumer Choice Health Plan. With or without enactment of these plans, there will always be a need for a publicly supported provider of last resort. I think appropriate contractual arrangements between government and hosptials are the best way to pay for this. Charity care should not be an unfair competitive burden on those hospitals that provide it. On the other hand, not all bad debts are for charity care. Whatever arrangements are made for charity and collection losses for teaching hospitals ought to be made on an equitable basis for all hospitals.

Colloton would like the *Fund* to provide institutional support for the unmeasured societal contributions of undergraduate medical education, new technology testing, clinical research, and the incremental cost of the highly intensive patient care mix common to most teaching hospitals. As Colloton notes, the Fund would be fixed in total amount, and not open-ended. This would represent a major advance over today's open-ended third-party reimbursement system from the point of view of fiscal control. Still, allocation methods that would reward the efficient and effective rather than the politically favored and the wasteful would need to be worked out.

Colloton estimates the average cost per patient day of unmeasurable societal contributions of teaching hospitals by subtracting the cost of measurable contributions from the difference between the daily charge in teaching hospitals and nonteaching hospitals. I would not be prepared to accept at face value the implicit assumption that all of the unmeasured difference is properly attributable to societal contributions, and that none of it is attributable to extra waste and inefficiency. As the proposal is refined, this possibilty would need to be addressed.

I have already commented on the problems of taxpayer support for medical education. The problem of financing undergraduate medical education is not unlike the problem of financing postgraduate training. Perhaps higher tuition and more loans would be part of the solution. In any case, I believe that appropriate financing arrangements can be worked out. It would be wrong to hold the reform of the entire health care delivery system hostage to a good financial deal for medical education.

Overall, with these and other modifications, I think a workable plan along the lines proposed by Colloton could be developed. Perhaps the question of designing the mechanism to determine which hospitals and specialties get the subsidized residencies is the most difficult. I think it would be appropriate for Colloton, the Council of Teaching Hospitals (COTH), and AAMC to develop expeditiously a proposal that would merit broad support.

COLLOTON ON COMPETITION

My preference would be to stop the analysis of Colloton's proposal here. This is the constructive part of the discussion, the part worth pursuing. However, I cannot leave unchallenged some of the points in Colloton's discussion of the competition strategy, lest by silence I appear to accept them.

Colloton's first pervasive error is to approach the competition strategy as if it were entirely an abstract theoretical proposition. One of his favorite terms is "It is theorized that. . . ." In fact, the competition strategy is based on empirical observation of demonstrated patterns of practical success involving millions of people over decades. The competition of organized systems of care exists in practice in Minneapolis and St. Paul, Minnesota, in Clackamas County, Oregon, in Hawaii, and in parts of California, and it does not exhibit the harmful effects he predicts on the basis of a priori reasoning.

For example, he says: "It is possible that competition may move providers too far from the focus on providing an adequate level and quality of service, especially for patients afflicted with complex diseases." Yes, it is *theoretically* possible. But I am not aware of documented evidence that such has been happening in the competitive markets just mentioned.

Or again, he says: "Disruption may occur in the administration and delivery of care when 150 million Americans are thrust into an altered medical marketplace personally seeking to understand, choose, and bind themselves to a particular plan for the delivery and payment of services. This experience should be of special concern because differences in health products are often technical, and price and quality information is difficult to obtain and assess." Before offering such a speculation, Colloton should have reviewed the experience of the Federal Employees Health Benefits Program, in successful operation for twenty years and now financing care for 10 million people. In this program, people are offered a multiple choice of health care financing or delivery plan and a fixed-dollar contribution toward the premium of the plan of their choice. More than eighty health care plans are offered. The program works with remarkable simplicity and effectiveness. There is nothing in this experience to support the fears expressed by Colloton. There was no disruption, no apparent inability of people to make choices and live with the conseqeuences. The same is true of the health care financing program for California state employees, which is similar to the federal program and also has been in successful operation for twenty years. The passage of pro-competitive legislation would not change all institutions and organizations overnight. Most ongoing relationships would not need to be interrupted. Change would be gradual and voluntary as people responded to changed financial incentives.

Or again, he says: "There is significant risk that competitive plans, which contract with community physicians and hospitals, would not be willing to establish appropriate referral arrangements with high cost, specialized tertiary care centers for their enrollees." That is not what generally happens in today's competing HMOs. For example, for many years, Kaiser-Permanente in Hawaii flew their open-heart surgery patients to Stanford. Then, after a local heart surgeon in Honolulu built up a substantial volume of cases and demonstrated high-quality results, they started referring to him instead. And they are under tough competitive pressure. We must allow a little credit for medical ethics and the ability of consumers to judge whether referral patterns make sense.

Again, he says: "It is theorized that individuals will opt for low-cost plans in making their selection." Not quite. It would have been more accurate to say: "When offered a choice on an economically fair basis, it is observed that consumers consider the cost, as well as other attributes of the alternatives, and that some, but by no means all, take the low-cost plans." The theory is that those who choose the more costly alternatives see extra value in them that, in their judgment, is worth the extra cost.

Colloton concludes by recommending research and experiments. "A more prudent approach would involve study of the effects of competition through evaluation of demonstration projects and other research." We don't need to wait for more research and demonstrations. We have the experience of millions of people over decades. What would be the point of gaining more experience if Colloton ignores the large amount of experience we already have?

Second, apparently Colloton is not well informed about the competition strategy and proposals. For example, he says, "There is a danger that deregulation of the health care system will be viewed as an opportunity to remove all governmental control of professional licensure so that some of the demand for health care can be satisfied by the unproved and possibly the unqualified." To the best of my knowledge, the authors of the competition strategy make no such proposals. Colloton attributes the competition strategy to Ellwood, McClure, and to me, but here he appears to confuse us with some libertarian economic theorists.

Colloton goes on to say: "Most proposals are based on the assumption that increased competition in the insurance market will lead insurers to shop for the least expensive providers and limit their purchase of services to these providers." That is not correct. The assumption is that the insurers will seek out *efficient* providers, that is providers who offer a good combination of quality and cost. Otherwise how could I explain the fact that all of the competing HMOs in my community, incuding the one to which I belong, sometimes use "expensive" Stanford Hospital?

Colloton goes on to cite as a major unresolved question the extent to which the American people would be willing to force individuals to live with decisions made in the marketplace. He quotes Kinzer, who asks:

> When you think about it, is it really conceivable that the American people will accept as public policy the idea that the consumer of health care can really be put "at risk," starting with the example of the person who chooses a coverage option that excludes dialysis and then develops kidney failure? . . . You either believe that a person should get all the care that professional judgment dictates he needs, or you don't.

Kinzer's statement is an unfair caricature of the competition proposals. None of them allow health insurance options that exclude dialysis or care for other serious illness. For example, in the Consumer Choice Health Plan, I proposed that a qualified health plan would be required to cover, at a minimum, the full list of services called "basic health services" in the HMO Act of 1973 (as amended). Gephardt-Stockman also includes a list of covered services that must be paid for by the health plan after the consumer's out-of-pocket spending limit has been reached. There is no room for Kinzer-like scenarios in these proposals. The idea of the competition proposals is to put *providers* at risk, not consumers. Colloton seems to have compiled his information on the competition strategy from the writings of commentators rather than from the writings of the actual authors of the strategy.

Third, Colloton does not show nearly enough recognition of the urgent need for cost control. The competition proposals are based on the premises that the size and growth of health care spending are creating a serious problem for our government and our economy, that a continuation of the status quo for many more years is untenable, and that the real choice is between a model based on fair economic competition in the private sector and a system of comprehensive regulation by the government. Colloton seems to think that indefinite continuation of the status quo is a realistic alternative. Many of his concerns about the introduction of economic competition, such as his fear of "system-wide quality of care erosion," would apply much more seriously to the regulatory strategy. I recommend that interested persons ask hospital administrators in New York what they think about the impact of state rate regulation on quality. Then they should ask hospital administrators in Minneapolis-St. Paul and Hawaii what they think about the impact of competition on quality. In the small sample I have observed, the answer is a negative for state rate regulation and a positive for competition.

Fourth, it is especially inappropriate for Colloton to raise the specter of poor quality in the context of competing HMOs. He offers no evidence to support his speculations, and there is much evidence to support the opposite point of view. Competing HMOs tend to do very well serving educated groups of consumers such as professors and other teachers, civil servants, and employees of high-technology companies. If the quality were poor, one would think that these people, all of whom have a free choice, would switch back to fee for service. Implicit throughout Colloton's paper is the assumption that teaching hospitals provide good quality care while other hospitals provide inferior quality care, so that a decision not to refer a patient to a teaching hospital is a decision for poor quality care. I simply would not accept this assumption without a substantial amount of evidence.

I believe the competition strategy will greatly improve the quality of care in many respects. It will make the system more responsive to the desires of consumers. It will promote improved organization and more rational patterns of care. In a study of surgical mortality and the annual number of operations performed in each hospital, Luft, Bunker, and I found that there is a great deal of complex surgery performed in this country in hospitals having volumes too low for proficiency.[3] The competing HMOs usually refer their complex surgical cases to centers having high volumes. HMOs find it in their interest to employ various quality controls that are often absent in the fee-for-service sector. In the competition of organized systems of care, the focus will shift from people attempting to pick a specialist when they are sick to people making a considered choice of health care organization when they are well.

Another misunderstanding is reflected in Colloton's claim that "competition would serve as a substitute for price and cost regulation; it would not be a substitute for regulation of availability and quality of health care." Not at all. HMOs traditionally compete on accessibility. That is usually their strongest selling point: guaranteed access. The experience with competition suggests that it will regulate availability and quality far better than today's noncompetitive system.

Fifth, Colloton expresses doubt that, "If consumers are given an incentive to save money on health insurance expenditures, they will have the expertise and desire to choose policies which provide maximum coverage for care needed in the future (and minimum coverage for care not needed), at a minimum total cost and at an appropriate level of quality." Again, his doubts would be alleviated if he reviewed the experience of the Federal Employees Health Benefits Program and similar large-scale, long-term successes with multiple choice systems.

Proponents of the competition model recognize that for a competitive market to produce a socially desirable result, it is necessary that buyers be reasonably well informed about the alternatives they are considering and be able to make intelligent choices for themselves.

The market will not work well if it is too costly for buyers to become well informed. Health care and health insurance are complex fields, poorly understood even by the experts. Insurance policies are often very complex because insurers rely on complicated limitations and exclusions to control their costs and because some insurers seek to avoid price competition by making their policies difficult to compare with others. For this market to work well, there should be a systematic program by employers and government to make it easy for consumers to understand and compare alternative health plans.

In the successful examples of competition already in place, the system has been designed to help consumers understand and compare. I think much more can and should be done. As a part of Consumer Choice Health Plan, I recommended standardization of the list of covered services to make it easier for consumers to compare health plans without having to master many pages of fine print or to make actuarial comparisons of one complex package with another.

Finally, in some parts of his paper, Colloton expresses fears that competition legislation will work too fast and too well: "Disruption may occur in the administration and delivery of health care when 150 million Americans are thrust into an altered medical marketplace." And: "It would be ill-advised, however, to rapidly convert a highly complex and pluralistic system . . . to a new system unproved on a national scale." But elsewhere he doubts that it will have any effect at all:

> Existing evidence that competitive plans will be successful in bargaining with providers to bring about the perceived need for change in style of practice and control of costs is not convincing. Illustrative of this fact is that HMOs, even with significant subsidies, have experienced quite limited success in establishing advantageous financial arrangements with providers and expanding enrollment. While the first HMO was developed in the United States in the late 1920s, only 4 percent of the general population is currently enrolled in these plans. In the Federal Employees Health Benefits Program, which has been a model for the consumer choice health plan, there was only a 9 percent enrollment in HMO-type plans during 1980, after twenty years of operation.

In other words, he is not sure whether competition legislation will have too big an impact or too little; he is just sure that it will be bad one way or the other. The authors of the competition proposals and legislation do not see them as sudden and disruptive; they see the proposals as mid-course corrections in the incentives that will have a gradual effect as people adapt voluntarily. If the proposed incentive reforms are not strong enough, stronger ones can be tried. But the idea is to solve the problem of cost through incentives reform in a decentralized private market, not by all-embracing federal economic controls.

Colloton's evidence that incentives reform will be ineffective is that HMOs have grown slowly "even with significant subsidies." Colloton is obviously unaware of a great deal of history. Federal outlays for HMO subsidies were budgeted at $22 million in 1978, $39 million by 1981, both very small amounts in our overall health care economy. The latter and larger amount is about 0.6 percent of the "societal contributions" of 270 teaching hospitals as estimated by Colloton, hardly "significant." Colloton ignores the very large subsidies to non-HMO hospitals, such as over $2.6 billion in Hill-Burton funds and access to tax-exempt financing. (For the most part, the hospital-based HMOs have financed their construction out of retained earnings and long-term borrowing at commercial rates.) Colloton ignores the decades of harassment, boycott, ostracism, and denial of hospital privileges to HMO doctors by organized medicine, practices that led to antitrust cases and went even to the Supreme Court. Colloton ignores the many anti-HMO biases and barriers to their growth contained in the Social Security Act and created by the tax laws. For example, studies show that, because it is based on cost reimbursement, Medicare systematically pays more on behalf of beneficiaries who choose fee for service than on behalf of actuarially similar beneficiaries who choose HMOs. Because the tax laws make it advantageous for the employer to pay 100 percent of the employee's health insurance premiums, employers frequently pay more on behalf of employees who choose fee for service than employees who choose HMOs.

It is not surprising that only 9 percent of federal employees chose HMO plans in 1980 when one considers the fact that most of them do not have the choice of joining one on a geographically convenient basis. I think a far better indicator of the potential is the experience in markets where strong HMOs are offered in sufficient locations to make them convenient choices. For example, roughly half the state and federal employees in Kaiser Northern California's service area belong to Kaiser. Or one might consider the experience of the Twin Cities reported to this conference by Paul Ellwood (see Chapter 4).

Finally, it would be a mistake to tie the success of competition to the growth of HMOs. As Ellwood's paper brings out, there is a great variety of "competitive medical plans," including "preferred provider organizations," " primary care networks," "health alliances," and other models that can be developed and put in place in a much shorter time than it takes to develop a multispecialty group practice. So the 4 percent market penetration by HMOs in a system designed in so many ways against them says very little about the prospects for a variety of "competitive medical plans" in a system that is designed to foster fair economic competition.

NOTES

1. "National Health Care Reform Act" (H.R. 7527, introduced by Richard Gephardt and David Stockman, June 9, 1980).
2. See Alain C. Enthoven, "Consumer Choice Health Plan (in two parts)," *New England Journal of Medicine* 298 (March 23 and 30, 1978): 650-58 and 709-20. Also *Health Plan: The Only Practical Solution to the Soaring Cost of Medical Care* (Reading, Mass.: Addison Wesley, 1980).
3. Harold S. Luft, John Bunker, and Alain C. Enthoven, "Should Operations be Regionalized? The Empirical Relation between Surgical Volume and Mortality," *New England Journal of Medicine* 301, no. 25 (December 20, 1979): 1364-69.

RESPONSE
by *David E. Rogers*

John Colloton has done us all a great service. He has put together an extraordinarily thoughtful and carefully documented analysis of proposed competitive health plans and their implications for teaching hospitals. Even more valuable, he has thought through and articulated a set of strategies designed to help teaching hospitals survive, should competition become our way of life. I learned a great deal from reading his paper and I would like to respond to his proposals, in the hope that he can put to rest my remaining fears.

I would also like to point out that teaching hospitals are now faced with a new threat, more dangerous and more immediate than the hazards of increased competition: proposed cutbacks in Medicaid reimbursement.

Most of the changes that our political process makes in our health care system are incremental. I believe that this will be the case with the implementation of proposals to expand competition. I suspect it will take four to seven years to implement those plans, should the nation decide to proceed in that direction. With people like John and Alain to guide us, we will have an early understanding of the problems and ample opportunity to alleviate or resolve them.

But the cutbacks in Medicaid are proposed for September. The adoption and implementation of these cutbacks will threaten the very survival of our teaching hospitals as resources capable of making the societal contributions so well described by John. Simply because of their locations (often in inner cities), their clientele (often a disproportionate share of the poor), and their heavy reliance on federal support for all their important work, any reduction in Medicaid support, no matter how small, would put our teaching hospitals at risk. I do not see how they can cope with the cutbacks that have been proposed.

Events have played a cruel trick on John and this conference. John was asked to examine our boat for potential leaks because of a storm somewhere over the horizon. This he has done, and done very well. But now a torpedo has been launched, and it threatens to sink us long before the storm arrives.

If the Medicaid cutbacks are adopted, teaching hospitals will face six months from now a very disagreeable choice, between alternatives equally unacceptable. They can choose to do business as usual, to continue treating charity and Medicaid patients, and to continue making their traditional societal contributions, secure in the knowledge that they are likely to incur staggering and potentially fatal losses in the process.

Alternatively, they can decide to begin turning away charity and Medicaid patients, to give up ambulatory care, to cut back on teaching and research, and to shrink their bed complements to keep their occupancy rates acceptable. Even if they adopt this strategy immediately and pursue it aggressively, they face serious immediate losses in the transition to greatly reduced revenues. Some may go under. Simply to survive, they will have to give up their uniqueness, much of their reason for being, and their claim to special treatment as semipublic institutions making national contributions.

Medicaid cutbacks pose an immediate and pressing problem for our teaching hospitals, and I would urge the members of this group to bring to its analysis the intelligence and vigor which John Colloton has invested in his examination of the hazards of competition. In one guise or another, you are all advisers to teaching hospitals. When they ask you how they should prepare for the Medicaid cutbacks proposed for this fall, what will you tell them?

Let me now, and more directly, comment on John's analysis and recommendations. Early on, John argues that, if teaching hospitals are to operate in a competitive market, we will have to shift to à la carte pricing. I agree. I believe that à la carte pricing will be absolutely essential to their survival. It worries me, as it worries John, that we have no experience with such pricing, for it will probably prove more complex than we realize. Putting the machinery in place will be a major effort, but we will have to undertake it because our teaching hospitals simply cannot survive in a competitive environment without à la carte pricing.

At another point, John argues that it is their societal contributions which force teaching hospitals to spend more than nonteaching hospitals. I agree, and here I feel on firmer ground. Over the last eight years, we have looked quite carefully at some of the differences in cost, and we have come to the conclusion—and with some evidence to support it—that the usual answers are the wrong answers. It is not inefficiencies in management, it is not lack of staff productivity, and it is not poor collection policies that make teaching hospitals more costly than community hospitals. It is the costs of their teaching, of their vastly more complex medical-surgical cases, of their research, and of their underfunded ambulatory care programs. In short, it is the cost of their societal contributions that makes teaching hospitals more expensive.

Agreeing on that point, I must also agree on the next: If we are to have an environment in which hospitals compete on price, then someone other than the patient must be found to pay for the societal contributions of teaching hospitals. John has obviously thought a great deal about this problem, and I think he has developed some interesting and imaginative suggestions for the recovery and allocation of funds that teaching hospitals spend for purposes other than patient care.

If you believe in rationality, in making clear and sensible that which is foggy and foolish, you have to like John's scheme. It seems reasonable to identify the societal contributions of our teaching hospitals and the amounts spent for each and to pay for them through rational mechanisms designed for this purpose. Indeed, that looks a lot more sensible than hiding the societal contributions and burying their costs in patient care charges.

John has designed several mechanisms appropriate to the purpose. He has specifically addressed the deficiencies of the program grant approach suggested in the Gephardt-Stockman bill. His alternative seems most imaginative and intriguing: develop institutional support grants, funded by an earmarked percentage surcharge on all health care premiums; set up a teaching hospital advisory council to allocate the funds; develop ways to reward for both the measurable and the unmeasurable contributions.

Here again rationality wins out. With a mechanism like this, we could treat expenditures by teaching hospitals for their societal contributions as specific public goods. We could then decide, more clearly than we can now, how much of these goods we need or want. When it came time to allocate the funds, we could evaluate the various institutions and decide which are most efficient and responsible. We could also decide which purposes most need funding and the places at which they are best funded. As John has suggested, we could then collectively ask some other perfectly appropriate questions: Is our health personnel output compatible with the needs of our society? Is our research effort of an appropriate size? Is there a reasonable balance between basic and applied research funding? In this way, we could deal more directly with these and other questions largely avoided by teaching hospitals and medical academe.

We could also help our teaching hospitals understand better their obligations to meet local, state, and regional needs, as well as national and international needs. That will inevitably lead us to consider carefully those issues which we now overlook. For example, New York City hospitals now train about one-sixth of all medical residents in the United States. We have never before viewed that fact with alarm or regarded it as deserving public policy analysis. In an era in which we believed we had a major shortage of physicians, nobody worried much about the geographic distribution of medical residents among teaching hospitals, so long as more got trained. But now, John suggests, we probably must. Certainly, if we employ the mechanisms that he proposes, we will have to, and that is a powerful argument for their adoption.

Even so, and despite all the other good things to be said for it, I must, with sadness, indicate that I do not believe the approach that

John has suggested will be good for medical education or research. Our government is appropriately preoccupied with an effort to reduce its expenditures anywhere it can, and health care would appear to be an area where reductions are certain. Those concerned with maintaining federal support at its current levels should recognize the fact that changes in the forms of federal support—whether by the substitution of block grants for categorical funding or some other— are sure to be accompanied by reductions in the level of support. Since we seem more likely to maintain government support at the current level for programs which remain otherwise unchanged, I think we should be very cautious about changing the forms of federal support at this juncture.

I would be afraid of what would result from an effort to restructure federal support for the societal contributions of teaching hospitals if it were to involve unbundling the patient care charges in which they are now buried. Given the current political context, identification of the various societal contributions and isolation of their costs are sure to lead to reduced federal support for basic and applied research, for graduate medical and dental education, and for new experiments in ambulatory care. The inevitable result will be erosion of the quality of medical practice as we know it in the United States.

I would also suggest that the creation of a mechanism that would allow us to isolate the costs of the societal contributions of teaching hospitals and to fund them separately from a pool created by a surcharge on health insurance premiums would not render the distribution of those costs more equitable than it is now. It may seem inappropriate and irrational to bury the cost of those contributions in patient care charges, but they wind up increasing the cost of health insurance just as surely as they would when added as a surcharge. Since following the approach that John has proposed seems certain to result in loss of funds and no gain in equity, I see no advantage to accepting the risk his strategy creates.

However else we may disagree, especially about strategies and tactics, the people in this room all wish to protect teaching hospitals and their critical role in medical research, education, and health care delivery. In this company, it is hard to remember that our belief is not held so strongly or so widely that we can be sure that teaching hospitals will not face a crisis six months from now. Our major political parties are both devoted to reducing the federal budget; indeed, they are competing to see which can come up with the largest cuts. The urgency and popularity of that effort will give it precedence over all but the most compelling causes, and the protection of institutions that make vaguely understood societal contributions, with payoffs five or twenty years hence, is not particularly compelling.

Reduced federal expenditures for health care may seem so unwise as to appear unlikely, but the facts are opposite. If, with President Reagan, one elects to preserve untouched Social Security and other directly or indirectly indexed transfer programs, one exempts more than 40 percent of federal spending from scrutiny and reduction. If one then increases defense spending, now 25 percent of the federal budget, and continues to pay the interest owing on the federal debt, at the rate of 10 percent of current spending, one is left with about 25 percent of the budget in which to find the cuts essential to spending increases elsewhere and to federal tax cuts. Those programs which are viewed as nice, but not essential—and the ill-defined contributions of our academic medical centers would fit comfortably in this category—are at massive risk. There are many sacred cows in the federal budget, and some of those may survive unscathed. But academic medical centers, medical schools, and teaching hospitals are not among them. When the expense of their social contributions is made highly visible, I believe that it will prove all too easy to decide that they can be reduced.

That is my major worry, for I believe that the social contributions of teaching hospitals are essential to the quality of medical research, medical education, and health care in this country. The fact that young physicians are trained in an environment in which they are hearing, seeing, touching, smelling, and working with research-oriented faculty every day is not a small matter. It is, I believe, the fact that physicians are trained in this atmosphere which prompts the majority of them to stay abreast of new advances, for it makes them vividly aware of the half-life of medical advances. It shapes them to take personal professional responsibility for keeping up to date. Indeed, this attitude becomes so ingrained that most physicians I know continue to read journals, to attend meetings, to talk with their colleagues, and to feel that their profession is first, foremost, and sacred. This attitude distinguishes our physicians, and they do not get this mindset from *Time* or a vocational journal. They get it from their exposure to that very precious, ill-defined environment which the social contributions of good teaching hospitals create.

If we make our expenditures for these social contributions visible, as John suggests, and put them in categories separate from our expenditures for patient care, we will be inviting their reduction. Indeed, the temptation to ax them would be virtually irresistable. The constituency which believes them important is relatively small, and the impact of the loss would not be felt for at least a decade.

We may have to go the route that John describes. If we do, I think we may soon see the end of the era in which American medicine was the best in the world. But the really dreadful part is that we will not know, and neither will those who make the cuts, until they have taken effect, and then the whole remarkable structure of biomedical science and biomedical education, so laboriously built over the past fifty years, may have to be rebuilt from scratch.

RESPONSE
by *Richard Egdahl*

Perhaps the most useful thing I could do would be to respond to John's paper as our critics might. Our critics will respond, of course, and those of us responsible for the management and survival of major teaching hospitals will have to confront the issues they will raise.

As spokesman for an academic medical center, I am involved in a continuing dialogue with professors of public health, medical sociology, statistics, and economics, on the one hand, and practicing physicians paid fee for service, on the other. It is not hard for me to imagine what such a group of professors and physicians might say about John's paper. Their issues are familiar, and we discuss them frequently in various interdisciplinary meetings and forums. My purpose in rehearsing them here is to make clear the risk of exposing the costs of subsidizing teaching, research, and the other societal contributions of teaching hospitals.

Let us not forget that this is a time of enormous pressure to cut social expenditures. We must be alert to the dangers of exposing these costs and prepare appropriate defenses—or change our behaviors. I'm going to go through John's paper and pick out points which our adversaries will use as an excuse to say: "Let's examine teaching hospitals, let's find out what they really do, and let's reform them."

John quotes Walt McNerney as asking, "How do we avoid the virtual exclusion from the market of the academic medical centers offering the best—and most expensive—care?'' Float that question to our critics and they will quickly ask, "Is care really better in the teaching hospitals?'' They will then point out that, for simple surgical procedures and much other secondary care, the rates of infection are lower and the interest of the staff in giving personal service is higher in good community hospitals. So the question is, "For other than tertiary problems, is care better in the teaching hospitals?'' We who represent teaching hospitals believe that it is, but the professors and physicians I meet with do not, and the question will continue to be raised.

Discussing it is often uncomfortable. I was at a panel not long ago where we were reviewing the performance of certain simple surgical procedures. The university medical center was sponsoring the session, and the discussion went along quietly until somebody pointed out that very few such procedures were actually done in the university hospital. At that point, a physician from a small town and a good community hospital said: "Listen, we do more of them, we do them faster, and we have an infection rate a fraction of the rate you would expect here or in any other academic medical center. Why would anybody in his right mind refer a secondary problem like this to a teaching hospital?'' There was a long silence. The moderator of the panel, a medical school professor, had to choose his words carefully in his answer.

At another point, John talks about the impact of increased competition on teaching hospitals, focusing on "three primary areas: patient referral patterns, financing, and retention of quality patient care throughout the system. Deterioration in any of these areas would detract from the sophisticated educational setting necessary to prepare the physicians and other health professionals of tomorrow.'' But our critics ask whether the academic clinicians who staff teaching hospitals are the right people to train future physicians. Dave Rogers spoke about the importance of exposure to inquiry, the search for new knowledge, and the ferment which that creates, and I think he is right to stress their value.

But our critics would say that immersion in the search for new knowledge is exactly what the physicians of tomorrow do *not* need. Training aspiring physicians in the sophisticated setting of the academic medical center makes many of them feel insecure, and like second-class citizens if they don't plan to specialize. It also leads them to practice in the style of their research-oriented mentors, many of whom have never been exposed to the realities of private practice. In response, our critics ask whether medical students are not best taught in community hospitals and other clinical settings where "true private practice" (whatever that is) is the model. Does not the Rockford experience demonstrate that a higher percentage of medical students go into primary care and do the things that most people want their doctors to do if they are not exposed to the massive numbers of research-oriented people who dominate academic health centers and teaching hospitals?

That is a difficult issue. On the one hand, I agree with Dave Rogers that exposure to the search for medical knowledge is valuable. On the other, I suspect that there is some truth to the argument that research-oriented physicians are less likely to give learners an example of the commitment to continuing personal service that our best clinical practitioners provide, and that most patients seem to want.

We can expect a similar response to John's discussion of faculty practice plans, which may have to be converted to private practice, "thereby curtailing their availability for support of academic programs." Whether or not they are converted, our critics will argue that many of the practice groups established at teaching hospitals are not true multispecialty group practices. Instead, their argument goes, they are the clinical sidelines of faculty members interested primarily in teaching and research. Placing learners in genuine group practices and in good community hospitals will give them useful and relevant experience. It will also strengthen the ties between medical schools and community hospitals, which are now seeking support for the instruction of medical students. The hospitals argue that they deserve support because they have real cost and because they are preparing students for the kind of practice into which the vast majority will go.

Elsewhere, John argues:

> The setting of teaching hospitals is necessary to insure that the student is challenged at the bedside and in regular conferences with the searching questions of academic clinicians actively engaged in the testing and discovery of new knowledge through current research. The case mix in tertiary teaching hospitals assures that all students and trainees are exposed to an appropriate range of challenging medical problems at each level of clinical education so that they can be trained systematically and efficiently.

But our critics point to the focus on research and to the interest in exotic and complicated cases which dominate our case mixes and ask whether teaching hospitals offer the right environment and the appropriate clinical experiences for the instruction of learners. In the course of their training at an academic medical center, students will see a very small percentage of the sexual and psychological problems, and of the lonely, tired, and "boring-to-treat" patients, that they will encounter most commonly. Instead, their exposure is to the rare and intellectually challenging patients who fill tertiary care hospitals. Because learners are not prepared for the situations which they will encounter, they are said to be very much ill at ease, particularly in the early stages of practice. Like Dave Rogers and Bill Anlyan, I am used to answering these criticisms with all the orthodox responses: "Once in practice, our learners quickly adapt. They have been exposed to high-quality thinking, and they know how to solve problems. They keep up with the literature and work constantly to improve their understanding and their treatment of patients." I think we can continue to hold our own in these conversations, but I do not look forward to defending our flanks at all these points simultaneously. Public discussion of John's proposal would force us to do that.

At another point, John proposes the deposit of a surcharge on health insurance premiums in a trust fund to be allocated "after mandatory consultation with an appropriate academically related advisory group, such as the Teaching Hospital Advisory Council." This arrangement "would have the benefit of not interjecting any further governmental regulation of decisions regarding the numbers and types of residency training programs in teaching hospitals or the scope of other programs in teaching hospitals." At that point, our critics will ask whether the fox is to be allowed to guard the chicken coop. They will describe the Teaching Hospital Advisory Council as a mechanism for continued control by the elite, by the same people who control the system which has "given us an excess of specialists." They will ask such questions as: Who knows what kinds of doctors this country needs? How many of each kind should be trained? Who should decide? Should it be a group composed entirely of academic clinicians? Or should it be a group dominated by the real world of practice, or by consumers, or by a combination thereof?

John points out that the introduction of competition on price into our health care system will work a "revolutionary change" in its structure, "the outcome of which no one can accurately predict." He goes on to advocate the creation of safeguards to protect us against unexpected and untoward consequences, including "a device to sustain the vigor of our nation's teaching hospitals which underpin the quality of the entire health care system." It is precisely on this point that attacks are increasing. Our critics argue that the greater administrative complexity, multiprofessional relationships, and concern for research that characterize academic medical centers make the services which they provide for patients requiring secondary care more expensive, less efficient, and perhaps of lower quality than those provided in good community hospitals. John Cooper, Dave Rogers, and I would like to argue that the quality of secondary care provided in an academic health center is at least as good as that provided in the outstanding community hospitals, but the evidence is fragmentary. If we make the subsidy for social contributions overt, we will have to defend it and justify its funding with evidence which may be inadequate to the task.

Meanwhile, our adversaries will see this as a golden opportunity to reduce tertiary care teaching hospitals to their "appropriate" size and role and to reorient medical education and residency training toward private practice and the community hospital. You can write their strategy as well as I: Pay hospitals the same amount for services rendered to comparable patients receiving the same, straightforward, secondary surgical procedures, such as choleocystectomies, or treatment of the same medical conditions, such as myocardial infarction. Because of their high costs, paying teaching hospitals at the community hospital rate for secondary care will force them to give it up. Secondary care patients will thus be driven into community hospitals—where they are better treated anyway, our critics would say. A simultaneous adjustment in the financing of medical education will result in the transfer of much medical student learning to smaller, less expensive community hospitals, where students can prepare themselves to cope with the situations and problems that they will confront in practice.

When you boil down the rhetoric of our several varieties of critics, you find four basic points: Care for secondary conditions is better done in good community hospitals than it is in major teaching hospitals. "Get your hernia fixed at a community hospital." That is first. Second, the academic clinicians who staff our major teaching hospitals are poor role models and teachers for the vast majority of the aspiring physicians. They teach the wrong kind of medicine in the wrong environment. Third, major teaching hospitals have the wrong case mix for teaching students, and it will grow even more wrong as competition draws into good community hospitals much of the secondary care now provided in tertiary facilities. Fourth, a research institute is the wrong place to train people to perform the work of practicing physicians.

So far, we have held our own in these arguments. But the promotion of organized competition in the health care community will create enough confusion and ferment that the critics of teaching hospitals may be able to make significant inroads. As I read John's paper, and as I think of all the discussions that will follow its publication, I worry that we will be put in an unfair and most difficult position at a time of immense budgetary cuts. Along with Dave Rogers, I am dubious about our ability to sustain the support of teaching hospitals in a time of extraordinary pressure to reduce government expenditures, particularly if that support will require the explicit approval of Congress and the administration.

John has given us a fine document. It raises all the issues and forces you to think them through. It offers a strategy for the protection of teaching hospitals and their social contributions which seems to me both sensible and reasonable. But I hope that the fate of our teaching hospitals does not hang on its public acceptance and approval.

DISCUSSION

John Colloton: Alain Enthoven has pointed out various deficiencies in my understanding of the competition proposals and health economics. All I can say is that, if I misunderstand, then there are many people in academic medical centers who misunderstand, and there is a huge educational job to be done.

Let me respond instead to his comments and suggestions about the approach outlined in my paper. His first objection was to rewarding inefficient teaching hospitals and to retrospective payments. I can understand his concern, but it seems to me unreasonable to risk the future of the academic medical centers on a new system constructed without a safety valve. The pool I discussed is not bottomless; it is limited, and it would provide the academic medical centers limited protection against the risks of a competitive environment. It would not protect the most inefficient. Elsewhere, he described $1.8 billion as a small price to pay for the implementation of a competitive system. I should make it very clear that we are not talking about $1.8 billion; we are talking about $6.7 billion. At another point, he said that unmeasurable societal contributions might not account for all the $2.7 billion which I claimed for them. I would agree, but I would ask how he proposes to sort those out and how radically he proposes to cut the funds available to the facilities which underpin our system of health care. He makes the point that we show too little appreciation of the importance of containing costs. I would remind him that, after years of work in this field, he recently produced a book about competition called *Health Plan* in which there is no reference to academic medical centers. If we seem to stress our own problems, it is because we want to make sure that they are understood by those who propose to redesign our system of health care. He charges me with engaging in speculation when I express the fear that the system which he proposes will lead to the inappropriate retention of patients requiring tertiary care in hospitals providing secondary care. He is right, I am speculating, but on the basis of common sense and considerable evidence. In many sections of this country, there is a very fuzzy line between tertiary care and secondary care, and it seems reasonable to believe that, if there is a powerful financial incentive to keep patients in hospitals providing secondary care, they will be kept there, even though some of them might receive better or more appropriate treatment in tertiary care facilities. None of the competition proposals which I have seen creates a special pool for tertiary care to protect against this risk.

Finally, he emphasizes that the plan must be responsive to society's needs and that we must therefore have a council dominated by users. They will be obliged to decide significant issues: whether medical students and residents must pay the full costs of their educations; how many physicians of various kinds we should be training, and so on. When you consider the complexity and sensitivity of these problems, you begin to wonder about the realism of a proposal that a user-dominated council decide them. Moreover, when you consider the record of the academic medical centers, when you examine their response to society's need for more physicians and for a changing mix of physicians, you discover that academic medical centers respond about as quickly as needs are identified, and you are led to the conclusion that we would be wise to leave the control of academic medicine where it is.

John Cooper: I am always awed by economic planners who give the appearance of having a special vision of the future which is somehow denied to us mere mortals.

Alain Enthoven asked who is to decide how many and what kinds of physicians should be trained. Given the long period of training which they face, to say nothing of their careers in practice, I think the students themselves can make choices as good as those which can be made by planners. In 1948, planners in New York were asked to estimate the need for additional beds to be devoted to the treatment of patients with tuberculosis. Their recommendation was to double the number of beds. Two years later, before their recommendations could be acted upon, beds were being closed. Who would have predicted that? Or any of dozens of other biomedical advances of the last thirty years?

His next question is, What kind of research should we do? And who should decide that? I am reminded of a meeting I attended in Washington several years ago. Every division of the Department of Health, Education and Welfare was represented. We were discussing research and how to make it more efficient. A planner from the Office of Education said he couldn't understand our confusion. "Look," he said, "If you want to cure cancer, develop a five-year plan and cure it." The lack of understanding of research displayed by people who have never been involved in it is truly amazing.

Perhaps the only effective interaction between the private and public sectors in this field occurs at the National Institutes of Health. There, decisions about the distribution of research funds are made by people who know something about it. The problem with most policy-makers is their perspective. In the House of Representatives, the horizon is two years or less; in the executive branch, four years or less. It is hard to take the long view in that environment.

I share John Colloton's concern about payment for charity care provided by teaching hospitals. That's what Medicaid and Medicare were established for, and yet we still have enormous numbers of patients for whom insufficient support is available. The resources of our teaching hospitals—obtained one way or another—are used to carry a social burden which has yet to be assumed by government at any level.

Alain and John talked about HMOs and the use which they make of teaching hospitals. I would remind you that the percentage of people enrolled in HMOs is relatively small, even in the Twin Cities and Northern California, and I think that perhaps the other parts of the system keep the HMOs honest. To see what may happen in the future, look at Washington, D.C., where the HMO pulled out of George Washington University Hospital and sent its patients to a hospital which soon went bankrupt because it could not attract patients other than those sent by the HMO. Even where their market share is small, there are examples of HMOs shopping for lower quality, low-cost care.

Finally, I should respond to a few of Dick Egdahl's points. I don't think he believes them all, but I want to be sure that the other side appears in the record.

Where should primary care be taught? In environments with no research? At the University of Washington Medical School, which receives more federal support than any other, 40 percent of the most recent graduates went into family medicine, and many of the rest chose internal medicine, pediatrics, obstetrics, and other specialties with heavy involvement in primary care. To say that a commitment to patient care cannot flourish in an environment filled with exciting research is plainly wrong.

What kinds of specialists should we be training? How many of each? Whatever we decide today, we are likely to be proved wrong five or ten years from now. Medicine has been transformed in the last thirty years, from a largely empirical to a largely scientific profession. Even in the last five years, our knowledge has simply exploded. Faced with that, the medical schools are trying to teach their students as much science as they can, to give them some way of coping with the flood of new information which the future will bring.

Uwe Reinhardt: No one will deny the substantial social contributions of academic medical centers and teaching hospitals. But it is legitimate to ask: How much is enough? Who should decide how much is enough? These are legitimate issues which we have swept under the rug for decades.

If your concern is to defend the teaching hospital, the question is: Who is the enemy and what do you shoot at? It is unfortunate that some people pick the competitive strategy, for that strategy is only a symptom of a widespread feeling that there is a need for economy in health care which the existing system cannot meet. It is a mistake to style the defense of academic medical centers and teaching hospitals as an attack on the competitive strategy. That is not only bad strategy—it will surely fail—but it is also intellectually wrong. John Colloton's assault on competition is unnecessary. It is quite unrelated to his point that we need a financial mechanism to preserve the social contributions of teaching hospitals in an era of diminishing resources.

David Rogers said that, if the competitive strategy—which is really just a budgetary assault—compels us to zero-base teaching hospitals and justify everything they do, they are sure to be cut. Instead, he argues, we should keep the expenditures for teaching and research jumbled up with expenditures for patient care so that they cannot be cut. As someone who watched the National Science Foundation budget go under Stockman's assault, I share these fears. On the other hand I am also concerned about the lack of faith in the democratic process implicit in our posture.

Monte DuVal: Our conversation this morning has turned on the unique role of teaching hospitals, and I sense that the way in which they are special is being defined too narrowly: that is, in terms of their teaching and research. The academic medical center is the court of last resort in medicine, and medicine is the only arena where the university functions in that role. Instead of arguing about the price structure, I would suggest that we price out tertiary care and put it in the marketplace. That would not bother me because I think every level of care has its price, and it would simply come back to a question of economics. If that thesis proves correct, it really isn't necessary to treat the academic medical center as a separate and special entity—except in the context of ethics. Should the physician at the court of last medical resort admit a patient when he knows perfectly well that the patient will be dead in two weeks and that the bill rung up will be in excess of $15,000? That is a tough issue.

My other question concerns the future course that universities will take. Given the economic stress facing teaching hospitals in the next few years, I think the question is whether universities will unbundle this function. It is quite possible that there will come a time when the universities will say: "Sorry, but the burden of maintaining a teaching hospital has now outstripped our capacities. Let's unbundle this function and put it in a separate, free-standing entity."

Dan Tosteson: It is becoming part of our awareness that medicine is unique among the professions in the extent to which the organization and practice of the profession are closely intertwined with education and research. That is not an accident. The academic medical center was a conscious creation, and it is a considerable achievement. The Reagan transition team paper on health said that the current situation is untenable, that we must have more competition or more regulation, but I think we have much to be proud of and that we should approach adjustments to the existing system with a spirit of conservatism. I am concerned that we not lose what we have, particularly in the following four areas:

First, care of the poor. It has been the principle for some time in this country that we are headed toward a one-class system of care, but a lot of what I hear from those interested in competition is focused on patients who can pay, and not on those who can't. Our little colloquy about Medicaid payments to teaching hospitals makes me wonder whether we are headed back to a two-class system.

Second, intelligent choice. I'm a strong believer in educating the public about health care and in promoting prudent buying of health care services, but I am not terribly optimistic about it. The over-the-counter health market is one in which the consumer now has the opportunity to act the prudent buyer, but I don't see much prudent buying going on. Let me ask about the insurance field: Are insurers providing solid and comparable data about their plans, or in fact are the plans pretty complicated and is their obfuscation part of the marketing? When I compare the over-the-counter health field, where there is a lot of competition, with the telephone industry, where there is very little, I'm not sure which serves the public better.

Third, the implications of these structural changes for the ethical tension in which physicians work. Up until now, the economic incentives and the professional incentives in the practice of medicine have been complementary. I see the introduction of more competition as putting those incentives in conflict. There are certainly problems that result from having economic and professional incentives complement one another, and we see those, but there are problems that will result from having them in conflict. I think those are problems that medical educators will have to consider with some care.

And fourth, the relationship between research and practice. My concern is that a great deal of what goes on at the frontier of research is directed at problems whose resolution will not have much impact on the economics of medical care. My view is that 70 percent or 80 percent of all expenditures for medical care are devoted to disorders which get better anyway and that doing less or nothing for these disorders would produce substantial savings. Most biomedical research, on the other hand, is directed at serious biological dysfunction which has relatively low incidence. That is not to say that those research efforts are not enormously important. Rather, it is to point out that to focus all the planning of the medical care system on the high volume items that drive costs up is to divorce the direction of development of the health care system from the direction of current research.

Rollins Hanlon: Alex McMahon talked with us about the importance of accepting the inevitable. What I see as inevitable is the deterioration in quality. I don't know whether it's because of scarce resources, antiscientism, or what, but I think we are headed for deterioration in quality, and I wish we could find some way to avoid that.

Paul Ellwood: Our experience shows that competitive medical plans are going to grow very slowly at first, but those curves in my graphs are exponential growth curves. That kind of growth has a way of hitting the system all of a sudden. Those curves show an impact in 1990, but they are based on national numbers. Academic medical centers in San Francisco, Denver, Boston, Seattle, Portland, the Twin Cities, Los Angeles, and other big cities are going to feel the impact in far less than ten years, perhaps in two or three years. And that makes me wonder whether these institutions are going to be able to cope. What I heard this morning was: "We don't like competition," and, "We certainly don't want the politicians allocating these resources." Well, who's going to do it? And when are the academic medical centers going to be ready to participate? This stuff hasn't come up very suddenly. John Cooper and I talked about this in 1970. I recall the preoccupation *then* was with the cost of medical care. And people were making the same kind of grave predictions then that they are now, except now the predictions are starting to come true. Academic medical centers are large institutions, and the lead time they require to make the sort of adustments they will need to make is very long. I'm just wondering how one gives them a sense of urgency, how one gets them to begin assuming that they have to make these changes, knowing that they have to adjust to the new competitive realities, and not just hoping that they can avoid them.

AFTERWORD

Did the conference meet our expectations and objectives?

It brought together a group of people from diverse backgrounds and a variety of perspectives to focus on a major problem of our society: the financing of health care. It was planned as a debate between adversarial approaches—regulation versus competition. Two days of discussion revealed that the competitive approach will not get rid of the shackles of regulation (or overregulation); instead, a new set of regulations will be required to foster fair competition. Colloton argued that these might cripple teaching hospitals. Enthoven disagreed vigorously, while Reinhardt sought a middle ground and compromise.

That was characteristic of the conference. People who need to hear one another took the opportunity to listen, challenge, and discuss. The dialogue was courteous, and wherever possible the participants sought common ground. Physicians, economists, and administrators found themselves on all sides of the questions. No solutions were discovered and no converts were made, but the discussion clarified the issues and seemed to modify some opinions.

The Seventh Private Sector Conference, to be held in March 1982, will focus on the financial support of health care for the elderly and the indigent. As the Reagan administration and Congress are concerned primarily with balancing the nation's economy, it is mandatory that the health issues of the poor and the elderly be examined in discussion arenas other than the political.

William G. Anlyan, M.D.

Duke University Medical Center

INDEX

231

ABOUT THE EDITORS

William G. Anlyan, M.D., is Vice President for Health Affairs at Duke University. He taught, practiced, and performed research as a professor of surgery until 1964, when he became Dean of the Duke University School of Medicine. Since then he has devoted most of his time to leadership roles in academic medicine, primarily at Duke, but also in national organizations like the Association of American Medical Colleges, the National Library of Medicine, the American Surgical Association, and the Association for Academic Health Centers. In October 1980 he was awarded the Flexner Award of the Association of American Medical Colleges.

Duncan Yaggy, Ph.D., is Director and Chief Planning Officer of Duke University Hospital and a professor at Duke's Institute of Policy Sciences and Public Affairs. Before coming to Duke in 1980, he served six years as an analyst and manager in the Executive Office of Human Services and two years as the Assistant Commissioner for Health Regulation in the Massachusetts Department of Public Health.